Andalus Press

AN ILLUSTRATED HISTORY OF
THE IRISH REVOLUTION
1916-1923

Michael B. Barry

Published by Andalus Press
Dublin, Ireland

info@andalus.ie
www.andalus.ie

AN ILLUSTRATED HISTORY OF THE IRISH REVOLUTION, 1916-1923
ISBN 978-0-9933554-7-9
© Michael B. Barry 2020
Michael B. Barry asserts the moral right to be identified as the author of this work.

All rights reserved. No part of this publication may be reproduced, stored in a retrieval system, or transmitted in any form or by any means, mechanical, electronic, recording, photocopying or otherwise, without the prior permission of the publisher.

By the same author:
Across Deep Waters, Bridges of Ireland
Restoring a Victorian House
Through the Cities, the Revolution in Light Rail
Tales of the Permanent Way, Stories from the Heart of Ireland's Railways
Fifty Things to do in Dublin
Dublin's Strangest Tales (with Patrick Sammon)
Bridges of Dublin, the Remarkable Story of Dublin's Liffey Bridges (with Annette Black)
Victorian Dublin Revealed, the Remarkable Legacy of Nineteenth-Century Dublin
Beyond the Chaos, the Remarkable Heritage of Syria
Homage to al-Andalus, the Rise and Fall of Islamic Spain
The Alhambra Revealed, the Remarkable Story of the Kingdom of Granada
Málaga, a Guide and Souvenir
Courage Boys, We are Winning, an Illustrated History of the 1916 Rising
The Fight for Irish Freedom, an Illustrated History of the War of Independence
The Green Divide, an Illustrated History of the Irish Civil War

Jacket Images
Author photograph: Veronica Barry.
Front cover: Dublin Fire Brigade/Micheál Ó Doibhlinn b. All other jacket images were colourised by John O'Byrne, adapted from original sources as follows — Front cover: Mulcahy family tl & mr, NMI tm, John Sweeney Archives tr, NLI ml; Back cover: NLI; Front flap: NLI; Back flap: NLI.

Jacket design by Anú Design
Book design by Michael B. Barry
Principal colourising services by NC & JO'B Photography

Printed by Białostockie Zakłady Graficzne SA, Poland

Contents

Acknowledgements and Illustration Credits — 5

Chronology — 6

Introduction — 9

Chapter 1 Freedom's Long Journey — 11

Chapter 2 1916 — 43

Chapter 3 War of Independence — 115

Chapter 4 Truce — 233

Chapter 5 Civil War — 259

Bibliography — 361

Glossary — 364

Index — 366

Dedicated to Eun Sun Barry and her two Michaels: Michael D. and Michael A.

Acknowledgements

The author is privileged to have had the services of John O'Byrne who painstakingly and with exceptional skill colourised many of the historical black and white photographs:

NC & JO'B Photography
3 Main Street, Rathangan Demesne, Rathangan, Co. Kildare, R51 DD23
johnobyrne.ellistown@gmail.com; telephone 085 1567879

This work benefitted from the help, insights and scholarship of many kind people. Thanks are due especially to: Dr Brian Kirby, Irish Capuchin Provincial Archives; Aoife Torpey, Kilmainham Gaol Archives; Commandant Daniel Ayiotis, Lisa Dolan, Adrian Short, Hugh Beckett and Noelle Grothier, Military Archives, Cathal Brugha Barracks; Aideen Ireland, National Archives of Ireland; Angus Mitchell; Anne Boddaert, Crawford Art Gallery; Audrey Whitty, Clare MacNamara, National Museum of Ireland; Bernard Minogue; Berni Metcalfe, Glenn Dunne, Bríd O'Sullivan, National Library of Ireland; Conor Dullaghan; Damian Murphy; Daniel Breen, Cork Public Museum; David Byrne; Derek Jones; Diarmuid O'Connor; Dónal Fallon; Dónal MacLynn; Dr Lydia Ferguson, TCD; Dr Margarita Cappock, Dublin City Gallery; Dr Mary Clarke, Dublin City Library & Archive; Edward Burke; Ernest McCall; Frank Twomey; Garry O'Brien; George Morrison; Gerald Burroughs; Geraldine McCarthy; Gillean Robertson Miller; Ivan Lennon; Jackie Dermody, Clare County Library; James Doyle; James Langton; Janet Murphy; Joe Gannon; Joe Maxwell; John Kirby; John R. Bowen; John Reidy; Joseph Scanlon; Las Fallon; Marcus Howard; Mark Humphrys; Mark Kennedy, Debra Wenlock; Mark Platts; Martin MacDevitt; Michael Fewer; Michael O'Connor 'Scarteen'; Mícheál Ó Doibhilín, www.kilmainhamtales.ie; Mick O'Dea; Mick O'Farrell; Nigel Curtin, Dún Laoghaire-Rathdown Libraries; Oisín Marsh; Revd Canon Professor Patrick Comerford; Paul Neilan; Peadar Collins; Pearse Lawlor; Peter McGoldrick; Peter Rigney, Norman Gamble, Irish Railway Record Society; Professor Davis Coakley; Professor Frank Imbusch; Ray Bateson; Richard McCormack; Risteárd Mulcahy family; Robert Ballagh; Robert Porter; Roger Wallsgrove; Séamus Ó Maitiú; Senator Mark Daly; Sharon O'Donovan, Mercier Press; Stephen Ferguson, An Post; Tom Harrington and Tommy Mooney.

A big thanks to Paddy Sammon. It is a privilege to have his kind advice, support and assistance during the preparation of this book. Lastly, but most importantly, my eternal muse: Veronica Barry.

Illustration Credits

Images on the specified pages are courtesy and copyright of the following (abbreviations for top, bottom, left, middle, right, respectively, are: t, b, l, m, r) — American Irish Historical Society: 140b; Angus Mitchell: 217t; Archiseek: 51b; *Bibliothèque nationale de France*: 150b, 161b, 201t; Board of Trinity College, The University of Dublin: 122t, 145t, 146b, 151b, 154b, 164b, 166t, 190, 193b, 254t, 358b; British National Archives: 335tr; British Newspaper Archives: 219t; Cashel Folk Museum: 88t; Central Catholic Library: 99t; Clare Co. Library: 239t; Cork Public Museum: 239m; Crawford Art Gallery: 162b; David Byrne: 333b, 337b; Davis Coakley: 77t; Debra Wenlock: 153m; Department of Special Collection, Hesburgh Libraries of Notre Dame University: 319bl; Derek Jones: 151bm, 157b, 180t, 196bl; Diarmuid O'Connor: 268-9t, 287, 339m, 349t; Dónal MacLynn: 337m; Dónal Fallon: 122bl; Dublin City Archives: 105b, 119t, 126tl, 133t, 145b, 148t, 150m, 151t, 152tr, 153t, 157ml, 161t, 169b, 170t, 172t, 172m, 173t, 174tl, 176, 177t, 178t, 186, 203b, 204br, 205b, 217t, 217b, 219bl, 221m, 230m, 230b, 231b, 236b, 240t, 249m, 250, 253b, 254bl, 254br, 255t, 256t, 256b, 258b, 258, 264tl, 264tr, 267t, 283b, 289m, 289br, 315b, 325b, 343b, 355tr; Dublin City Gallery The Hugh Lane: 324m; Dublin Fire Brigade/Mícheál Ó Doibhlinn: 220t; Edward Burke: 281b; Ernest McCall: 210t; Frank Twomey: 131m; George Morrison: 252b, 314b, 322t, 355tl; Geraldine McCarthy: 342br; Gerard Burroughs: 183t; Iarnród Éireann: 328b, 329m; Imperial War Museum: 39m, 201br, 232t; Irish Capuchin Provincial Archives, Dublin: 56b, 57t, 81m, 81b, 82t, 84b, 97t, 97b, 112t, 124b, 129b, 139t, 163t, 168tr, 171tl, 171tr, 171br, 174tl, 208b, 240b, 267m, 286t, 307t, 307b, 308tl, 308tr, 316b, 341b, 350b; Irish Independent: 47t, 110b, 248m, 252t; Irish Labour History Society: 244tl; Irish Railway Record Society: 56m, 326b, 332t; Joe Maxwell, Max Decals Publications: 309m, 309b, 310m; Joe Scanlon: 337tl, 338br; John Kirby: 41t; John R. Bowen: 318br; John Ward-McQuaid: 335tl; Joseph McGarrity Collection, Digital library@ Vilanova University: 20b, 24t, 53m, 109t, 110t, 111t, 119b, 134b; Kerry Library Archives: 282t; Kilmainham Gaol Museum: 32t, 33t, 64bl, 64br, 99b, 101bl, 122br, 125b, 167t, 169tl, 182t, 191b, 227tl, 227tr, 241m, 245b, 268b, 271b, 278b, 279t, 279b, 287b, 293b, 341mm, 341mr, 350tr; Las Fallon: 107b, 298b; Library of Congress, Washington DC: 18b, 20tl, 21m, 22t, 23t, 23b, 31b, 37b, 60b, 73br, 107t, 172b, 178b, 266b; Limerick City Archives (courtesy of George Imbusch collection): 304-305t; Mark Humphrys: 138b; Marsh's Library: 113b; Mercier Press and Dún Laoghaire-Rathdown Libraries: 294t, 295b, 299b; Michael Curran: 147m; Michael Fewer: 231b, 272br, 288b, 358m; Michael O'Connor 'Scarteen': 312t; Michael O'Donohoe Memorial Heritage Project (Janet Murphy): 347b; Mick O'Farrell: 94t; Mick O'Dea: 157t, 218t, 225t, 226t; Military Archives, Cathal Brugha Barracks: 25m, 27b, 35b, 38t, 46t, 51t, 51bl, 70t, 71b, 73t, 75tl, 77m, 143b, 83m, 83b, 88, 89b, 90b, 105bl, 106m, 118t, 118b, 120, 126tr, 127t, 131t, 132m, 132b, 135b, 136t, 142t, 142b, 143, 150t, 151bl, 163b, 175b, 179t, 180m, 181b, 183t, 182t, 189b, 193t, 196t, 197t, 203m, 221t, 221b, 228t, 228b, 232t, 237t, 247b, 251t, 280b, 285bl, 310t, 324t, 325t, 326t, 332b, 344mt, 344mb, 354b, 356tr, 359t; Military Museum, Collins Barracks, Cork: 146t; Military Museum, The Curragh: 62b, 242m, 242b; Moss Hannon: 353br; Mulcahy family: 21t, 57b, 79tl, 124t, 344b; Museum of Technology, Lincolnshire: 243m; National Archives of Ireland: 257, 272bl, 289bl, 351b; National Library of Ireland: 17t, 22b, 25tl, 25b, 26t, 28t, 31t, 34t, 37t, 38b, 41b, 42t, 48b, 53b, 54t, 58b, 59t, 62t, 69t, 70b, 78br, 86-87, 91b, 92, 92t, 98t, 98b, 100t, 123b, 125t, 128b, 132t, 135t, 167b, 171m, 173b, 179b 180b, 187b, 188b, 194b, 195b, 196bm, 199b, 200t, 230t, 249b, 251b, 262b, 264b, 264t, 266t, 269b, 270b, 273m, 282b, 287t, 291m, 292b, 304b, 305b, 306b, 308b, 310b, 316b, 317b, 323b, 324b, 330t, 330, 333t, 333b, 334b, 337tr, 339b, 340t, 342t, 348t, 354, 356bl; National Maritime Museum: 39t, 52t; National Monuments Service, Department of Culture, Heritage, and the Gaeltacht: 223t, 223b; National Museum of Ireland: 26b, 84t, 95b, 152t, 155b, 181t, 204t, 225m, 238b, 241b, 243b, 267b; National Portrait Gallery, London: 277b; National Print Museum, Dublin: 48t; New York Public Library: 105br; Osprey Publishing (illustrations by Peter Dennis): 50, 74t, 85b; Ó Dúlacháin Collection (colourised by John O'Byrne): 40b; Patrick Comerford: 205b (inset plaque); Paul/PJM_warrelics.eu: 40b; Pearse Lawlor: 166b; Pearse Museum/OPW Rathfarnham: 33b, 35t, 36b; Peadar Collins: 330m, 330b; Peter Rigney: 83t; Police Museum, Belfast: 159t; Ray Bateson: 104tl; Rifles (Berkshire & Wiltshire) Museum: 158t; Rijksmuseum, Amsterdam: 16t, 19b; Robert Ballagh: 29t; Robert Porter: 160b; Roger Wallsgrove, MMP books (illustrations by Maurizio Brescia): 311t, 311bm; Royal Hampshire Regiment Museum: 224t, 224b; Séamus Ó Maitiú: 58t; South Dublin Libraries: 27t, 30b, 42t, 49b, 64bm, 73bl, 76t, 94, 108br, 121b, 129t, 136b, 209t, 209m, 222b, 245tl, 246t, 278t, 345b; Swedish Military Museum: 242t; The Honourable Society of King's Inns: 114t; Tommy Mooney: 239b, 356br; UCD Archives: 136m, 137t; Ulster Museum: 15b; Veronica Barry: 11, 43, 102t, 115, 197bl, 233, 249; www.buildingsofireland.ie, National Inventory of Architectural Heritage: 342bl; www.irishconstabulary.com: 147t, 153b, 243tr; www.irishpapermoney.com: 137b, 181m; www.thewildgeese.com: 121t; www.thehistorybunker.co.uk: 159b; www.irishvolunteers.org: 197bl, 213br.

Wikimedia Commons: 24(309) British Library, 133b; A. & R. Annan & Sons, 128t; Am1ki_National Gallery of Ireland, 14t; Andrew Parnell_Trim Castle, 14b; Askild Antonsen_Luger, 242m; Bhalalash/Kanchelskis, 213t; Btm0330, 213bl; Dronepicr, 66t; Family Archives, 341ml; www.fionnbarcallanan.com/archive-McGuinness, 216t; Henry Doyle_Project Gutenberg, 20tr; Kate-Mulkern, 79r; Keogh Brothers, 196ml; Leitrim Observer, 32b; Magpie66, 248b; MrPenguin2, 157mr; PD-USGov-Military-Navy, 21b; QS:P571_British Library, 17br; Rama_www.archive.org/de, 243tl; Robert Emmett_National Gallery of Ireland, 18t; Stephen Gwynn, 25tr; www.thewildgeese.com/Kilmainham Gaol Museum, 196mr; William Orpen_NPG, 284t; www.cairogang.com, 171bl.

Colourised: copyright John O'Byrne and Michael B Barry © 2020, adapted from original work with their respective copyrights — An Post: 113t; Angus Mitchell: 217t; Author's collection: 281t; *Bibliothèque nationale de France*: 155t, 162t, 191t; Bob Porter: 218b; Cork Public Museum: 141t, 206b; Diarmuid O'Connor: 288t, 339tr; George Morrison: 299t, 313t, 315t, 328t, 339tl, 343t, 316t; Iarnród Éireann: 327b, 327t; Imperial War Museum: 189t, 202t, 207t, 212t, 212b, 226b, 237b; Irish Capuchin Provincial Archives, Dublin: 75b, 139b, 148t, 174tl; Irish Independent: 93b, 138t, 276t; John Sweeney Archives (James Doyle) www.duckettsgrove.ie: 238t; Kilmainham Gaol: 26t, 55t, 85t, 89t, 211b, 219br, 277t, 341t; Library of Congress: 28b, 108t; Limerick City Archives: 302b, 302-303t; www.mediaworldhub.com: 297b; Mercier Press and Dún Laoghaire-Rathdown Libraries: 297t, 298t; Military Archives, Cathal Brugha Barracks: 123t, 127b, 245t, 253t, 280t, 290t, 309t, 319m, 319b, 356tl; National Library of Ireland: 24b, 98t, 130b, 134t, 126b, 144t, 194t, 215b, 222t, 249t, 263b, 265b, 270t, 272t, 273t, 274t, 274b, 284b, 289t, 293t, 295t, 301, 306t, 317t, 318t, 318bl, 320t, 320b, 334t, 345t, 351t, 357t, 357b, 188t; National Museum of Ireland: 30t, 175t, 195t, 205t, 229b, 241t; Old Photos of Cork: 227b; Pearse Museum/OPW Rathfarnham: 36t; Paul/PJM_warrelics.eu: 40t; Royal Fusiliers: 208t; South Dublin Libraries: 75t, 154t, 160t, 229t, 236t, 285t, 292t; UCD Archives: 140t, 276b, 303b, 344t.

Colourised: copyright Tom Marshall, PhotograFix © 2020, adapted from original work with their respective copyrights — Military Archives, Cathal Brugha Barracks: 104tr; Mulcahy family: 103, 105tl, 105tr. Colourised: copyright © 2020, Adept Data Services and Michael B Barry © 2020, adapted from original work with their respective copyrights — Author's collection: 244bl, 247t, 248t; Dublin City Archives: 244tr; George Morrison: 255b; Kilmainham Gaol: 246bl; Military Archives, Cathal Brugha Barracks: 253t; National Library of Ireland: 244m, 244br; South Dublin Libraries: 164t.

All other photographs and maps not mentioned here are copyright Michael B Barry © 2020. Every effort has been made to establish copyright, but if a copyright holder wishes to bring an error or omission to the notice of the publishers, then an appropriate acknowledgement will be made in any subsequent edition.

Chronology

1916

24 April	The Easter Rising begins in Dublin. The Irish Republic is declared. On 29 April Patrick Pearse surrenders to Brigadier-General Lowe.
3–12 May	Executions of leaders of the Rising.
3 August	Sir Roger Casement is hanged.
23 December	Staged release of first internees begins with the Volunteers interned at Frongoch camp.

1917

3 February	Count Plunkett wins North Roscommon by-election.
March	National Executive of Irish Volunteers re-established.
9 May	Joseph McGuinness wins South Longford by-election.
10 July	Éamon de Valera wins East Clare by-election by a landslide.
25 July	Opening of an Irish Convention to discuss how Ireland is to be governed. Discussions end in April 1918 with no agreement.
10 August	WT Cosgrave wins Kilkenny by-election.
25 September	Death of Thomas Ashe in Mountjoy Gaol after a hunger strike. It is followed by a huge funeral procession in Dublin.
25 October	Éamon de Valera is elected President at the Sinn Féin annual convention.

1918

4 January	Two soldiers from Donegal, arrested for desertion, are rescued by Irish Volunteers.
March	The GHQ of the Irish Volunteers is established; Richard Mulcahy is Chief of Staff; Michael Collins is Adjutant-General.
17 March	Volunteers raid the RIC barracks at Eyeries, Co. Cork and seize rifles.
16 April	There is universal opposition to conscription proposed for Ireland. Two million people sign a national pledge against conscription.
11 May	Lord French, appointed as Lord Lieutenant, arrives in Dublin.
17 May	Sinn Féin leaders are rounded up as part of a supposed 'German Plot'.
11 November	An Armistice is signed. WWI hostilities cease.
14 December	In the General Election, in Ireland, Sinn Féin win 73 seats; Unionists 26 and the previously dominant Irish Parliamentary Party, 6.

1919

21 January	The first meeting of Dáil Éireann is held at the Mansion House in Dublin. The same day an ambush at Soloheadbeg results in the shooting dead of two RIC constables.
3 February	De Valera and two others escape from Lincoln Gaol.
6 April	An attempt to free a prisoner from a prison hospital in Limerick results in an RIC man and the prisoner being killed. The Limerick 'Soviet' (workers council) calls a general strike on 13 April, in protest against military restrictions.
13 May	Seán Hogan is rescued from a train at Knocklong, Co. Limerick: two RIC men are killed.
11 June	De Valera arrives in the USA intending to marshal support for Irish independence.
July	Michael Collins, now IRA Director of Intelligence, forms a 'Squad' to carry out preemptive assassinations.
30 July	Detective-Sergeant Smyth is mortally wounded in Drumcondra by the 'Squad'. Detective Hoey is shot dead on 12 September.
7 September	An IRA unit led by Liam Lynch attacks a military party at the Wesleyan Chapel in Fermoy. The military loot the town.
Autumn	Isolated RIC barracks in the south and west are evacuated. The larger barracks are transformed into bastions.
October	A British Cabinet committee is established to draft a new Home Rule Bill. In December a 'Government of Ireland' bill is introduced in the House of Commons, with provision for northern and southern parliaments.
November	Approval is given to reinforce the RIC with ex-servicemen recruited in Britain.
26 November	Dublin Castle proscribes Sinn Féin and associated organisations.
19 December	There is an attempt to assassinate Lord French near Ashtown railway station. Volunteer Martin Savage is killed in the ensuing gunfight.

1920

3 January	Carrigtwohill RIC Barracks are attacked. This is followed by a wave of attacks on barracks across the country.
15 January	In local elections, Sinn Féin (and supporters) gain control of 172 out of 206 borough and urban districts.
21 January	Assistant-Commisioner Forbes Redmond, sent to reorganise the 'G' Division of the DMP, is shot dead at Harcourt Street, Dublin.
20 March	Tomás Mac Curtain, Lord Mayor of Cork, is assassinated in his home at Blackpool by men with blackened faces.
26 March	Alan Bell, successfully investigating Sinn Féin finances, is shot dead in Ballsbridge.
early April	The IRA burn 180 barracks recently abandoned by the RIC.
5 April	Republicans arrested in mass round-ups in January go on hunger strike In a confused move, the authorities release the prisoners.
April	A review of the Irish administration leads to a shake-up: Sir Hamar Greenwood is appointed Chief Secretary in early April.
May	The 'Munitions Crisis' starts as railway workers refuse to transport soldiers and equipment. It continues until December.
28 May	A large attack is made on Kilmallock RIC Barracks. Two RIC men and one Volunteer are killed.
June	Courts are authorised by the Dáil and become established all over Ireland.
26 June	Brigadier-General Lucas is captured near Fermoy by the IRA. He escapes weeks later.

May	Ex-officers are recruited and trained for the Auxiliary Division of the RIC and in the months that follow are deployed across Ireland.
17 July	Lieutenant-Colonel Gerald Smyth is shot in Cork. This followed the RIC mutiny at Listowel on 19 June 1920, where Smyth told the constables that no policeman would get into trouble for shooting any man.
12 August	Terence MacSwiney, Lord Mayor of Cork, is arrested and begins a hunger strike. He dies 74 days later in Brixton Gaol.
20 September	Volunteer Kevin Barry is arrested at an ambush. He is court-martialled and sentenced to hang. On 1 November Barry is executed.
20 September	Balbriggan is sacked and burned by Crown forces. Two Volunteers are arrested, bayonetted and their bodies dumped.
22 September	An RIC patrol is ambushed at Rineen, Co. Clare. Five RIC men are killed. Brutal reprisals ensue in Ennistymon, Milltown Malbay and Lahinch.
28 September	Volunteers capture the military barracks at Mallow and seize weapons. The following night Mallow is torched by Crown forces.
October	Reprisals at Listowel, Tralee, Tubbercurry, Tuam and other towns.
17 November	Killing of an RIC sergeant in Cork city. It results in a wave of 'tit-for-tat' killings.
18 November	Sir Hamar Greenwood, in the House of Commons, alleges that the IRA were considering spreading typhoid among British troops.
21 November ('Bloody Sunday')	The IRA assassinate suspected British spies across Dublin. Later Crown forces fire on a crowd at a football match at Croke Park. Three prisoners are murdered in Dublin Castle that evening. There was a massive roundup of Republicans in the following weeks.
28 November	Ambush at Kilmichael, Co. Cork, where 17 Auxiliaries are killed, with three IRA dead.
11 December	Cork city centre is burned and looted.
23 December	The 'Government of Ireland' Bill comes into force.
27 December	Martial law is proclaimed in Cos. Cork, Tipperary, Kerry and Limerick – later extended to Clare, Waterford, Kilkenny and Wexford.
29 December	The first official reprisal occurs in Midleton after an ambush. Other official reprisals soon follow.

1921

28 January	An ambush laid at Dripsey, Co. Cork is foiled. Two Volunteers die and eight are captured. Mrs Mary Lindsay, who had informed, was later killed (with her chauffeur) after five of the Dripsey prisoners are executed.
3 February	An attack on RIC men in tenders at Dromkeen, Co. Limerick, results in eleven RIC dead.
15 February	An attack on a train carrying troops at Upton, Co. Cork, results in eight civilian and three IRA deaths.
20 February	At Clonmult, Co. Cork, a house where the IRA are billeted is surrounded. Twelve Volunteers are killed.
7 March	The Mayor of Limerick and his predecessor are shot dead at their homes by men in civilian dress.
11 March	Crown forces attack an IRA training camp at Selton Hill, Co. Leitrim. Seán Connolly and five other Volunteers are killed.
14 March	Six Volunteers are hanged in Mountjoy Gaol. Three more are hanged over the following months.
19 March	A large British sweep at Crossbarry is resisted by the IRA under Tom Barry. Ten British soldiers and four IRA men are killed.
21 March	The IRA mount an ambush at Headford Junction, Co. Kerry. Eight British soldiers, two civilians and two IRA men are killed.
11 April	Attack on 'Q' Company base at the Railway Hotel, North Wall, Dublin. One Volunteer is killed.
23 April	The RIC encircle a farm near Clogheen, Co. Cork. Six Volunteers are shot dead.
3 May	The IRA ambushes the RIC at Tourmakeady, Co. Mayo, resulting in four RIC dead. As British troops make a sweep over the Partry Mountains, the IRA Adjutant is killed in an exchange of fire.
14 May	The IRA hijack an armoured car in a daring but failed attempt to rescue Seán Mac Eoin from Mountjoy Gaol.
15 May	The local IRA lay an ambush and shoot Detective Inspector Biggs and Winifrid Barrington at Coolboreen, near Newport, Co. Tipperary.
24 May	Elections are held under the 'Government of Ireland Act'. Unionists win 40 of the 52 seats for the 'Northern Ireland' Parliament. No polling takes place for the 'Southern Ireland' Parliament – all candidates are returned unopposed. Sinn Féin win 124 of the 128 seats.
25 May	The IRA seize the Custom House in Dublin, which is burnt, as planned. Four Volunteers as well as four civilians are killed.
31 May	A mine explodes as the band of the 2nd Battalion Royal Hampshires march at Youghal. Seven bandsmen are killed.
2 June	At Carrowkennedy, Co. Mayo, eight RIC men (including a District Inspector) are killed in an ambush.
22 June	King George V makes a conciliatory speech at the opening of the Northern Ireland Parliament
24 June	A troop train (carrying Hussars and horses) is derailed at Adavoyle, Co. Armagh. Three soldiers and many horses are killed.
4 July	Discussions begin at the Mansion House, Dublin, between Éamon de Valera and southern Unionists on a call by Lloyd George for talks in London. Another meeting is held with General Macready on 8 July. Terms for a truce are agreed.
10 July	On the eve of the Truce, an ambush at Castleisland, Co. Kerry, leaves four British soldiers and three Volunteers dead.
11 July	A Truce comes into force. Under its terms, the British were to end manoeuvres, raids and searches. The IRA were to cease attacks on Crown forces.
12 July	De Valera and a delegation arrive in London. He later meets with Lloyd George. There is little meeting of minds.
11 October	Irish plenipotentiaries arrive at Downing Street and weeks of negotiations ensue.
6 December	The plenipotentiaries, under severe pressure to sign the Treaty or face renewed war, fail to consult Dublin and sign the document. There is limited freedom, but no Republic.

1922

3 January	Dáil Éireann meets and resumes the Treaty debate. On 7 January it approves the Treaty.
10 January	De Valera and other supporters leave Dáil Éireann. Arthur Griffith elected as its President.
14 January	Parliament of 'Southern Ireland' meets and sets up Provisional Government.
31 January	New Provisional Government army sets up HQ at Beggar's Bush Barracks.

26 March	An IRA Convention at the Mansion House repudiates the Treaty and appoints an Executive.
14 April	Takeover of the Four Courts, in the early hours, by anti-Treaty forces.
20 May	De Valera and Collins announce a pact for an election planned for June.
5 June	British forces shell Provisional Government army positions in Pettigo, Co. Donegal.
14 June	Collins, at an election meeting in Cork, repudiates the election pact.
16 June	Election in 26 Counties. Results are: 58 pro-Treaty seats; 36 anti-Treaty; 34, Labour and others.
22 June	Sir Henry Wilson assassinated in London.
26 June	JJ O'Connell, Deputy Chief of Staff, Provisional Government Army, is kidnapped and held at the Four Courts.
28 June	The Four Courts garrison issued with a demand to surrender at 3:40 am. Artillery bombardment starts shortly afterwards.
29 June	Following continuous shelling, pro-Treaty troops storm the Four Courts. On 30 June there is a large explosion. The Garrison surrenders.
30 June	Fighting intensifies around the 'Block' in Upper Sackville Street. After days of fighting, the 'Block' is in ruins.
6 July	Republican forces assemble in Blessington, but disperse several days later on the approach of large numbers of pro-Treaty forces.
11 July	Clashes begin in Limerick. By 20 July Anti-Treaty forces withdraw after their barracks are shelled.
12 July	A 'War Council' of three is created by Michael Collins.
24 July	Provisional Government forces land at Westport.
2 August	Pro-Treaty troops land at Fenit and take Tralee.
8 August	The Provisional Government Army under General Dalton lands at Passage West. Cork City is captured days later.
12 August	Arthur Griffith dies of a cerebral haemorrhage.
22 August	Michael Collins, on tour of West Cork, is ambushed and shot dead at Bealnablath.
25 August	WT Cosgrave is appointed Chairman of the Provisional Government.
16 September	Seven pro-Treaty soldiers (including Colonel-Commandant Tom Keogh) are killed by a trap mine near Macroom.
20 September	Pro-Treaty troops mount a sweep through the Sligo area. Six Republicans are captured and shot dead on Benbulben.
10 October	The Roman Catholic Bishops issue a pastoral condemning the anti-Treaty side.
15 October	The Public Safety Act comes into effect. It includes powers for military courts to issue death sentences.
10 November	Erskine Childers is arrested at Annamoe, Co. Wicklow and charged with possession of a revolver.
24 November	Childers, sentenced by a military court, is executed at Beggar's Bush Barracks, Dublin.
30 November	Liam Lynch, the IRA Chief of Staff, issues a general order to assassinate those who approved the Public Safety Act.
6 December	The Irish Free State comes into being.
8 December	Four Republican prisoners (O'Connor, Mellows, McKelvey, and Barrett) are executed in Mountjoy Gaol as a reprisal for the killing of Seán Hales the previous day.

1923

13 January	WT Cosgrave's house in Rathfarnham is burnt down. In later months similar action is taken against pro-Treaty supporters.
9 February	After being captured in January, Liam Deasy, Officer Commanding First Southern Division, IRA, issues a call to his comrades for immediate and unconditional surrender.
11 February	Thomas O'Higgins (father of the Minister of Justice, Kevin) is shot dead during an attack to set his house on fire.
18 February	The IRA leader, Dennis Lacy, is shot in action at the Glen of Aherlow, Co. Tipperary.
6 March	Six National Army soldiers are killed at Knocknagoshel Co. Kerry after being lured to a trap mine.
7 March	Nine Republican prisoners are brought to Ballyseedy, near Tralee, tied together and blown up by a mine. Eight die, one escapes.
26 March	A meeting of the IRA Executive in the Nire Valley, Co. Waterford votes narrowly in favour of continuing the war.
10 April	Liam Lynch, fleeing from Free State troops in the Knockmealdown Mountains, is mortally wounded.
16 April	Siege of Republicans begins at Clashmealcon Caves, North Kerry.
24 May	Frank Aiken, the new IRA Chief of Staff, issues orders to cease fire and to dump arms.
20 July	The Free State Government requests the British to set up a Boundary Commission.
15 August	De Valera is arrested in Ennis while attending a Sinn Féin meeting for the General Election announced for later in August.
27 August	In the General Election, anti-Treaty Sinn Féin win 44 seats; pro-Treaty Cumann na nGaedheal, 63; Labour and others, 46.
13 October	A six-week mass hunger strike by Republican prisoners ends. Prisoner releases follow, up to mid-1924.

Introduction

It was a mere seven year period, 1916 to 1923. However, these years constitute the elemental founding stage of the Irish State. It started abruptly, at Easter 1916, when advanced nationalists rose up and proclaimed an Irish Republic. The War of Independence that followed was the infinitely more difficult and bitter undertaking of trying to secure that Republic, to wrest independence from what was still the most powerful empire in the World. When that empire was finally forced to negotiate, it would grant only a flawed form of independence, not a Republic. This led to an even more bitter struggle between the pragmatists and the idealists of Irish independence. It has taken a journey approaching a century for the 26-county Irish State to find its mature place as a Republic amongst the world's nations.

I have now spent around a decade researching this period while writing my trilogy which covered, respectively, Easter 1916, the War of Independence and the Civil War. Things have moved on over that time. With the advent of the so-called 'Decade of Centenaries', new research has emerged. So with some additional information and a wealth of new images, I decided that it was worthwhile to draw together the historical strands of this formative era into one illustrated volume.

In the years leading up to 1916, and grasping the opportunity of a Britain sunk in the morass of war, Republican leaders developed a coherent strategy and plan. On Easter Monday 1916, they mobilised their forces and seized strategic positions across Dublin. However, they did not have enough men. Small numbers held off large bodies of British troops. Without the disaster of the failed arms landing and particularly the confusion of the countermanding order, they would have had a much fuller complement in Dublin. Nevertheless, the British would have eventually prevailed. Only the events at Ashbourne demonstrated the effectiveness of the 'flying column' tactic, a harbinger of what was to come.

General Maxwell, unrestrained by any political control, made the colossal mistake of ordering the execution of 15 of the rebels, principally leaders. The new public sympathy led to significant support for Sinn Féin, now with 1916 veterans in the leadership. It won a majority in the 1918 general election, thus allowing these advanced nationalists to consider establishing an independent Irish parliament, Dáil Éireann.

Coincidentally, on the same day as the first Dáil met in January 1919, the ambush at Soloheadbeg resulting in two RIC deaths took place. This ambush is significant as it marked a loss of innocence, and in essence triggered the start of the War of Independence. From this point on, the struggle was countrywide and more ruthless, in contrast to the simpler narrative of the week-long, Dublin-centred Rising.

The IRA, as the Volunteers became known, were fortunate in having exceptional leaders at GHQ, such as Richard Mulcahy and Michael Collins. Collins saw clearly the overriding importance of intelligence and the need to maintain security by eliminating spies, who had dashed every previous Irish attempt at independence. Throughout the country the principle of subsidiarity applied to the IRA as an organisation: the local units decided most of their own actions, albeit within a framework of directives from GHQ in Dublin – which were sometimes ignored. Guerrilla warfare has been called the method of the weak versus the strong. Through trial and error, the IRA developed an ad hoc form of guerrilla war that proved to be particularly effective in the areas that actually saw the fighting.

As 1920 dawned, the news from Ireland got worse for the British. The RIC had come under severe assault. Thousands of ex-servicemen were recruited in Britain – the 'Black and Tans' soon arrived in Ireland. In addition, an elite paramilitary force of ex-officers, the Auxiliaries, was recruited.

There was a post-war deadline on the parliamentary front – the all-Ireland Home Rule Act, passed into law in 1914, was due to come into force. Lloyd George responded to Unionist pressure and the British Cabinet crafted a new Orange-tinted Home Rule bill which specified the partitioning of Ireland. It became law in December 1920. Thus, by an Act of the British Parliament, for the first time in history, Ireland was partitioned.

In 1921 the IRA mounted increasingly sophisticated ambushes. Reprisals marked a new low in the campaign on the part of the Crown forces. The British began to earn an international reputation for brutality. By mid-1921, oscillating between a policy of flooding Ireland with troops and instituting peace talks, the British opted for talks. The Truce was duly signed. In the months that followed, negotiations led to the Treaty of December 1921, which resulted in a limited form of independence for the 26 counties. It was this status — agreed under the Treaty — as a Dominion as opposed to a Republic, which was the principal cause of the Civil War that broke out six months later.

The seizure of the Four Courts, in the heart of Dublin, by the non-compromising wing of the IRA was a visible gesture of defiance towards the new Provisional Government, then at its most fragile. The Wilson assassination and the kidnapping of the Deputy Chief of Staff of the Provisional Government Army proved to be the tipping point, and a hastily-arranged bombardment of the Four Courts began.

On the anti-Treaty side, there had been no strategic planning in the event of conflict. In the early days the Republicans set up in containable, easily besieged, locations. Intense set-piece battles in Dublin, which favoured the pro-Treaty side with its artillery and armoured vehicles, were followed by similar actions in Limerick City and the region around it.

After landings by the Provisional Government forces in the south and west, the anti-Treaty side resorted to guerrilla encounters, coupled with attacks — disastrous for the economy — on the soft targets of railways and roads. The Free State Government responded with ruthless executions of captured Republicans to the continual sniping and trap-mine attacks on pro-Treaty troops which had resulted in a never-ending death toll. As the months progressed it was able to plan and prosecute the war in a systematic manner, using its ever-growing army. It also had the benefit of plentiful military matériel, provided by the ever-watchful Great Power across the water.

The IRA Chief of Staff, Liam Lynch, was a diligent and honourable man. Nevertheless, despite his reputation for competent command during the War of Independence, he was not able to see the big picture and give decisive command and control to the sprawling network of IRA divisions — a very difficult task. This is sharply illustrated by his failure to comprehend in early 1923 that the war was lost – and the war effectively came to an end when he was mortally wounded on a bare mountain in April 1923.

Estimates of the casualty figures of the Irish Revolution fluctuate greatly: more research is required. The 1916 Rising in Dublin was a small insurrection – estimates of the total of those killed (rebels, civilians and Crown forces) do not exceed 500. The War of Independence was bloodier. One approximation gives a figure of around 1,450 killed (comprising 261 British Army, 428 Police, including Auxiliaries, 550 IRA Volunteers and around 200 civilians). Equally bloody was the Civil War. Estimates at the lower end (probably the more reliable) are at around 1,400 deaths (350 Republicans, 730 National Army and 300 civilians).

Despite the necessary constraints of space in this book, I aimed to tell the story of such a wide range of events in a comprehensive yet nuanced way. The inclusion of a chronology and a glossary is intended to add to the comprehension. If further detail is needed, readers can check out my trilogy or source more information from the veritable mountain of books published during the Decade of Centenaries – a helpful guide on books worth consulting in the first instance has been included in the bibliography.

I have endeavoured to present the history in a rich visual manner, using old, as well as contemporary, photographs and specially created maps, sourcing old documents and periodicals from Ireland and abroad. I used some illustrations from continental magazines that depicted the Irish conflict in full colour (although in an imaginative style of derring-do, that may not be totally accurate).

The quality — and availability — of images matters when preparing a book which narrates history through illustrations. Over the seven years in question, photographic technology moved on: from the poor-quality photographs of Volunteers in the GPO, to the higher-quality ones of the Civil War, sometimes taken by photographers embedded with the National Army. Given the clandestine nature of rebellion and guerrilla warfare, there are few extant photographs of Republicans engaged in their struggle, relative to those of the authorities' armed forces.

In the course of preparing this book, I was able to source many new images. In addition I was privileged to secure the assistance of John O'Byrne, who has developed a special expertise in colourising photographs from that period. Included in the book is a selected range of impactful photographs that he has painstakingly colourised. This adds an extra dimension, which helps bring the events and figures of that era to life.

As we move towards the end of the Decade of Centenaries, many of the principal disagreements that all the protagonists fought over a century ago have long since evaporated – in the 26 counties we now have independence, in the form of a Republic, albeit not a perfect one. Nevertheless, the Irish Revolution is not over. The issue that in reality they did not fight about in the Civil War has still not been resolved: the partition of Ireland. Resolving this will take much change, both in Northern Ireland, and in the present 26-county Republic, needing maturity and wisdom in making a 32-county Ireland a fair and welcoming place for the culture and aspirations of all.

Michael B. Barry
In a time of Coronavirus, Dublin, Summer, 2020

Chapter 1
Freedom's Long Journey

The road to the Rising of 1916 was long and painful. It began in 1169 when the Normans landed in Wexford. A year later, they seized Dublin. The Normans initially settled in the prosperous eastern lowlands, an area known as the Pale, named after the fortified boundary. In the century after their invasion the Normans also seized large swathes of territory beyond the Pale. However, over time, the native Gaelic lords expanded their domains and the extent of Norman control had contracted. By 1450, the (by now) Hiberno-Norman lords controlled most of the south and the south-west. They had become hibernicised, having assimilated Gaelic language, customs and culture. Beyond, in the more remote parts of the country, were the native Gaelic lords who were organised in an intensely fragmented system. In the 1530s the English King Henry VIII developed the policy of 'Surrender and Regrant'. The concept was that a Gaelic lord would submit to the authority of the King and in return get title to his lands.

The conquest continued under the Tudors – punctuated by rebellions that were harshly suppressed, with a particularly bloody period in 1588 when Spanish survivors from wrecked Armada ships were summarily executed. The 'Flight of the Earls' in 1607 marked the end of the power of the Gaelic lords and a consolidation of English power. There was extensive confiscation of land and, in turn, the importation of colonist settlers. These early plantations across Ireland were followed by the large settlement in Ulster of Protestants from Scotland.

It was a pioneering enterprise: the practices of colonisation and plantation were first developed in Ireland, including the techniques of scorched earth and clearance as well as the mechanics and administrative procedures for settlement. With the expertise garnered using these methods, the Jacobean English were able to establish flourishing colonies in the New World over the course of the seventeenth century.

Cromwell flashed like a blood-red comet across the Irish firmament after he landed in 1649 to enforce the rule of the English Parliament against Catholic opposition. In a ruthless and sanguinary campaign he rapidly overran Irish towns and cities. More land was confiscated and additional penal laws were enacted against Catholics. In 1690, Ireland came to be at the epicentre of conflict between the kingdoms of Europe, manifested on Irish soil by the clash between King James II of England and King William III. At the Battle of the Boyne in July, William decisively won. The Franco-Jacobite army continued their fight in Ireland until they surrendered under the Treaty of Limerick of October 1691. Thousands of Irish Jacobite soldiers left for France, led by the prominent commander Patrick Sarsfield – this became known as the 'Flight of the Wild Geese'. Articles in the treaty were not honoured and more land confiscations followed, amounting to around one million acres by December 1699.

By the 1700s, Ireland, subjugated, had become a perfect colony under the British Crown: a place where the Anglo-Irish Protestant Ascendancy could peacefully enjoy their estates and attend their Parliament in Dublin. The rise in agricultural prices during the eighteenth century resulted in great wealth and allowed them to build the grand squares and townhouses of Dublin. However, Ireland was much different from the neighbouring island. It was agricultural, poorer, disaffected, and its population predominantly adhered to a religion different from the bedrock of the Crown, the Established Church. This resulted in assertive and intolerant persecution of Catholics, and, for good measure, of Dissenters.

Dissatisfaction bubbled in Ireland at England's interference in Irish affairs and also the discrimination against Catholics and Presbyterians. The United Ireland movement was founded by Protestants in Belfast in 1791. The recent French Revolution proved an inspiration for the United Irishmen, who in time, sought to end the English king's rule and establish a sovereign republic in Ireland. Wolfe Tone, leader of the

United Irishmen, went to France and met Napoleon in late 1797 to discuss an invasion of Ireland. However, each of the French expeditions to Ireland failed. In May 1798 a rebellion by the United Irishmen flared up across the eastern part of the country and was bloodily suppressed. Atrocities abounded on both sides and the death toll reached 30,000.

This bloody rising struck fear in the ruling elite and in 1800 an Act of Union was enacted to unite Ireland to Britain and its Parliament. Catholic Emancipation in 1829 unleashed a rising Catholic tide, which prompted the Dublin Castle administration to centralise its power and control. The Great Famine of 1845-49 exposed the administration's incompetence. The mixture of Providentialist ideology and laissez-faire policies contributed to widespread death by starvation and disease of the Irish masses. These deaths, combined with emigration, caused the Irish population to fall by one fifth between 1845 and 1851.

There was an unsuccessful rebellion by the Young Irelanders in 1848. It was followed by the emergence of the secret Irish Republican Brotherhood (IRB, also known as the Fenians) which sought a republic by force of arms. Strong in North America, the Fenians made an audacious attempt to invade British Canada in 1866, but failed. Riven with spies, their rising in Ireland the following year also failed. Militancy took a back seat as parliamentarianism flourished under Charles Stewart Parnell and his Irish Parliamentary Party (IPP). However, his Home Rule proposal was defeated.

At the turn of the twentieth century there was a strengthening of Irish national consciousness, both cultural and political. A third Home Rule Bill was introduced in 1912. The Unionist population, predominantly northern, could not accept the concept of even limited Home Rule. In the following year the Ulster Volunteer Force (UVF) was formed to prevent this. The Irish Volunteers were founded in response. In April 1914 the UVF imported 25,000 rifles purchased in Germany. As news of the event came through, membership of the Irish Volunteers surged. In turn, the Irish Volunteers imported a total of 1,500 old Mauser rifles the following July and August. When the Great War broke out, IPP leader John Redmond offered the services of the Volunteers. The remaining minority, now under IRB control, prepared for a rising, believing it was opportune. The IRB were steely protagonists in keeping the dream of Irish independence alive. As the British sank into the morass of war, the maxim 'England's difficulty is Ireland's opportunity' came into sharper focus. The activists of the IRB decided to go ahead with a rising. A Military Council was established to draw up plans and the Germans were requested to send help. A German arms ship was intercepted by the Royal Navy on 21 April 1916; at the same time Roger Casement was arrested after landing from a German submarine. As news of these events filtered through, Eoin MacNeill, Chief of Staff of the Irish Volunteers, countermanded the orders for a rising on Easter Sunday 1916, planned without his knowledge.

Above: one of the most popular paintings in the National Gallery of Ireland is 'The Marriage of Strongbow and Aoife' by Daniel Maclise. The centuries-long subjugation of Ireland began in 1169 when the Normans landed in Wexford. A year later, led by Richard FitzGilbert de Clare (Strongbow), they seized Dublin.

The Normans initially settled in the eastern lowlands of Ireland, an area known as the Pale, named after the fortified boundary. Left: Trim Castle, built by the Normans to defend the fertile plains of Meath.

Above: the Lord-Deputy sets out from Dublin Castle. By the 1560s, English rule only extended to parts of Ireland. The rest remained under the control of Gaelic chieftains.

The Tudors began to strengthen their control over this unruly colony. In 1588 Queen Elizabeth I feared that the retreating Spanish Armada would land and seize control in Ireland. In the event, prompt slaughter of Armada survivors eliminated that threat. English control was consolidated after the 'Flight of the Earls' in 1607 following their defeat at the Battle of Kinsale.

Right: the shipwreck of the Armada galeass, 'Girona', near the Giants Causeway.

Above: King William's victory at the Battle of the Boyne in 1690 further enhanced English control of Ireland, already well established by the seventeenth century Cromwellian settlements. During the eighteenth century high agricultural prices meant that many wealthy landowners could build townhouses in Dublin, which blossomed and became the second city of the Empire.

Left: the House of Lords in College Green, Dublin. The houses of parliament there represented the Anglo-Irish in Ireland. Meanwhile Catholics had to endure the restrictive Penal Laws.

The Society of the United Irishmen, founded in 1791, wished to free Ireland, embracing Catholic, Protestant and Dissenter. Right: Wolfe Tone, leader of the United Irishmen, depicted meeting Napoleon in late 1797 to discuss an invasion of Ireland. Each of the French expeditions to Ireland failed. Tone was captured, but cut his throat after being sentenced to death.

In May 1798 the rebellion of the United Irishmen flared up across the eastern part of the country. It was bloodily suppressed. Atrocities abounded on both sides and the death toll reached 30,000.

Below right: the 1798 battle of Vinegar Hill in Co. Wexford, where a British military force defeated around 20,000 lightly-armed rebels.

Below: coffins of the executed leaders of the rebellion, Henry and John Sheares, in a crypt of St Michan's Church, Dublin.

17

Left: Robert Emmet, born in Dublin, kept the flame of liberty alive. Only 25, he made plans for a rising in Dublin. His rebellion of July 1803 proved to be a shambles and failed to capture Dublin Castle. Emmet was captured. At his trial, after being found guilty, he ended his speech with the resonant plea: 'When my country takes her place among the nations of the earth, then, and not till then, let my epitaph be written'.

Below: retribution was vengeful and gory – a depiction of Emmet's execution by being hung, drawn and quartered.

Frightened by the rebellion, the British resolved to tighten control and campaigned for a union of the two kingdoms. The Irish Parliament was induced to vote for an Act of Union, which came into force on 1 January 1801. Irish parliamentarians now sat in London. Right: in Dublin Castle, an allegory of the union. King George III receives from a kneeling 'Peace' the olive branch and the crowns of the two kingdoms.

Below: a ribald view of the corpulent King George IV being received by the 'ultra-loyal' Lord Mayor of Dublin during his Irish visit in 1821.

SIGNAL FIRES ON THE SLIEVENAMON MOUNTAINS.
IRELAND, 1848.

The Great Famine occurred in 1845-49 when blight attacked the potato, staple diet of the Irish masses. Death by starvation and disease, along with emigration (above), resulted in the Irish population falling by one fifth between 1845 and 1851.

Above left: signal fires in Tipperary during the uprising. The Young Ireland movement attempted an insurrection in 1848. Swamped by British troops, it collapsed.

Left: Fenian engravings. The growing Irish presence in the United States resulted in New York being where the Fenian movement emerged in 1858. The Fenians believed that the British presence had to be removed by force. They grew into a sizeable organisation with branches in Ireland, North America and Britain. 'Fenian' is a term that embraced the Fenian movement and the Irish Republican Brotherhood, (IRB).

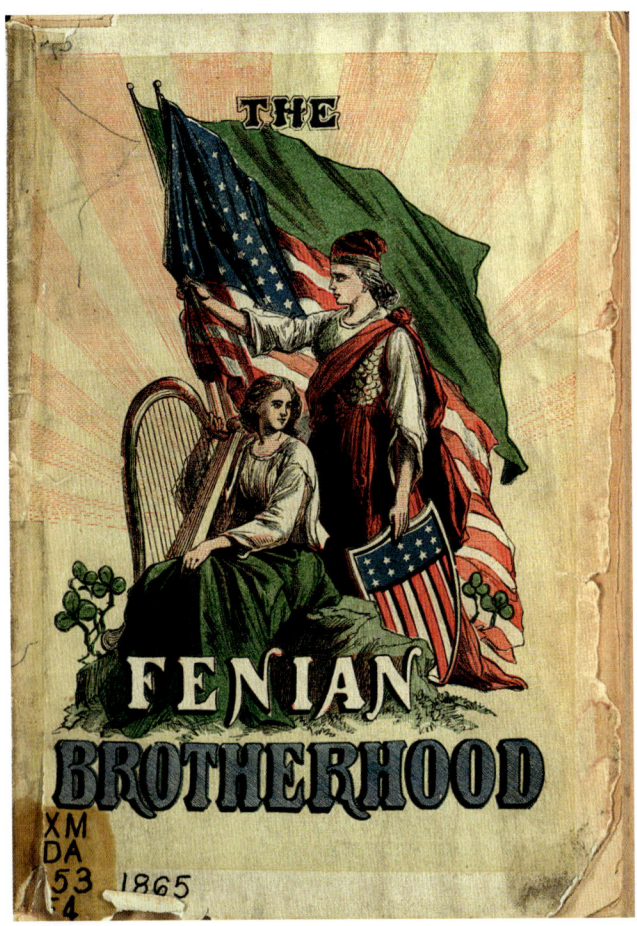

In Ireland, the Fenians rose in 1867 and were quickly suppressed. There were skirmishes across the country, as depicted in this engraving (right) of the Tipperary Flying Column, 'set up by authority to put down the rebellion'.

Below right: the Battle of Ridgeway. The Fenian movement in North America was nothing if not ambitious. After the Civil War, a Fenian army, including many experienced veterans, assembled in June 1866 near Fort Erie in British Canada, across the Niagara river from Buffalo. The intent was to temporarily seize Canada to force the British to grant independence to Ireland. The Fenian army initially put the local Canadian militia to flight, but retreated when substantial local and British forces advanced towards them.

More ambition: the Fenians funded the Irish engineer, John Holland (who later built the first submarine for the US Navy) to develop a submarine that could be used against the British. Dubbed the 'Fenian Ram' (right), it was launched at New York in 1881. Holland fell out with the Fenians and the submarine never went into service.

In mid-December 1870, the British Prime Minister William Gladstone announced a general amnesty for Fenian prisoners held in English jails. Five prominent Fenians chose to travel to America. They sailed there on the 'SS Cuba' (and they became known as the 'Cuba Five'). The US House of Representatives approved a resolution of welcome and the five received a tumultuous reception when they arrived at New York. All continued their Fenian activities in North America. Left: engraving of the five. John Devoy is on the left and Jeremiah O'Donovan Rossa is seated, second from right. The Fenians or IRB were steely protagonists in keeping the dream of Irish independence alive. The IRB provided the impetus and core planning for the rising in Dublin in 1916.

Left: a prison mugshot of John Devoy, known as the 'greatest of all the Fenians'.

Ireland chafed under the Union, and the dynamic became a political one for the rest of the nineteenth century. Right: Charles Stewart Parnell. In the 1880s he marshalled land agitation and the desire for Home Rule (where Ireland would have self-rule under the British Crown) into a formidable political force. His Irish Parliamentary Party promoted the Home Rule cause at Westminster, adroitly forming alliances there.

Below right: a cartoon in the reliably anti-Irish US magazine, 'Puck' depicts John Bull dancing to the Home Rule tune, as played by the monkey and master, Parnell. Prime Minister Gladstone drafted the first Home Rule Bill in 1886. The possibile break-up of both Union and Empire was anathema to most members of parliament and the bill was defeated. Ulster Unionism emerged as a growing force in alliance with the Conservative Party. In 1890 Parnell became embroiled in a divorce scandal and his power collapsed. In 1893, Gladstone got a second Home Rule Bill through the Commons. However, it was defeated in the Conservative-dominated Lords.

"CHANGE ABOUT"—THE MONKEY THE MASTER.

Towards the end of the nineteenth century there was a strengthening of Irish national consciousness, both cultural and political. The Gaelic Athletic Association was founded in 1884. The Gaelic League, founded in 1893, espoused restoring Gaelic, the Celtic language of Ireland.

Fianna Éireann was an Irish nationalist youth organisation. Left: Ardfheis, Mansion House, Dublin, 1913.

Below: Fianna members practising field dressing in Dublin.

Above: 'No Home Rule' – a postcard of the happy four nations.

Right: John Redmond, leader of the Irish Parliamentary Party, which held the balance of power after 1910. He induced Prime Minister Herbert Asquith to introduce a Home Rule Bill in 1912. The Unionist population, predominantly northern, could not accept the concept of even limited Home Rule.

In September 1912, around half a million Unionists assembled across Ulster to sign a covenant pledging to defeat Home Rule. *Above right: a covenant.*

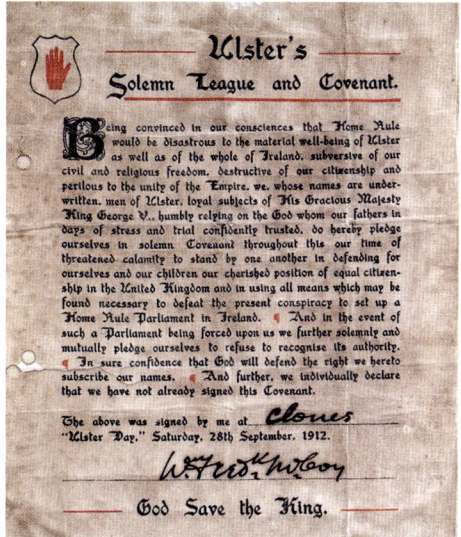

The Ulster Volunteer Force (UVF) was formally established in January 1913. It re-introduced the gun into Ireland at a time when most of nationalist Ireland was focussing on peaceful politics. Paradoxically, the loyalist militiamen were prepared to defy the laws of their Parliament.

Right: the Unionist leader Sir Edward Carson presents colours to the Central Antrim UVF.

25

Left: a humorous postcard depicting the Dublin Metropolitan Police (DMP). The caption runs 'Deeds that won the Empire, the capture of the Poles'. It refers to an incident before the King's visit in 1911. The DMP removed poles that had been erected in Grafton Street in protest against a royal visit.

Things were less jolly when, in August 1913, the DMP baton-charged striking workers in Dublin. This was during the lock-out of strikers by employers, primarily William Martin Murphy. In the aftermath the Irish Transport and General Workers' Union decided to set up a workers' militia, the Irish Citizen Army (ICA), as defence against police attacks.

Left: the ICA assemble at Croydon House in Fairview. Unlike the UVF (or later the Irish Volunteers) the ICA was not initially driven by constitutional issues but by self-defence in the struggle for workers' rights. By late 1914, James Connolly was in command of the ICA.

Left: this example of the ICA's flag, the Plough and the Stars, was flown during Easter 1916 over William Martin Murphy's Imperial Hotel in Sackville Street.

In direct response to the challenge from Ulster, Irish nationalists set up their own militia. At the inaugural meeting of the Irish Volunteers on 25 November, 1913 (poster, right), at the Rotunda Rink in Dublin, 3,000 men signed up. The stated objective was to 'secure and maintain the rights and liberties common to all the people of Ireland'. Eoin MacNeill later became Chief of Staff. The IRB secured key roles and control of the Volunteers, thus harnessing and controlling the forces of the nationalist tide.

Right: presentation of colours to the Irish Volunteers at Tralee Racecourse. By the end of 1913, national membership amounted to 10,000 and numbers kept expanding into 1914.

There was sensation on 25 April 1914. In a well-planned night-time operation, the UVF imported – principally through Larne (left) – 25,000 rifles purchased in Germany. As news of the event came through, membership of the Irish Volunteers surged, reaching 130,000 by May.

Below: a Colt Browning machine gun is reverentially paraded at a UVF rally.

Anglo-Irish nationalist sympathisers met in London to plan the import of arms for the Irish Volunteers. A tug brought 1,500 old Mauser rifles and ammunition from Hamburg to a rendezvous off the Belgian Coast. On 12 July 1914 the arms were transshipped to yachts: Erskine Childers' 28-ton 'Asgard' and Conor O'Brien's 20-ton 'Kelpie'.

Right: Robert Ballagh's depiction of Molly Childers and Mary Spring Rice with rifles and ammunition on board the 'Asgard'.

Right: the 'Asgard' on display at the National Museum of Ireland.

On 26 July 1914, the 'Asgard' sailed into Howth Harbour. The Volunteers and Fianna Éireann were there to receive the weapons – 900 rifles and 26 boxes, each with 1,000 rounds of ammunition were off-loaded. A further 600 rifles and ammunition were taken off another yacht and landed on Kilcoole beach in Co. Wicklow early on the morning of 2 August.

Above: the Mausers were off-loaded near the lighthouse on the south pier at Howth.

Left: Fianna Éireann members on the quayside help off-load weapons from the 'Asgard'.

Left: the weapons consignment at Howth was quickly spirited away. The King's Own Scottish Borderers and the DMP attempted an interception at Clontarf but the Volunteers managed to escape with their guns. After marching back, the British troops fired on a crowd, that was jeering them, at Bachelor's Walk. Three civilians were killed.

On 4 August 1914 Britain and Germany went to war. Leader of the IPP, John Redmond, stated that the Volunteers should fight for the British (Redmond allowed this poster to be issued, right). The underlying assumption was that the British would honour their promise to implement Home Rule. The Irish Volunteers split. A majority followed Redmond's advice. A minority, about 12,000, remained, and continued under the designation 'Irish Volunteers'.

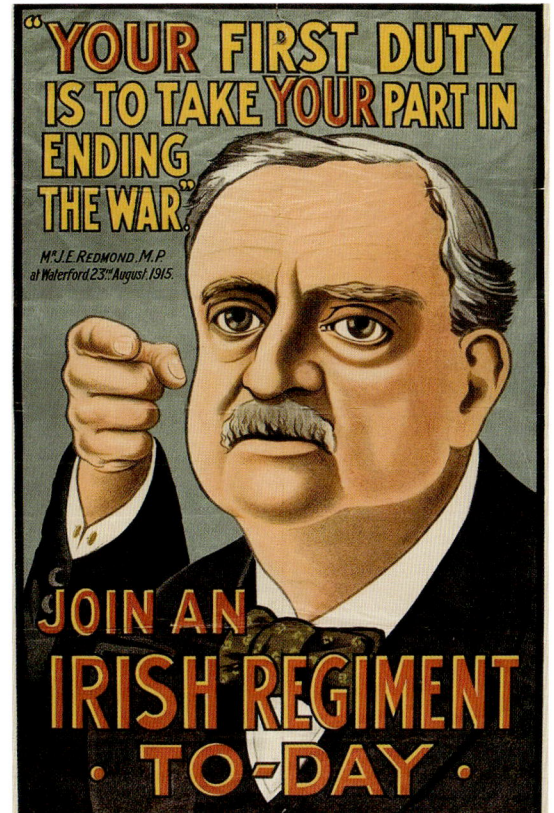

The British authorities published an array of clever and emotive posters encouraging Irishmen to enlist in the British forces (example, right).

Left: Thomas Clarke, in front of his shop at the corner of Parnell Street and Upper Sackville Street. Clarke had been active in the Fenian dynamite campaign in Britain and spent 15 years in British gaols. After a time working for Clan na Gael in the USA he returned to Dublin in 1907. Although of a different generation, he had a youthful demeanour and was full of enthusiasm. He proved inspirational to the younger members of the IRB.

The IRB kept the dream of Irish independence alive. They had gained new wind and a mix of new and seasoned adherents combined to propel advanced nationalist Ireland towards insurrection.

Left: Leitrim-born Seán MacDermott was national organiser for the IRB and protégé of Clarke. He brought a youthful dynamism to the planning and organisation for a rising. Both he and Clarke were executed in May 1916.

Right: Patrick Pearse, although he came late to militarism, became one of the most important protagonists in the run-up to the 1916 Rising.

On occasion, Pearse's prolific writings verged on the mystic. Belying his gentle and introverted manner, he wrote about the sanctifying power of bloodshed in the struggle for Ireland's freedom. Pearse made the transformation from the metaphysical to the practical. By December 1914 he was made Director of Military Organisation of the Irish Volunteers.

Right. Patrick's English-born father, James, ran a successful stone-carving business here at 27 Great Brunswick (now appropriately renamed as Pearse) Street.

An Claiḋeaṁ Soluis

[An Claidheamh Soluis.]
agus Fáinne an Lae.

[Registered as a Newspaper.]

Leabhar V. Uimhir 14.
Vol. V. No. 14

Baile Átha Cliath, Meitheamh 13, 1903.
Dublin, June 13, 1903

Pingin.
One Penny.

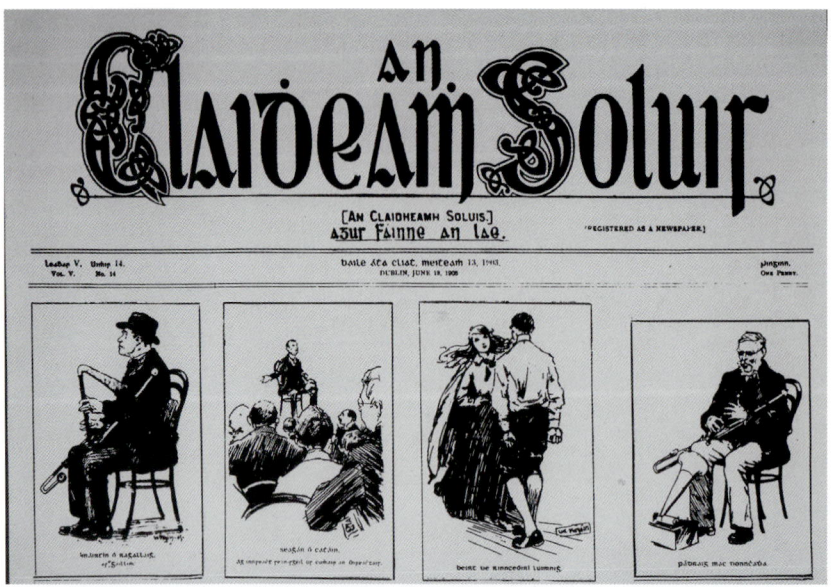

Patrick Pearse edited the Gaelic League's journal 'An Claidheamh Soluis' (left) from 1903. He later produced a series of books in Irish. Spending time in Connemara, he bonded with the people there and their language.

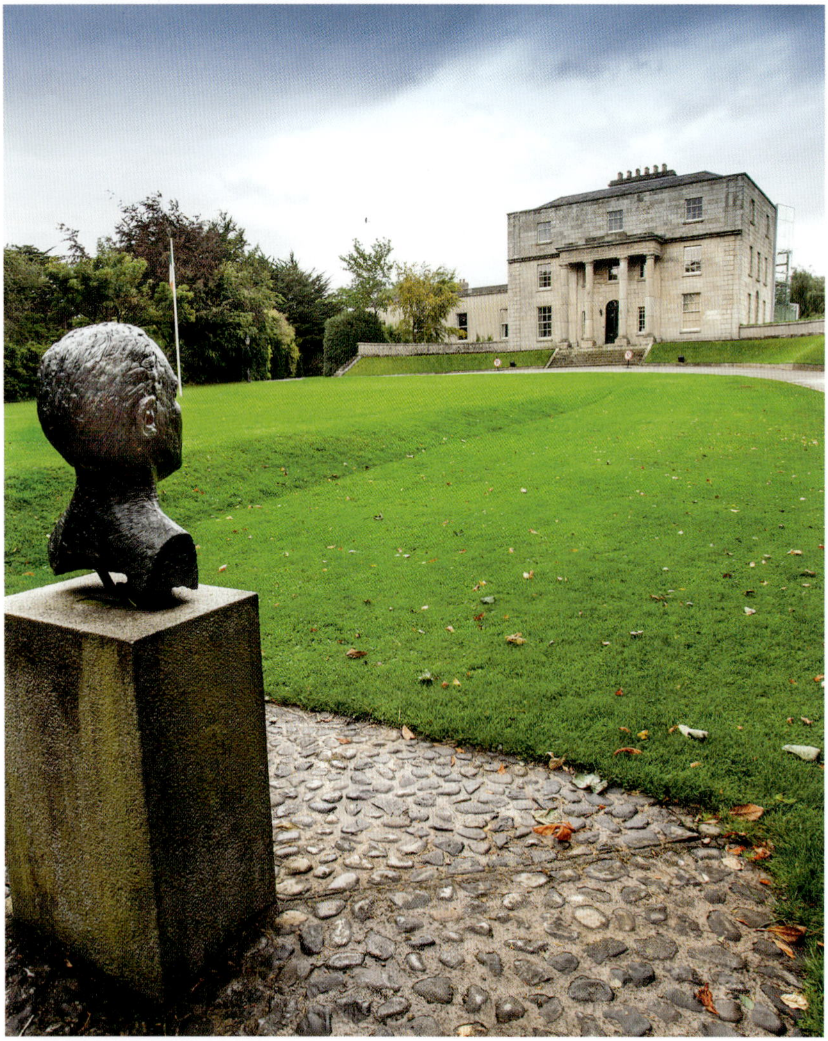

To provide a distinctly Irish and bilingual education, Pearse founded St Enda's School in 1908, initially in Ranelagh. In 1910 it moved to the more spacious 'Hermitage' in the southern Dublin village of Rathfarnham. This Georgian mansion (left) is situated in 50 landscaped acres, with streams and rocky outcrops. Fascinated by Robert Emmet and his rebellion, he named, in the grounds, a path 'Emmet's Walk' and a lodge 'Emmet's Fort'.

Right: Patrick Pearse's younger brother, William. He also threw his energies into the Irish Volunteers and the cause of Irish freedom. A talented sculptor and very involved in the arts and theatre, he helped run St Enda's School.

Right: a postcard of a group at an annual Christmas fair promoting Irish goods in 1909. Seán MacDermott is standing at the left. Veteran nationalist and journalist, Arthur Griffith, is seated on the right. His Sinn Féin movement played no direct part in the Volunteers, or indeed the later rising, yet the authorities dubbed them all 'Sinn Féiners'.

Left: 'A' Company of the 4th Battalion, Dublin Brigade, Irish Volunteers at Larkfield, in Kimmage, in September 1915. The Volunteers carried out much training and large exercises during 1915.

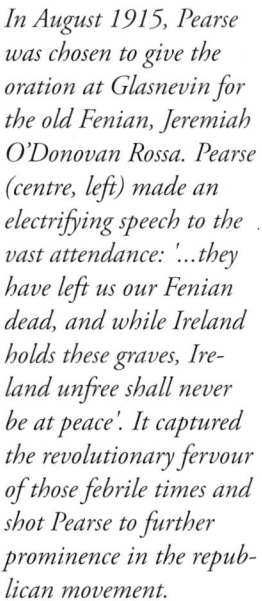

As the British sank into the morass of war, the maxim 'England's difficulty is Ireland's opportunity' came into sharper focus. Now was the time and the activists of the IRB decided to go ahead with a rising. A Military Council was established to draw up plans and secure arms. The council had essential ingredients including Tom Clarke's gravitas, Seán MacDermott's dedication and Pearse's inspirational energy.

In August 1915, Pearse was chosen to give the oration at Glasnevin for the old Fenian, Jeremiah O'Donovan Rossa. Pearse (centre, left) made an electrifying speech to the vast attendance: '...they have left us our Fenian dead, and while Ireland holds these graves, Ireland unfree shall never be at peace'. It captured the revolutionary fervour of those febrile times and shot Pearse to further prominence in the republican movement.

Right: Sir Roger Casement who was born in 1864, near Dublin. In his time in the Belgian Congo he brought to light the atrocities being perpetrated there. He served in Brazil in the British consular service, where he campaigned against the oppression of rubber workers – for which he received a knighthood in 1911. He joined the Gaelic League in 1904 and increasingly embraced the cause of Irishness and freedom. Casement helped finance the Howth gun-running. In mid-1914, he met with German diplomats in New York to seek support for an Irish rising and travelled to Germany in October that year.

The Germans were ready to stir unrest in Britain's backyard. They allowed Casement to recruit Irish prisoners of war to join an 'Irish Brigade' to fight for Irish independence, but only a handful joined up.
Right: members of the brigade at their camp at Limburg, in their specially designed uniforms. Sergeant Daniel Bailey is fourth from the left, beside a German interpreter. He later travelled to Ireland with Casement.

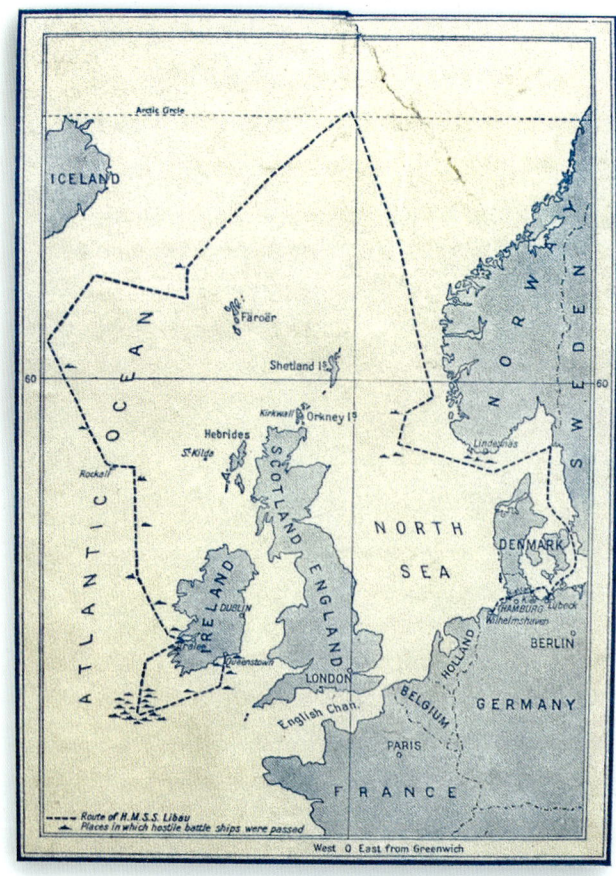

Poet, nationalist and IRB member, Joseph Plunkett (left) travelled to Germany, where he and Casement requested weapons and troops. The Germans, unenthusiastic about sending troops, agreed to dispatch weapons. The coordination (such as it was) moved to America. In March 1916 the veteran Fenian John Devoy informed the Germans of the date of the rebellion.

The German Admiralty arranged for a steamer to be fitted out in Norwegian colours and renamed the 'Aud'. On board were 20,000 Russian Moisin Nagant rifles, captured after the battle of Tannenburg in 1914. It set out for Fenit, near Tralee, to arrive on the eve of the planned rising.

On 20 April, the 'Aud' reached Tralee Bay as scheduled. It moored just off Inishtooskert and gave its pre-arranged green signal. No signal light came from shore. The ship had no wireless and, unknown to the captain, the date had been changed via a message in New York. There was no local Volunteer lookout.

Left: the long looping voyage, touching the Arctic Circle, of the 'Aud', from Germany to Ireland.

The 'Aud' headed southwest. It was intercepted late on 21 April by Royal Navy warships and escorted towards Queenstown (now Cobh).

On reaching the approaches to Cork Harbour, at around 9:30 am on 22 April 1916, the captain raised the German colours and scuttled the 'Aud', (sketch, right).

Right: the Imperial naval ensign of the 'Aud', now in the Imperial War Museum in London. Naval divers salvaged this soon after the ship sank.

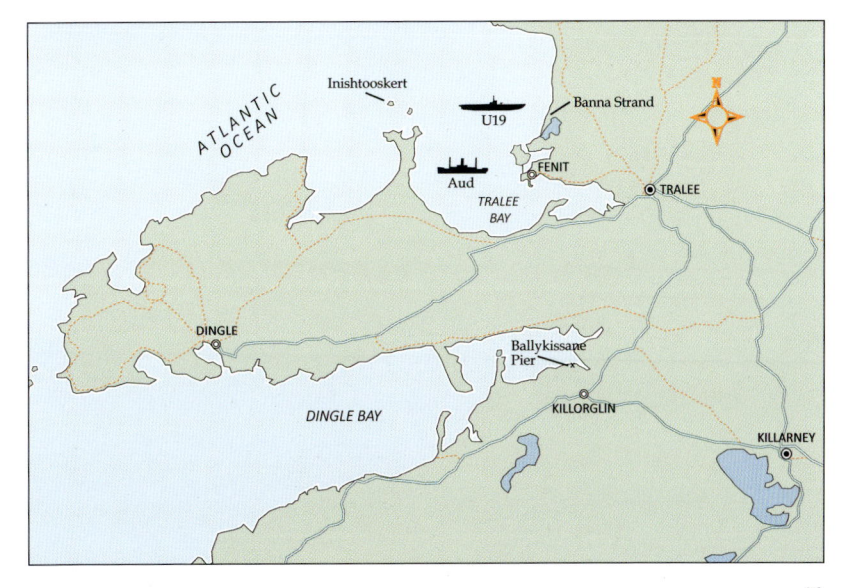

Right: multiple failures – map showing the location of the 1916 maritime events in Kerry.

Roger Casement departed on a submarine from Wilhelmshaven on 12 April 1916, destination Kerry. It is likely that Casement intended to stop the planned rebellion as he thought that it would fail. The submarine had engine trouble and he was transferred to the U19. This arrived in Tralee Bay late on the night of 20 April 1916.

Left: Pictured with the U19's officers, on the conning tower en route – from left, Robert Monteith, (a Volunteer and military instructor of the Irish Brigade), Casement (bareheaded), and fourth from left, Daniel Bailey (Irish Brigade) with soft hat.

There was no sign of the 'Aud'. The captain decided that his passengers should go ashore that night. The Casement party rowed ashore in a collapsible dinghy, and landed at Banna Strand. An exhausted Casement rested as his two companions headed for Tralee, seeking help. Alerted by news of the abandoned boat, two RIC officers came across Casement and arrested him.

Left: the U19 and its deck gun.

Casement was identified and escorted to imprisonment in London, arriving on Easter Sunday, 23 April 1916.

The final part of these poorly-coordinated events occurred here at Ballykissane pier (right). On Good Friday evening, Volunteers from Dublin travelled in two cars towards Caherciveen to seize equipment from the wireless college there, planning to use it to communicate with the arms ship. The driver of the second car missed a turn and drove off the pier. Three Volunteers were drowned.

Meanwhile, in Dublin, pre-Easter Week, tension was building up. On Wednesday 19 April, a purported Government plan was disclosed, showing intent to carry out mass arrests, including senior Volunteers. A sympathiser in Dublin Castle had seen details and memorised the contents. The document may have exaggerated the intent, but it persuaded Eoin MacNeill to issue a general order to the Volunteers to resist being disarmed.

Right: MacNeill, officially the Chief of Staff of the Irish Volunteers, had been sidelined by the IRB leaders who were planning a rising.

41

> 22 apl 1916
>
> WOODTOWN PARK,
> RATHFARNHAM,
> CO. DUBLIN.
>
> Volunteers completely deceived. All orders for special action are hereby cancelled, and on no account will action be taken.
>
> Eoin MacNeill

MacNeill only heard of the plans for the Rising on the night of Holy Thursday, 20 April. As news of the failure of the 'Aud' arms expedition filtered through, after a meeting on the Saturday night, he issued an order (left) that 'Volunteers completely deceived. All orders for special action are hereby cancelled'.

NO PARADES!
Irish Volunteer Marches Cancelled
A SUDDEN ORDER.

The Easter manoeuvres of the Irish Volunteers, which were announced to begin to-day, and which were to have been taken part in by all the branches of the organisation in city and country, were unexpectedly cancelled last night.

The following is the announcement communicated to the Press last evening by the Staff of the Volunteers:—

April 22, 1916.

Owing to the very critical position, all orders given to Irish Volunteers for to-morrow, Easter Sunday, are hereby rescinded, and no parades, marches, or other movements of Irish Volunteers will take place. Each individual Volunteer will obey this order strictly in every particular.

EOIN MACNEILL,
Chief of Staff,
Irish Volunteers.

GRUESOME STORIES
Result in a Girl Killing Her Lover and Attempting Suicide.

To remove her lover from the further dangers of the war, a Prague servant girl named Erna Putzmann shot him and then tried in half a dozen ways to commit suicide. The young man, the son of a Prague professor, had been fighting in the Carpathians and Serbia, and had written the girl most gruesome stories of seeing prisoners' heads chopped off and like horrors.

These tales seemed to have preyed on the girl's mind, and when her lover's leave was expiring she was unable to bear the thought of his going back to the trenches, so she killed him. Next she made a...

ARMS SEIZED
Collapsible Boat on Kerry Coast
"MAN OF UNKNOWN NATIONALITY."

A collapsible boat containing a quantity of arms and ammunition was seized at Carrahane Strand, Tralee Bay, on Friday morning.

A man of unknown nationality found on the shore close by was arrested and kept in custody.

It is not known where the boat came from or for whom the arms were intended.

TWO MEN ARRESTED.
Realm Act Case in Kerry—Well-Known G.A.A. Man in Custody.

(From Our Correspondent.)
Tralee, Saturday.

During last night the rooms of Mr. Austin Stack, Tralee, were searched by the police and some time afterwards himself and Mr. Cornelius Collins, a Post Office official, Dublin, and a native of Abbeyfeale, were arrested and kept in the police barracks overnight.

They were charged to-day, before Mr. Wynn, R.M., under the defence of the Realm Act, and remanded for eight days, without bail.

The Irish Volunteers had a special mobilisation last evening, and marched to Mr. Stack's lodgings. They afterwards proceeded to their headquarters, where an armed sentry was posted, and relieved at intervals during the night.

WANTED UNITY AT HOME.

THREE DROWNED
Tragic Motoring Affair in Kerry
A WRONG TURNING.

Tralee, Saturday.

A sensation was caused in Tralee to-day by the news of a tragic motor accident at Killorglin, which resulted in the deaths of three men unknown.

Details to hand indicate that a party travelling in a Limerick registered motor car from Killarney to Tralee stopped en route at Killorglin for a supply of petrol.

On leaving the town the chauffeur inquired as to the road to the Tralee road. He was told to take "the first turn on the left." He unfortunately obeyed the direction to the strict letter, and turned the car down towards Ballykissane quay, which is locally regarded as a "bohereen." His informant was under the impression that he would continue until meeting the main road and overlook the "bohereen."

The car, which was occupied by three passengers and the chauffeur, sped down the by-road and plunged into the River Lane, which at that point is of great depth. In some unexplained fashion the driver extricated himself from the steering wheel and got ashore, but the other occupants of the car were not so fortunate.

Contradictory rumours are afloat as to the identity of the unfortunate passengers, the chauffeur, it is alleged, disclaiming all knowledge of who they were.

The chauffeur gave the alarm to people living in the vicinity, and dragging operations immediately started for the recovery of the bodies.

ALLEGED SHOPBREAKER.

Jumped Through a Plate Glass Window to Evade Arrest.

Left: alarming news for an Easter Sunday morning — the 23 April 1916 'Sunday Independent' sets out the series of dramatic events.

The leaders planning the Rising, the Military Council, held a meeting at Liberty Hall early on Easter Sunday morning. After much debate they decided to carry on with the Rising. It was deferred to noon on Easter Monday, to allow for the remobilisation of Volunteers.

Chapter 2
Easter Rising

Despite the loss of the arms shipment and MacNeill's countermand, the IRB Military Council decided to proceed with the Rising on Easter Monday 24 April 1916. A mixed force of Irish Citizen Army (ICA) and Irish Volunteers duly assembled in front of Liberty Hall on Easter Monday where they lined up before James Connolly. Just before noon the main formation (designated the Headquarters Battalion) headed for the GPO. Detachments also set off for St Stephen's Green (under Michael Mallin) and the Mendicity Institution (under Seán Heuston). At the GPO, Patrick Pearse read the Proclamation of the Republic to a few bemused onlookers, followed by Connolly shaking his hand saying: 'Thanks be to God, Pearse, that we have lived to see this day!' Volunteer battalions and the ICA took over strategic locations at compass points around the city. The British military soon reacted: troops were rushed to Dublin Castle and reinforcements ordered to the city. At the GPO, after an early skirmish with Lancers, the first days were generally quiet. The fight became intense in other locations. City Hall was taken by troops who charged from Dublin Castle. On Tuesday, British soldiers, ensconced in the Shelbourne Hotel, cleared St Stephen's Green park of the ICA, who then retreated to the College of Surgeons. There were clashes at the South Dublin Union (SDU) and around the Four Courts. By Tuesday evening the British military had set up inner and outer cordons in the city. They decided to ignore the SDU, the Jacob's factory, and St Stephen's Green positions and concentrate on the GPO and the Four Courts. Trinity College, in the heart of the city, was transformed into a staging post on a grand scale for the British. On Wednesday morning the fishery-protection vessel *Helga* anchored by the Loop Line Bridge in front of the Custom House, and peppered Liberty Hall with 12-pounder shells. Seán Heuston fiercely defended the Mendicity Institution, which was taken by Wednesday. On the same morning Captain Bowen-Colthurst ordered that the captured pacifist Francis Sheehy-Skeffington, with two others, be summarily shot in Portobello Barracks. A detachment of Sherwood Foresters arrived by ship from Britain and landed at Kingstown. They marched to central Dublin and attacked lightly-manned outposts near Mount Street Bridge, and suffered heavy casualties. On Wednesday evening most of the Republican forces were still in place, but British troops were flooding the city as they completed the cordoning off of Dublin.

By then the number of British troops came to around 10,000 (and more were on the way); against these were around 1,400 of the Republican forces. Heavy fighting flared up at some Volunteer garrisons, while the GPO headquarters (and nearby outposts) were now being continuously raked with rifle and machine-gun fire. British artillery, which had arrived from Athlone on Tuesday, began to tip the balance. On Thursday, Republican positions around Sackville Street were shelled. James Connolly is reputed to have argued that the British would never employ artillery in Dublin: a capitalist government would not choose to destroy property. This maxim proved to be wrong. General Maxwell had free rein militarily and was also unhindered by any real political restraints. Faced with insurgents embedded in a built-up area, the military single-mindedly resorted to whatever weapon was effective, in this case 18-pounders. Their shrapnel shells caused fires to start in the tinderbox that was Sackville Street, much of which was in flames by Thursday evening. The British tightened the noose around the area and as outposts became untenable, Volunteers withdrew to the GPO. By Friday afternoon the GPO itself had been hit and went on fire. By evening the roof was collapsing and the building had to be abandoned.

As smoke billowed from the GPO, the O'Rahilly was tasked with pushing through to a new HQ location. As he led a party down Moore Street, they were raked by bullets and he fell, mortally wounded. The headquarter forces retreated from the GPO, weaving through laneways, and punched through into a terrace on Moore Street. Moved by the sight of civilian deaths, Pearse proposed to end the Rising. The members of the Provisional Government held a final council of war at a premises on Moore Street. They agreed that they would have to treat with the British.

An unconditional surrender was agreed on the afternoon of Saturday 29 April. Patrick Pearse was driven to meet General Maxwell at the British HQ in Parkgate Street, where he signed a surrender order. The brave Elizabeth O'Farrell brought Pearse's surrender message to his commandants across the city. By Sunday the only prospect in sight was a march into captivity. Most of those captured were brought to Richmond Barracks. In the days and weeks that followed, the bulk of the prisoners, those not selected for trial, were sent to Britain, where they were interned.

As the Republican outposts surrendered, the citizens of Dublin took stock of their shattered city centre. There was devastation all around in one of the principal cities of the supposedly 'United' Kingdom. The GPO and other buildings around Sackville Street were blackened ruins. With Ireland under martial law, General Maxwell was given carte blanche to deal with the aftermath of the rebellion – he proceeded in a draconian manner. He set up a regime of punishment, untrammelled (at least initially) by any effective political control or nuanced consideration of the impact on opinion across Ireland. To deter future insurgency, his priority was to punish the rebel leaders quickly, both for association with the German enemy and for the loss of life and damage to property. Field general courts martial were rapidly set up. The trials were rushed and lacked any semblance of justice. The leaders of the Rising, as well as less prominent figures, were sentenced to death. There was a power vacuum in Dublin and Maxwell filled it – he confirmed sentences without any real hindrance from the unassertive Prime Minister Asquith. The condemned men of 1916 were brought to Kilmainham Gaol. The executions were carried out with military expeditiosness in the grim Stonebreakers' Yard. All the condemned men faced their executions bravely. Connolly's execution was particularly ghastly. On 12 May, the wounded leader was conveyed by ambulance to Kilmainham. As dawn broke, he was placed on a chair and shot. The most obscure and secret location possible was chosen for burial. The bodies were interred at the rear of a yard at Arbour Hill Detention Barracks in Dublin. The trial of Sir Roger Casement formed a kind of coda to these events: at the end of June 1916 he was found guilty of treason and was hanged at Pentonville Prison on 3 August.

A *Royal Commission on the Rebellion in Ireland* began hearings in May 1916. Among its conclusions on the causes of the rebellion were: tolerance of militias, poor intelligence, and a dysfunctional system of government in Ireland. The Volunteers had been a tiny minority in Easter 1916 – they had been jeered at as they were being marched to captivity, but as the executions rolled on a shift in mood occurred. This change in public support helped propel the War of Independence that followed.

In the light of MacNeill's countermanding orders, a flurry of messages was sent to all units in an effort to reschedule the rising to Easter Monday. A mixed force of Irish Citizen Army (ICA) and Irish Volunteers duly assembled in front of Liberty Hall on Monday morning 24 April where they lined up before James Connolly. Just before noon the main formation, (designated the Headquarters Battalion) headed for the GPO, followed by carts carrying ammunition, weapons and other supplies. Detachments also set off for St Stephen's Green (under Michael Mallin) and the Mendicity Institution (under Seán Heuston).

Left: the 'Leaders in the Insurrection', most of whom were executed within little over a week from the end of the Rising.

On Easter Sunday night copies of a document, the Proclamation of an Irish Republic, were printed at Liberty Hall. Left: set in bronze — signatories of the proclamation (together with The O'Rahilly).

Right: trams terminate at the General Post Office and Nelson's Pillar – a busy scene on Sackville Street as it was before the Rising. The Post Office then played an important role in Irish life; the GPO was the communications hub and a focal point of Sackville Street.

On Easter Monday, just after midday, James Connolly led his column of Volunteers and ICA to halt outside the portico of the GPO, ordered 'Left turn!', then 'Charge!' They swarmed through the main doorway and took over the building. They proceeded to occupy buildings on both sides of Sackville Street, especially those buildings at the southern end that dominated the approaches to O'Connell Bridge.

Right: the public area today. After the Rising, the only part of the GPO more or less intact was the facade. The rest of the building was completely reconstructed during the years 1924-29.

47

POBLACHT NA H EIREANN.

THE PROVISIONAL GOVERNMENT
OF THE
IRISH REPUBLIC
TO THE PEOPLE OF IRELAND.

IRISHMEN AND IRISHWOMEN: In the name of God and of the dead generations from which she receives her old tradition of nationhood, Ireland, through us, summons her children to her flag and strikes for her freedom.

Having organised and trained her manhood through her secret revolutionary organisation, the Irish Republican Brotherhood, and through her open military organisations, the Irish Volunteers and the Irish Citizen Army, having patiently perfected her discipline, having resolutely waited for the right moment to reveal itself, she now seizes that moment, and, supported by her exiled children in America and by gallant allies in Europe, but relying in the first on her own strength, she strikes in full confidence of victory.

We declare the right of the people of Ireland to the ownership of Ireland, and to the unfettered control of Irish destinies, to be sovereign and indefeasible. The long usurpation of that right by a foreign people and government has not extinguished the right, nor can it ever be extinguished except by the destruction of the Irish people. In every generation the Irish people have asserted their right to national freedom and sovereignty; six times during the past three hundred years they have asserted it in arms. Standing on that fundamental right and again asserting it in arms in the face of the world, we hereby proclaim the Irish Republic as a Sovereign Independent State, and we pledge our lives and the lives of our comrades-in-arms to the cause of its freedom, of its welfare, and of its exaltation among the nations.

The Irish Republic is entitled to, and hereby claims, the allegiance of every Irishman and Irishwoman. The Republic guarantees religious and civil liberty, equal rights and equal opportunities to all its citizens, and declares its resolve to pursue the happiness and prosperity of the whole nation and of all its parts, cherishing all the children of the nation equally, and oblivious of the differences carefully fostered by an alien government, which have divided a minority from the majority in the past.

Until our arms have brought the opportune moment for the establishment of a permanent National Government, representative of the whole people of Ireland and elected by the suffrages of all her men and women, the Provisional Government, hereby constituted, will administer the civil and military affairs of the Republic in trust for the people.

We place the cause of the Irish Republic under the protection of the Most High God, Whose blessing we invoke upon our arms, and we pray that no one who serves that cause will dishonour it by cowardice, inhumanity, or rapine. In this supreme hour the Irish nation must, by its valour and discipline and by the readiness of its children to sacrifice themselves for the common good, prove itself worthy of the august destiny to which it is called.

Signed on Behalf of the Provisional Government,
THOMAS J. CLARKE.
SEAN Mac DIARMADA. THOMAS MacDONAGH.
P. H. PEARSE, EAMONN CEANNT,
JAMES CONNOLLY. JOSEPH PLUNKETT.

The Proclamation of the Irish Republic (left) was clear and inspirational. God is invoked. It sets out the central role of the IRB, and (over-optimistically, as it turned out) refers to the support of the 'gallant allies in Europe'. Continuity with the centuries of revolutionary separatism is stated. Thought to be mainly written by Pearse, Connolly's hand can be seen in the assertion of the right of the Irish people to the ownership of Ireland. It was progressive, claiming the allegiance of Irishwomen as well as Irishmen. With an eye on the North, it offered religious as well as civil liberty – and decried the differences 'fostered by an alien government', which it said divided the minority from the majority.

Left: rare actuality from Easter Monday 1916. Seeing a copy of the proclamation posted on railings at 86 St Stephen's Green (now Newman House), Dr Edward McWeeney took it to the garden at the back. McWeeney, a University College Dublin academic, is photographed there, reading the proclamation.

Right: the portico of the GPO. Soon after the takeover of the building, Commandant-General Patrick Pearse stepped out here and read the Proclamation of the Irish Republic to a small and bemused crowd of bystanders. Then Connolly shook his hand and said: 'Thanks be to God, Pearse, that we have lived to see this day!'

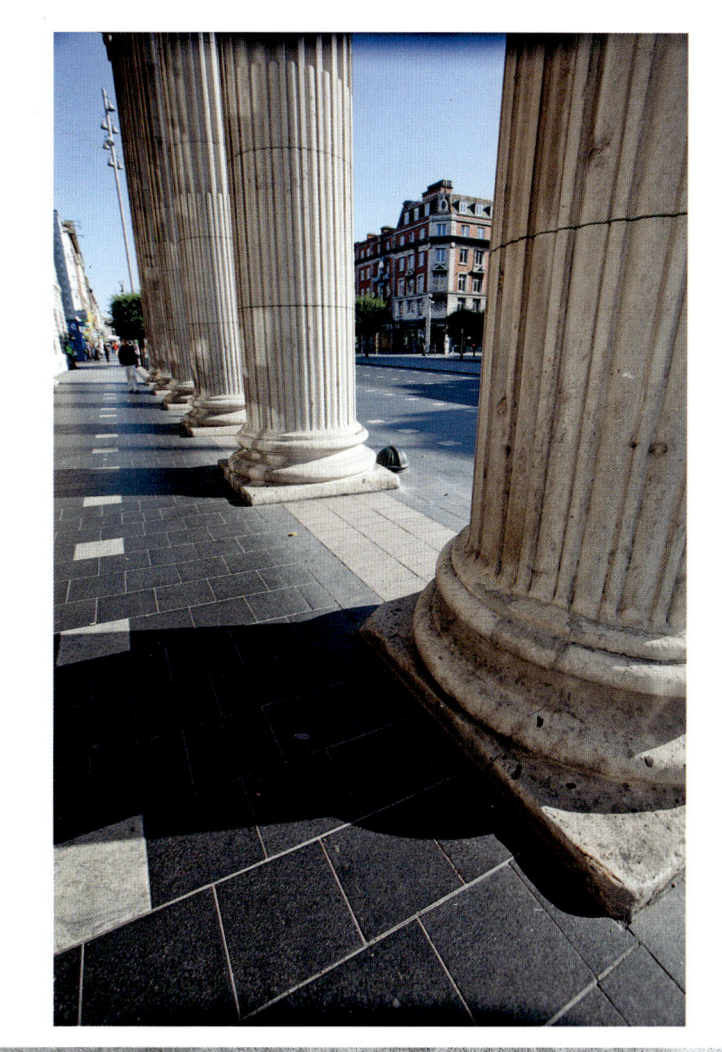

At around 1:15 pm on Easter Monday there was the first encounter with the British Army. A detachment of Lancers had been assigned to investigate reports of insurgency in the city centre. They rode south along Sackville Street in perfect order, lances at the ready. As the first of the Lancers passed Nelson's Pillar, some Volunteers opened fire with a scattered volley. Four soldiers toppled over; three were dead (depiction, right). The colonel in charge ordered them to pull back and they retreated.

50

Right: the 'Irish War News' was issued on Tuesday. It included a communiqué that the Irish Republic had been proclaimed. Two similar news sheets were issued later in the week.

More communication – Volunteers reactivated a transmitter at the School of Wireless on Sackville Street and broadcast news of the Rising. On Tuesday a naval ship at Kingstown intercepted the message 'Irish Republic declared in Dublin today...Irish troops have captured city...'

Left: schematic drawing of the GPO as it was early in the week:
1. public office
2. arms store
3. sick bay
4. entrance door
5. barricaded windows
6. office
7. message arrangement to other side of street (made of twine and a can)
8. snipers on roof
9. van yard.

A sketch of Pearse in the GPO, on Tuesday evening (near right). He reminds the Volunteers that Dublin had now regained its honour, lost by not supporting Emmet's 1803 Rising.

Far right: the Hotel Metropole, adjacent to the GPO. On Tuesday night Connolly ordered its occupation.

IRISH WAR NEWS

THE IRISH REPUBLIC.

VOL. 1. No. 1.   DUBLIN, TUESDAY, APRIL 25, 1916.   ONE PENNY

"IF THE GERMANS CONQUERED ENGLAND."

In the London "New Statesman" for *April 1st*, an article is published—"If the Germans Conquered England," which has the appearance of a very clever piece of satire written by an Irishman. The writer draws a picture of England under German rule, almost every detail of which exactly fits the case of Ireland at the present day. Some of the sentences are so exquisitely appropriate that it is impossible to believe that the writer had not Ireland in his mind when he wrote them. For instance :—

"England would be constantly irritated by the lofty moral utterances of German statesmen who would assert—quite sincerely, no doubt—that England was free, freer indeed than she had ever been before. Prussian freedom, they would explain, was the only real freedom, and therefore England was free. They would point to the flourishing railways and farms and colleges. They would possibly point to the contingent of M.P's, which was permitted, in spite of its deplorable disorderliness, to sit in a permanent minority in the Reichstag. And not only would the Englishman have to listen to a constant flow of speeches of this sort ; he would find a respectable official Press secretly bought over by the Government to say the same kind of things over and over, every day of the week. He would find, too, that his children were coming home from school with new ideas of history. They would ask him if it was true that until the Germans came England had been an unruly country, constantly engaged in civil war. . . . The object of every schoolbook would be to make the English child grow up in the notion that the history of his country was a thing to forget, and that the one bright spot in it was the fact that it had been conquered by cultured Germany."

"If there was a revolt, German statesmen would deliver grave speeches about "disloyalty," "ingratitude," "reckless agitators who would ruin their country's prosperity. . . . Prussian soldiers would be encamped in every barracks—the English conscripts having been sent out of the country to be trained in Germany, or to fight the Chinese—in order to come to the aid of German morality, should English sedition come to blows with it."

"England would be exhorted to abandon her own genius in order to imitate the genius of her conquerors, to forget her own history for a larger history, to give up her own language for a "universal" language—in other words, to destroy her household gods one by one, and put in their place

Left: 'HMY Helga', a Dublin-built fishery protection vessel, was used as an anti-submarine patrol vessel during WWI.

At 8 am on Wednesday, the 'Helga' anchored by the Loop Line Bridge in front of the Custom House, where, reportedly, a Guinness ship was moored. Using its QF 12-pounder, it opened fire on Liberty Hall, the perceived rebel HQ, now abandoned. Its log records 24 high explosive (HE) rounds being fired.

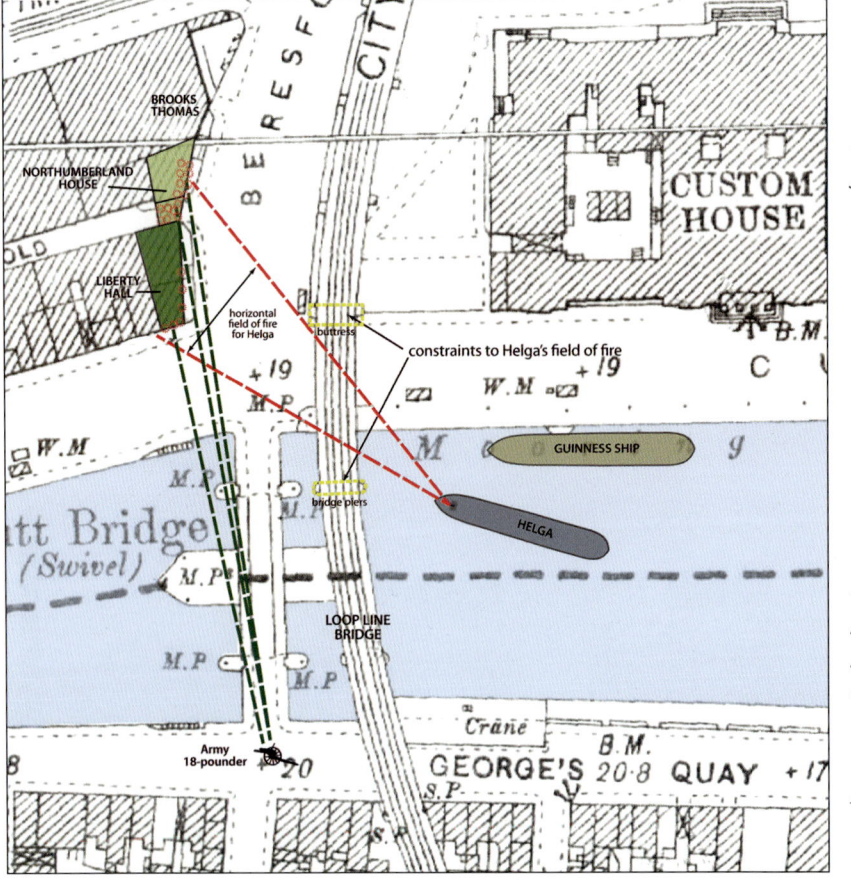

In a hurriedly arranged joint army-navy exercise, the British Army placed two 18-pounders on Tara Street and shelled Liberty Hall, using shrapnel shells (which would have acted like cannon balls) – all they had at the time.

Left: map of the engagement. The Helga's gunners did not have an easy task. They were constrained horizontally by the Loop Line Bridge pier and abutments and vertically by the soffit of the bridge.

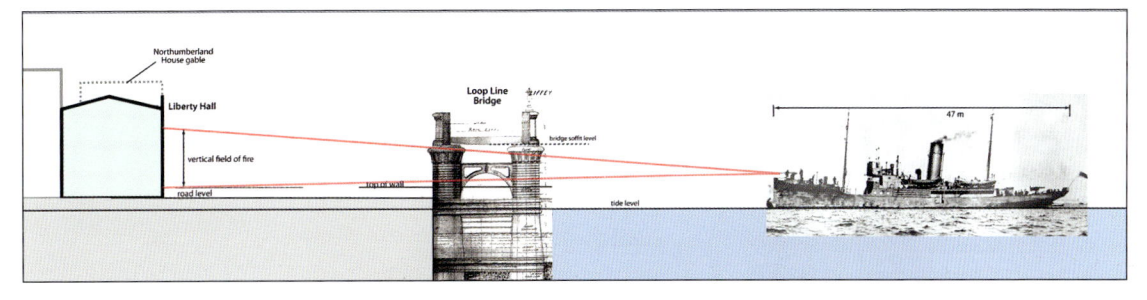

Above: cross-section showing possible trajectories. The ship's gun fired under the bridge at Liberty Hall and reportedly initially hit the bridge. There were probably a few strays but there is no evidence that the 'Helga' deliberately shelled the rebels in Sackville Street. One account suggests that there was an attempt to hit the hall by firing over the bridge from further downriver – possible but unlikely due to the probability of even more widespread damage.

Above right: Liberty Hall in the aftermath, damaged, but still structurally intact. The artillery did not inflict much external damage. Shrapnel shells coming from the Tara Street direction punched the relatively small holes as seen on the left gable. The adjacent Northumberland House, on the right, suffered more: the more extensive damage there was likely due to HE shells from the ship.

Right: the relatively scattered internal damage inside Liberty Hall.

On Easter Monday an ICA column under Captain Seán Connolly (an Abbey actor, as depicted in a role, sketch, left) headed from Liberty Hall towards Dublin Castle.

An unarmed Constable, James O'Brien of the Dublin Metropolitan Police (DMP), attempted to stop the column at the upper Castle gate at Cork Hill. As O'Brien put out his arm, Connolly raised his rifle and shot him.

An assault party charged the guardroom by the entrance gate (below left) and overpowered the six startled soldiers within. Not knowing it was lightly guarded, the ICA did not occupy the Castle. They took over City Hall and other buildings near the entrance. The British soon recovered. Troops from Portobello, Richmond and the Royal Barracks were ordered to Dublin Castle. By 2 pm troops had reached the Ship Street entrance. They set up on roofs and towers and fired on the ICA positions.

Seán Connolly was on the City Hall roof when he was shot by a British sniper. Dr Kathleen Lynn, medical officer of the ICA, attended him as he lay dying.

Right: in uniform, the unfortunate Constable O'Brien. The DMP was an unarmed force. Withdrawn after the beginning of the Rising, they took no direct part in the fighting.

The British launched a fierce assault on City Hall on Monday evening, forcing their way into the ground floor through a back window. Surrounded, Kathleen Lynn and her comrades surrendered. The party on the roof held out until dawn on Tuesday.

Below right: the ICA were still in occupation of the 'Mail' and 'Express' offices (on the left of the intersection with Parliament Street) and the Henry and James premises on the right.

At around 2 pm on Tuesday, waves of troops attacked the remaining rebel positions. Fire was also poured from the roof of City Hall, now in British hands. The troops broke through the front doors and stormed the stairs. Just before 3 pm, it ended: the survivors of the ICA garrison had climbed out the rear windows and slipped away.

The Volunteers had seized the telegraph exchange in the GPO. However, contact was established between the telegraph office at Amiens Street Station and the Post Office in London via a cross-channel cable that ran through the station. The insurgents did not, however, seize the Crown Alley central telegraph exchange (left). The British response was rapid. By just after 5 pm on Monday, 1,600 men had arrived at Kingsbridge Station by train from the Curragh. Orders were sent for artillery from Athlone; Dublin Fusiliers from Templemore; and more men from the Curragh, as well as a composite battalion from Belfast. Later that day troops in England were mobilised.

Left: telegraph sent to Belfast from Amiens Street requesting troops.

Left: Brigadier-General W. Lowe, 3rd Reserve Cavalry Brigade, the Curragh, was given command of the British forces in the Dublin area. He detrained at Kingsbridge station early on Tuesday morning. By now around 4,600 British troops had been assembled in the city.

56

Right: map from a post-Rising booklet. It shows the cordons set up by Lowe: heavy red line – inner cordon; lighter red – outer cordons; Republican positions are circled in red. As troops arrived, the outer cordons were set up. By Tuesday evening Lowe had decided to ignore the SDU, Jacob's, and St Stephen's Green positions and concentrate on the GPO and the Four Courts.

Right: troops man an armoured train fabricated for the military by the Great Northern Railway (Ireland).

Apart from Westland Row and Harcourt Street stations, the Volunteers did not capture any other railway termini. British reinforcements from the north, west and the south were rapidly funnelled by train to Dublin without any interference.

Early in the week, British soldiers sniped at rebels from the roofs of Trinity College.

Right: by mid-week, troops and artillery had poured into Trinity's Front Square. This grove of academe, in the heart of the city, was transformed into a staging post on a grand scale for the British military.

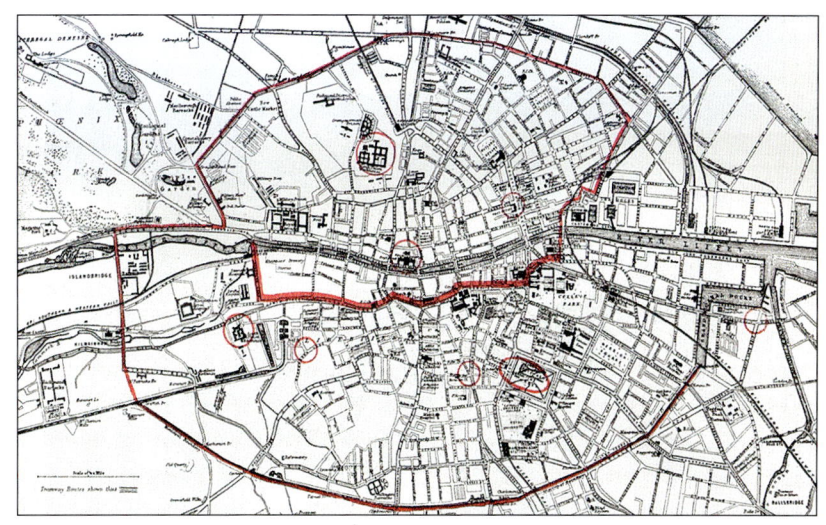

Just before midday on Monday Commandant Thomas MacDonagh assembled his 2nd Battalion at St Stephen's Green and marched with around 150 men to occupy the Jacob's biscuit factory complex at Bishop Street (left). Men were placed on roofs and towers. By Tuesday evening the British had decided to ignore Jacob's and concentrate on the GPO.

As it turned out, the 2nd Battalion position at Jacob's biscuit factory, large and impregnable, did not much affect the military outcome. Firing continued, however, from roofs and the high tower at the factory. In turn the British shot at the Volunteers here from high positions such as the Bermingham Tower in Dublin Castle.

Left: Thomas MacDonagh. Poet, playwright, and friend of Patrick Pearse, he taught at St Enda's, and lectured at University College Dublin. A founder member of the Volunteers, he had latterly joined the IRB and was a signatory of the Proclamation.

Right: Countess Markievicz arrived at St Stephen's Green and joined the ICA garrison there.

A unit of the ICA under Commandant Michael Mallin had arrived on Monday and occupied St Stephen's Green. They dug shallow defensive trenches covering the main entrances and erected barricades on adjacent roads. The Royal College of Surgeons of Ireland (RCSI) was taken over on Monday afternoon.

The original plan was to occupy the Shelbourne Hotel, dominating the north-east corner of the park. However, Mallin was short of men. As it turned out, it would have been better to assign forces there than to leave them exposed in the park.

After midnight on Monday, British troops took over the hotel and also the United Services Club (at the western end of the street). In the hotel, snipers were deployed and a Vickers machine gun was installed. At 4 am the British opened fire from both the hotel and the club. A hail of bullets lashed the ICA in the Green. Over the next hours, they fell back to the RCSI, having endured losses.

Right: map of the St Stephen's Green area

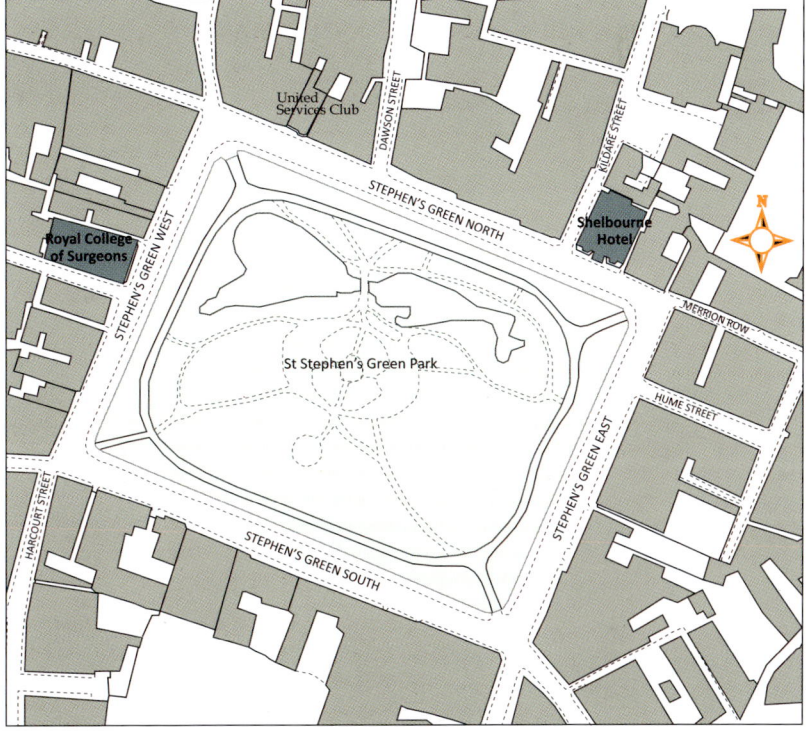

From the RCSI roof the ICA took aim at the British on the other sides of St Stephen's Green. There was a continuous exchange of fire, but the British never mounted an assault. On Thursday an ICA party was assigned to occupy Russell's Hotel (corner of Harcourt Street). They came under heavy fire while underway. One man was shot dead and ICA member, Margaret Skinnider, was seriously wounded. Left: the park and RCSI as seen from the Shelbourne.

Above: a present-day fish-eye view from the roof of the RCSI.
On Monday a unit of the ICA had been assigned to temporarily seize southern positions to allow the main force to set up in St Stephen's Green. They took over Harcourt Street Station (right) and spread out along the elevated railway line as far as the Grand Canal. To provide flanking support an ICA unit was assigned to occupy Davy's public house, along the canal to the west.

Just after midday on Monday, an ICA unit occupied Davy's public house (above), located by Portobello Bridge.

Soldiers from Portobello Barracks were on the way to relieve Dublin Castle when they were fired on from Davy's. Riflemen were deployed along the south bank of the canal, bringing along a Maxim machine gun. The British then directed heavy fire on the public house. The ICA slipped out the back and withdrew to St Stephen's Green.

Left: a Maxim machine gun (the predecessor of the Vickers).

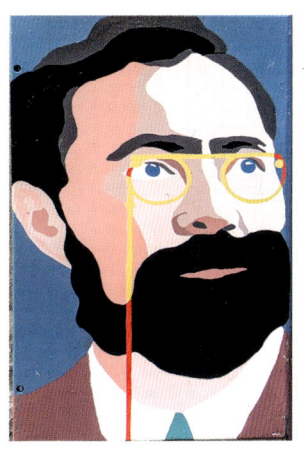

Above: 'Skeffy'. The quixotic pacifist Francis Sheehy-Skeffington as artfully depicted on a a telecoms equipment box at Rathmines Road Lower.

On Tuesday, Sheehy-Skeffington had put up posters in central Dublin calling for a meeting of citizens to band together against looting. As he approached the Portobello Bridge by the harbour (top right), he was arrested by a picket there and brought to Portobello (now Cathal Brugha) Barracks (parade ground, right).

Captain John Bowen-Colthurst was in the barracks, having suffered shell shock in France. After 10 pm on Tuesday, he charged into the guardroom and demanded that Sheehy-Skeffington be handed over. He set off with a raiding party from the barracks with a bound Sheehy-Skeffington in tow.

Right: cell in the guardroom at the barracks.

63

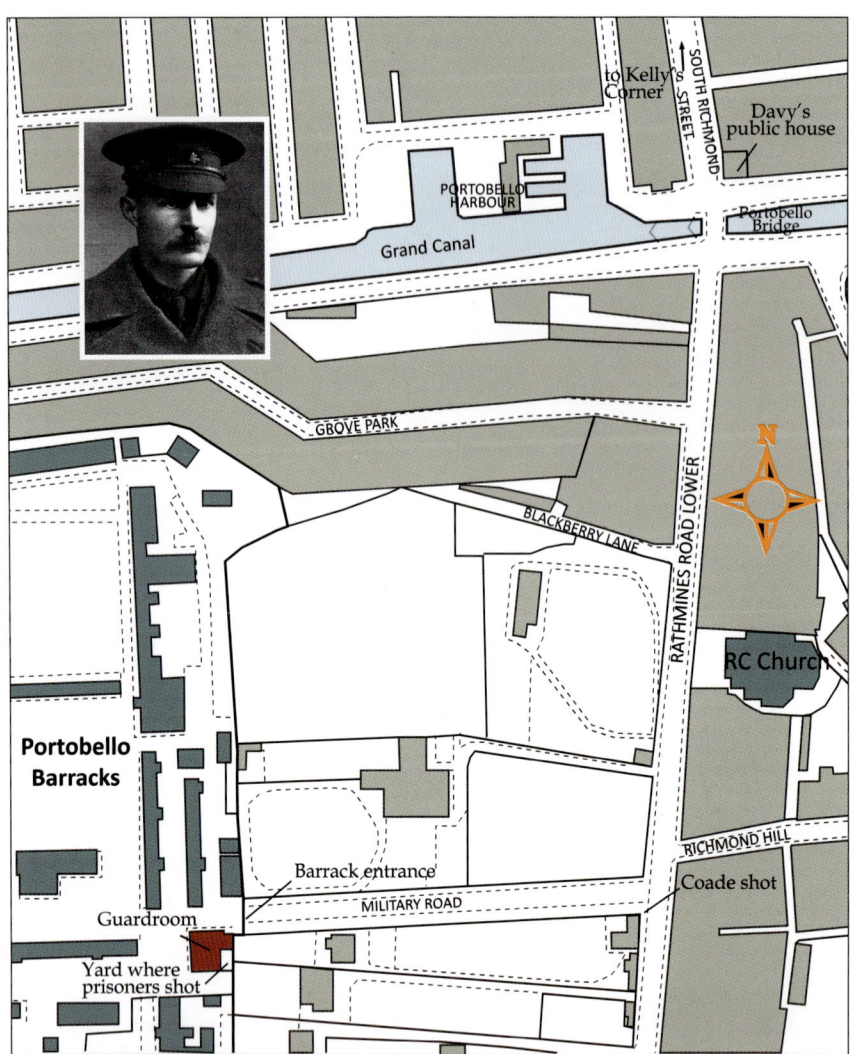

Left: the Rathmines area (inset: Bowen-Colthurst). At Rathmines Road, the captain intercepted three youths and shouted that martial law had been proclaimed. He shot and mortally wounded one, James Coade.

The party continued northwards. Bowen-Colthurst shot and mortally wounded the trade unionist, councillor and Volunteer, Richard O'Carroll, who had reportedly been pulled from his motorcycle in Camden Street. Next they raided a tobacco shop at Kelly's Corner (mistaking the proprietor for a 'Sinn Féiner') and seized four men, bringing them back to the barracks.

Below: some of the victims – from left: James Coade; Richard O'Carroll and Thomas Dickson.

64

At 10:20 am on Wednesday Bowen-Colthurst arrived in the guardroom, after spending the night reading the Bible. He gave an order that Sheehy-Skeffington and two men seized at Kelly's Corner, Thomas Dickson and Patrick MacIntyre, be brought to the yard. He said he was going to shoot them as it seemed 'the best thing to be done'. The prisoners were ordered to the wall (right). Bowen-Colthurst summoned seven soldiers and ordered them to fire at the prisoners, who were neither blindfolded nor bound. Sheehy-Skeffington was shot again after movement was seen. The bodies were buried in the barracks, the yard was scrubbed and the bricks with bullet holes were replaced.

After some prevarication by the Army authorities, a court martial was held. Bowen-Colthurst was found guilty of murder but (conveniently) deemed a 'criminal lunatic' – he was then sent to Broadmoor. Released from there in little over a year, he soon emigrated to Canada, where he lived up to his death in 1965.

Right: the Sheehy-Skeffington memorial at the barracks gate.

65

Left: the Magazine Fort, Phoenix Park, dating from 1738, where army ordnance was stored. The fort, with sides around 60 metres in length, has four demi-bastions and a moat.

Just after midday on Easter Monday, around 30 men arrived here, led by Paddy O'Daly, who was later a member of Collins' Squad, and gained notoriety as a pro-Treaty general in Civil War Kerry. Using the ruse of playing football, the Volunteers disarmed the guards and rushed in (entrance, left). Unable to access the main magazine, they set their explosive charges against its wall. As well as soldiers, prisoners included the wife and family of the fort's commander, who was abroad.

The prisoners were allowed to leave but told not to raise the alarm. Gathering a quantity of arms and ammunition, the Volunteers headed back to their battalion at Church Street. As they left, they saw George Playfair (23), son of the fort's commander, dashing away. Volunteer Garry Holohan followed him on a bicycle. Playfair ran out the Islandbridge Gate (left) and spoke to a policeman.

Playfair ran to nearby Park Place, where there were military residences. He frantically knocked on the door of this house, (right). As the door was being opened, Garry Holohan came up and shot him. Playfair fell, mortally wounded.

Right: George Playfair's grave, Hibernian Military School, Phoenix Park.

Below: Garry Holohan

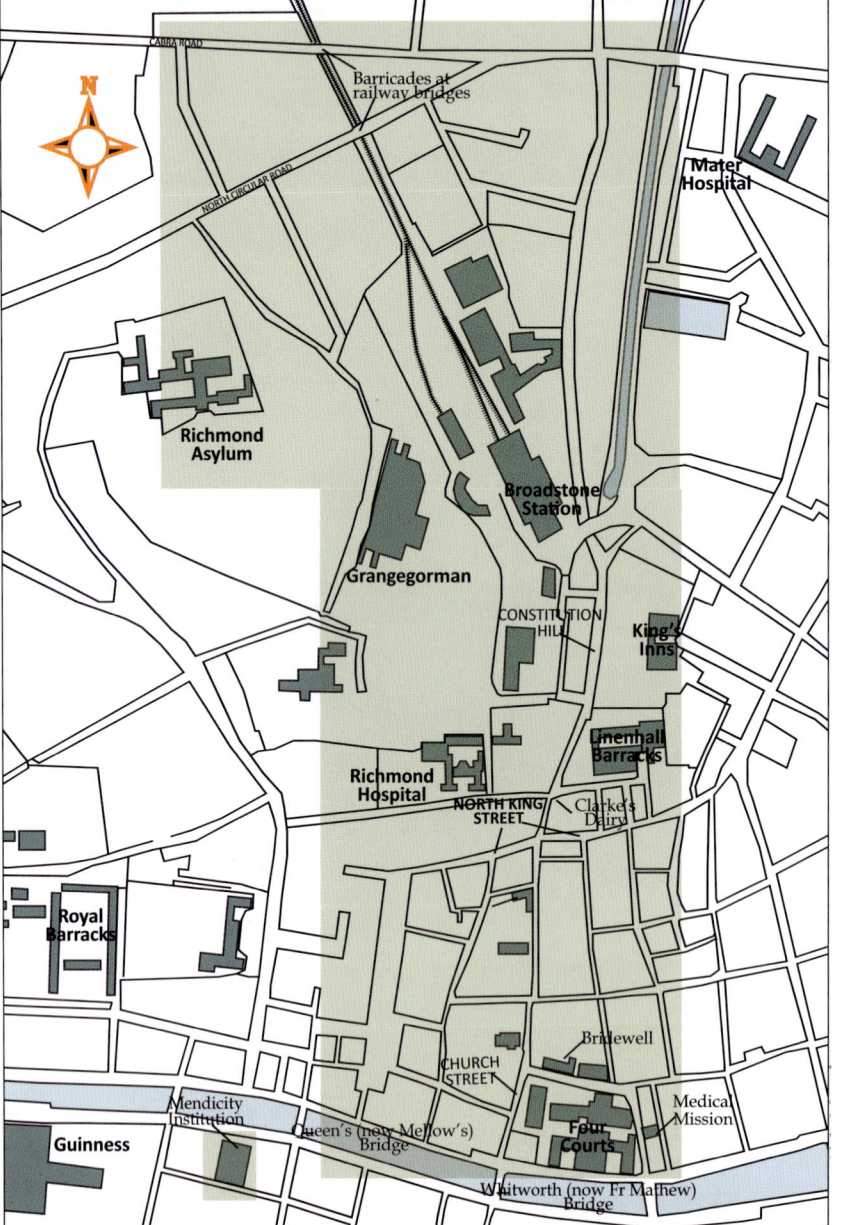

Above: granite fortresses – the Four Courts (left); Broadstone Station (right).

The 1st Battalion assembled at Blackhall Street at 11 am on Monday: objective – to occupy a line from Cabra to the quays. Commandant Daly assigned his men: one company to occupy the Four Courts; another Brunswick and Upper Church Streets. Others were to take over the Broadstone. They decided to occupy tenement houses in North King Street instead. Barricades were set up around Church Street.

On Tuesday afternoon the British shelled barricades on the railway bridges at North Circular and Cabra Roads. The Volunteers withdrew and the British were able to complete their northern cordon to North Wall.

Left: the sprawling 1st Battalion area.

Just after midday on Monday, Lancers were escorting military supplies (right, Lancers after the Rising). As they passed the Church Street intersection they came under fire; the lead soldier was killed. The Lancers took shelter in the nearby Medical Mission building where they held out until being rescued by armoured lorries on Thursday.

The British encircled the rebel positions in the Four Courts and Church Street areas. On Thursday evening, troops were deployed along the south quays, from where an 18-pounder shelled the Four Courts.

Right: Commandant Edward Daly, with companions. Aged only 25, he was the youngest of the 1916 commandants.

Left: Clarke's Dairy, at a narrow point along Church Street, which the Volunteers occupied. The South Staffordshires had been tasked with pushing a cordon west along North King Street. Early on Saturday morning, in an effort to advance on the major rebel stronghold at Reilly's public house (at the western corner of Church and North King Streets), troops charged into houses along North King Street. A hard battle ensued. Later it emerged that, after entering the houses that night, they had picked out 15 men and summarily killed them.

By 9 am on Saturday, with ammunition and food running low, the defenders evacuated Reilly's. As Volunteers still commanded nearby positions, the fighting went on all day. By 8 pm Daly ordered all men on the barricades to fall back to the Four Courts, where news came of Pearse's order to surrender. The men at Clarke's Dairy held out and didn't surrender until Sunday morning.

Left: the burnt-out Linenhall Barracks. On Wednesday, Volunteers blew a charge at the wall and those within surrendered. Unable to hold it, the Volunteers set it on fire.

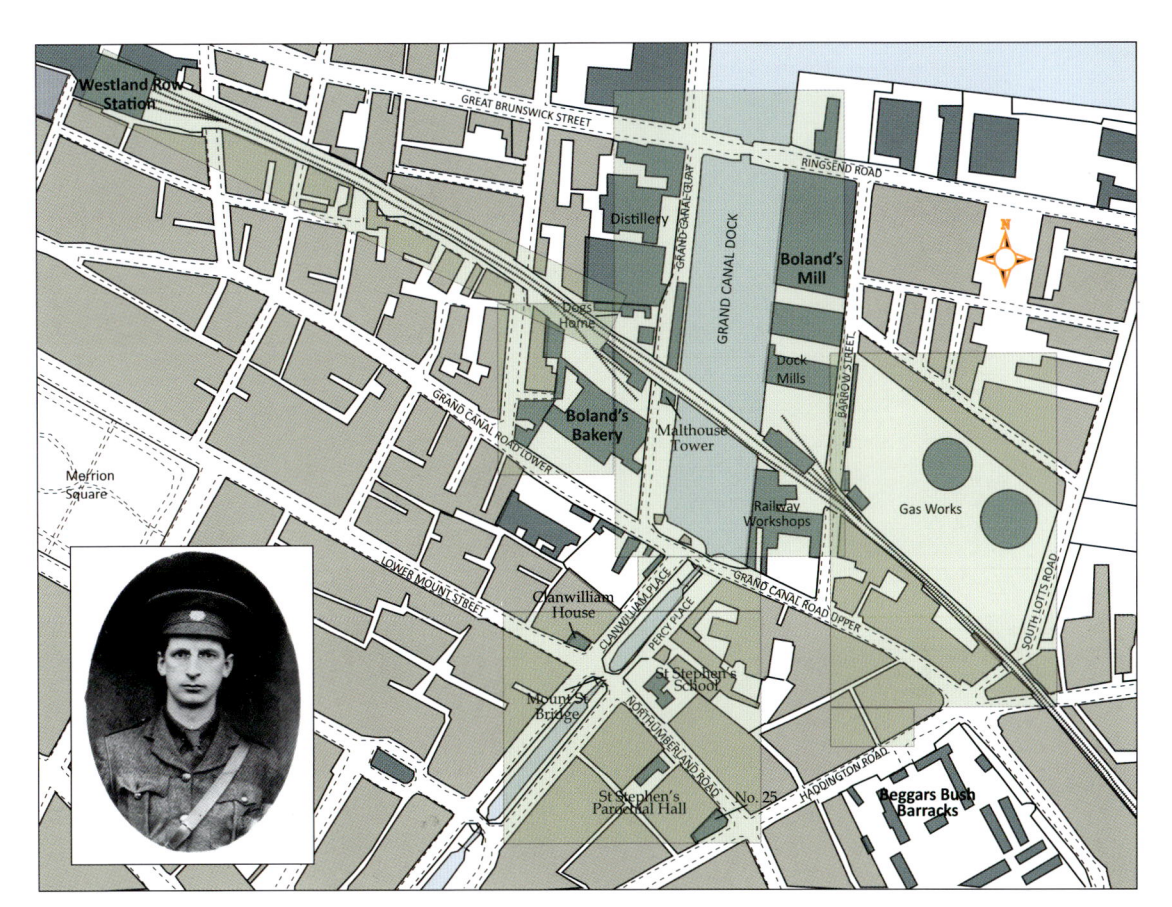

Above: map of the 3rd Battalion area. Inset: Commandant de Valera.

Around 120 men of the 3rd Battalion, commanded by Éamon de Valera, assembled at Earlsfort Terrace on Monday.

Just after noon they set up at Boland's Bakery. They established control in various places including the mills, gas works and railway workshops. Other outposts were set up around Mount Street.

Right: a 1950s view of Boland's Bakery at Grand Canal Place, with the Malthouse tower to the right.

71

On Monday, Volunteers seized Westland Row Station (left). They stopped trains, ripped up the tracks and damaged signalling equipment.

Fearful of an attack from the Beggar's Bush Barracks and reinforcement from Kingstown, de Valera had ordered his men to guard the southern approaches. A unit of the 3rd Battalion, under Lieutenant Michael Malone, was assigned to take over buildings in the Mount Street area, including Clanwilliam House, which commanded the bridge over the Grand Canal.

Volunteers occupied positions on Northumberland Road (left). No. 25 is on the left. Buildings occupied included St Stephen's School (below left) and the parochial hall.

At around 4 pm on Monday, a veteran defence force, the 'GRs' marched back to Beggar's Bush Barracks from exercises. Although 120 strong, they had just a few rifles, but no ammunition. As they came near they were fired on from Volunteer positions on the railway embankment and 25 Northumberland Road. Four died; the rest managed to reach the barracks.

Right: a view up Haddington Road (Beggar's Bush Barracks is in the middle distance), from South Lotts railway bridge. The Volunteers were able to snipe on the barracks from here.

On Tuesday, the 'Helga' had sailed upriver and fired two rounds at Boland's mills. De Valera ordered that a green flag be placed on a tower of an adjacent distillery, to attract the British fire. This ruse worked, as on Thursday when the 'Helga' returned, it fired 14 shells at the distillery building. On Thursday the area was pounded by another 88 shells from a naval six-pounder (taken from an armed trawler), reportedly set up at Percy Place.

Right: the Malthouse tower, another stronghold near Boland's Bakery. Immediately adjacent to the railway line, it still bears its 1916 pockmarks.

Troops were hastily mobilised in Britain to help quell the rebellion. The Sherwood Foresters sailed (near right, on ship) from Liverpool to Kingstown (far right), arriving on Wednesday morning.

73

This vivid sketch (left), depicts the charge on 25 Northumberland Road as being towards the south; in reality the attack was in the opposite direction.

At around 10:30 am on Wednesday, the Sherwood Foresters headed towards Dublin in two columns, one via Ballsbridge, the other inland. After midday, as the Ballsbridge column marched along Northumberland Road a volley rang out from No. 25, occupied only by Lieutenant Malone and Vol. James Grace. Many soldiers fell. In another charge they were again cut down by heavy fire from the house as well as from nearby positions. Brigadier-General Lowe sent orders that they push forward at all costs. After 5 pm, the troops mounted more assaults on No. 25, finally taking the position. Malone was killed on the stairway but Grace escaped.

Continuous assaults were made on nearby three-storey Clanwilliam House (which dominated Mount Street Bridge) but the troops were repelled, suffering heavy casualties. Later they received consignments of hand grenades from military stores.

Left: a close-up view of No. 25 Northumberland Road, today.

Above: valiant defender at No. 25 Northumberland Road, Lieutenant Michael Malone.

The Mount Street area was now heavily surrounded by the military (right, troops at Northumberland Road). Making a final assault, the Sherwood Foresters stormed Clanwilliam House using grenades, and took it after 8 pm on Wednesday. Several Volunteers were killed, the rest escaped. The British suffered 234 casualties in total (including four officers killed), all in one day's fighting.

Right: Clanwilliam House, the 3rd Battalion's 'Thermopylae', in ruins, after Easter week.

75

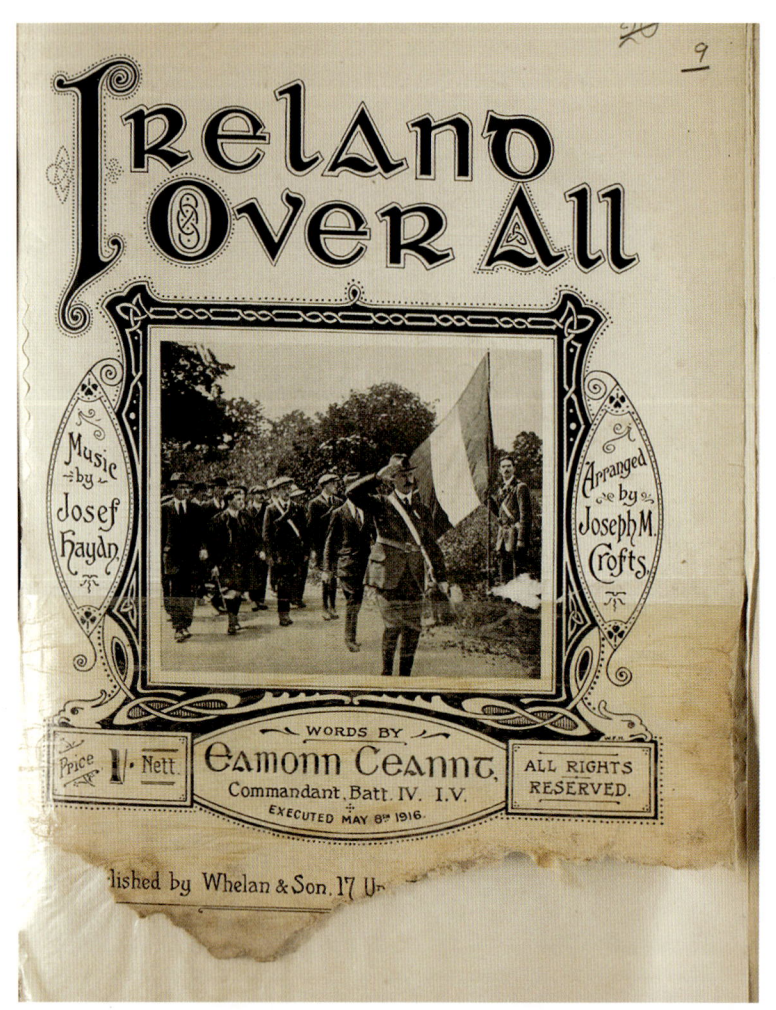

Left: songsheet, music by Haydn, words by Éamonn Ceannt. An accomplished uileann piper, he was very involved in the Gaelic League. Ceannt was at the revolutionary core – he was a member of the Military Council of the IRB.

The 4th Battalion under Ceannt mobilised at Dolphin's Barn at 11 am on Monday. They set out with Ceannt leading one unit and Lieutenant WT Cosgrave the other. Their destination was the South Dublin Union (SDU, now St James' Hospital). En route, parties were assigned to occupy strategic outposts: Watkins' brewery at Ardee Street; Jameson's distillery at Marrowbone Lane and Roe's distillery at Mount Brown.

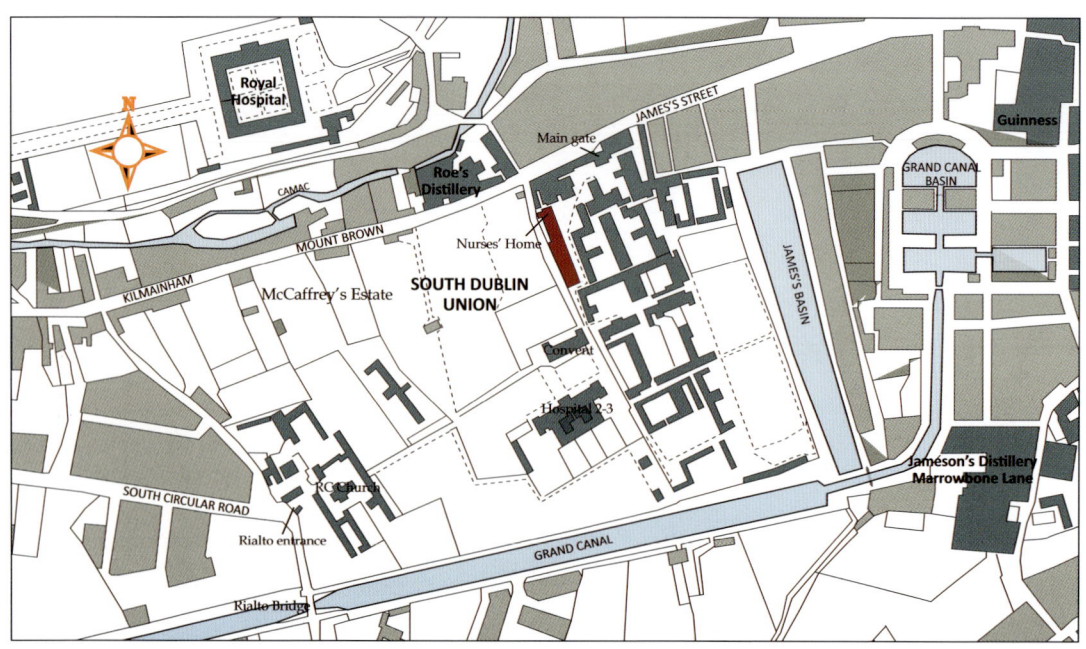

As their Volunteers occupied the SDU, Ceannt and his second-in-command, Cathal Brugha, set up HQ in the three-storey Nurses' Home (right). Centuries-old, the SDU had grown by 1916 to be a sprawling complex with hospitals, churches and 3,000 patients and staff.

After midday on Monday, soldiers of the Royal Irish Regiment set out from Richmond Barracks. Fired on by the Volunteers, the soldiers surrounded the SDU and then attempted to gain entry. After a series of hide-and-seek battles, the British occupied most of the SDU apart from the front area around the Nurses' Home. Later on Tuesday, the British HQ ordered the troops to withdraw from the SDU, for some 'extraordinary reason', according to the regimental history.

Above right: view from the distillery at Marrowbone Lane, with the SDU boundary on the right canal bank. The Volunteers, under the command of Captain Con Colbert, sniped from here.
Right: sketch of Volunteer at Marrowbone Lane.

On Thursday the British returned to the SDU. After an unsuccessful frontal assault on the Nurses' Home, troops entered the adjacent long building (left). Moving forward, they punched a hole into the entrance lobby of the home, where there was a barricade. Chaotic scenes ensued, to the sound of rifle fire and exploding grenades.

The Volunteers on the landing, hearing shouts, mistakenly thought these were orders to retreat, and withdrew. Vice-Commandant Brugha had been on the second floor. Not having heard the shouts, he went down the stairs, and was badly wounded by shrapnel from a grenade. He dragged himself to the barricade and fired an intense barrage from his Mauser C96 semi-automatic pistol. Realising that Brugha was managing to hold the position, the Volunteers mustered and as they returned to the Nurses' Home, they heard him singing 'God save Ireland'. Under the new assault, the British withdrew.

Far left: the stairs and landing of the Nurses' Home. Near left: Cathal Brugha.

The 5th Battalion under Thomas Ashe (above) mobilised on Monday near Swords. They ranged across north Co. Dublin attacking barracks. On Friday, as they attacked Ashbourne RIC barracks (above right, map; right, memorial), a convoy of around 50 RIC arrived. The Volunteers encircled and attacked the RIC, who surrendered, suffering eight dead.

The rising in the country failed, due to confusion and the countermand. To a greater or lesser degree, Volunteers in Louth, Cork, Kerry, Limerick and Ulster assembled and later went home.

Enniscorthy was an exception. Volunteers took it over on Thursday and held out until after the surrender in Dublin.

Volunteers under Liam Mellows (near right) ranged around eastern Co. Galway. 'HMS Laburnum' (far right) shelled the approaches to Galway city on Wednesday. By week's end, the rebels had disbanded.

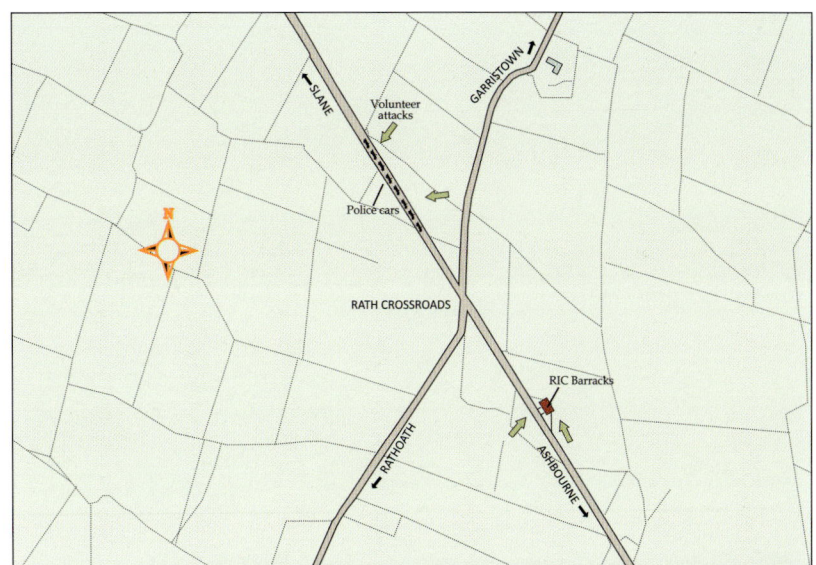

79

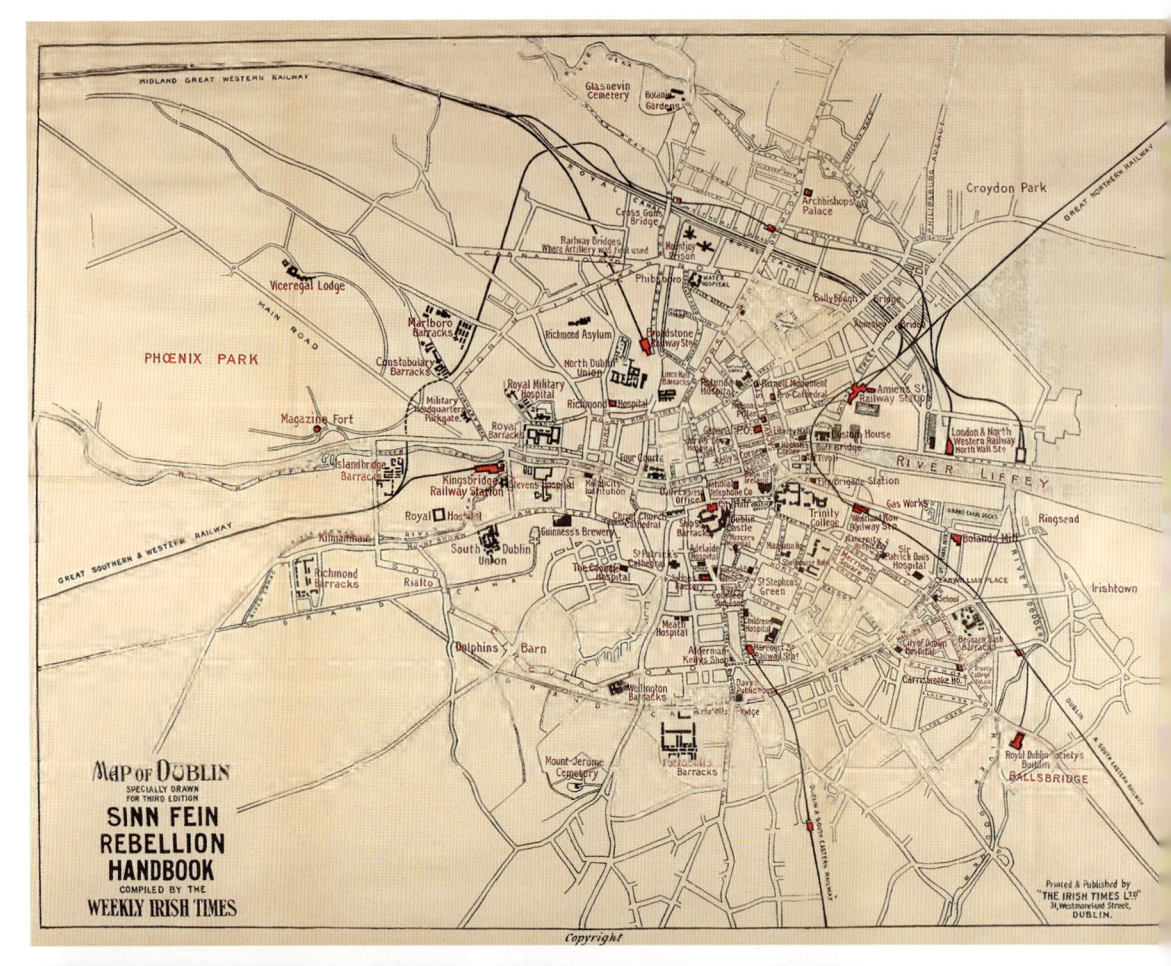

Above: map of the rising according to the 'Sinn Féin' Rebellion Handbook.

The British had put in place outer cordons north and south of the river, as well as an inner line from Kingsbridge to Trinity College.

Left: a posed photograph showing troops at a barricade of beer barrels on the Dublin quays.

Above: as British troops established their cordons and steadily advanced on Republican positions, they also built barricades. Carts and drays were useful components.

Right: the twin-arched bridge of the Great Northern Railway line over Clontarf Road. Soldiers man a barricade, made of sandbags. The machine gunner sits by his Vickers. The ladder behind allows access to their colleagues, positioned on the railway line above.

Right: soldiers at their ablutions in Trinity College, now transformed into a British military bastion.

Three days into the Rising, the Volunteers had established outposts in buildings on the east and west sides of Lower Sackville Street. Vastly outnumbering the insurgents, the British began tightening the noose on the central area around the GPO. On Thursday morning 18-pounders were wheeled from Trinity and promptly opened fire on the Sackville Street outposts.

Left: Dublin was in lock-down, swamped by British troops.

Below: a bird's-eye view of the actions of the 'Sinn Féiners'.

BIRD'S EYE VIEW OF DUBLIN LOOKING WESTWARD UP THE RIVER LIFFEY.

Right: an artist's depiction of improvised armoured lorries scurrying along O'Connell Bridge, as flames envelop buildings.

Five Daimler flatbed lorries, provided by Guinness, were armoured for the military at the Inchicore Works of the GS&WR. Three of these had locomotive smoke boxes fitted. Gun slits were cut, with some decoy slits painted on to confuse snipers.

Right: two versions of a photograph of one of these armoured lorries at Inchicore in 1916. The upper image shows the team that built it, proudly posing. In the lower image, issued in 1951 by the CIÉ Chief Mechanical Engineer, there is a curious case of redaction. Other than the soldier, all the other people have been excised from the photograph.

83

Left: this green flag was raised over the GPO, at the Prince's Street end. A tricolour was also hoisted over the Henry Street end.

At 10 am on Thursday a shell landed on the 'Irish Times' printworks on Lower Abbey Street, where large newsprint rolls went on fire. The fire spread rapidly along a barricade (partly composed of newsprint rolls) to the other side of the street. A huge blaze ensued and Wynn's Hotel caught fire. The Royal Hibernian Academy, next door, was soon enveloped in flames.

The Sackville Street area was a potential tinder-box, with stores of oil, paint and newsprint. On Thursday night, as fires raged, masses of oil drums, stored at Hoyte's chemists (Sackville Place corner), exploded. The frontage of Clery's and the Imperial Hotel collapsed. As outposts became untenable, Volunteers withdrew to the GPO.

Left: a depiction of the spectacular flames over Sackville Street on Thursday evening.

Above: one of two rare photographs, taken by photographic chemist Joseph Cripps inside the GPO. It shows the Volunteers' miscellany of equipment and weapons. The men appear to range in age from their teens to their thirties.

The GPO came under direct shell fire late on Friday afternoon (British gunners at work, right). The roof quickly caught fire and began to collapse.

The Walter Paget print (overleaf) depicts the desperate scene in the GPO.

85

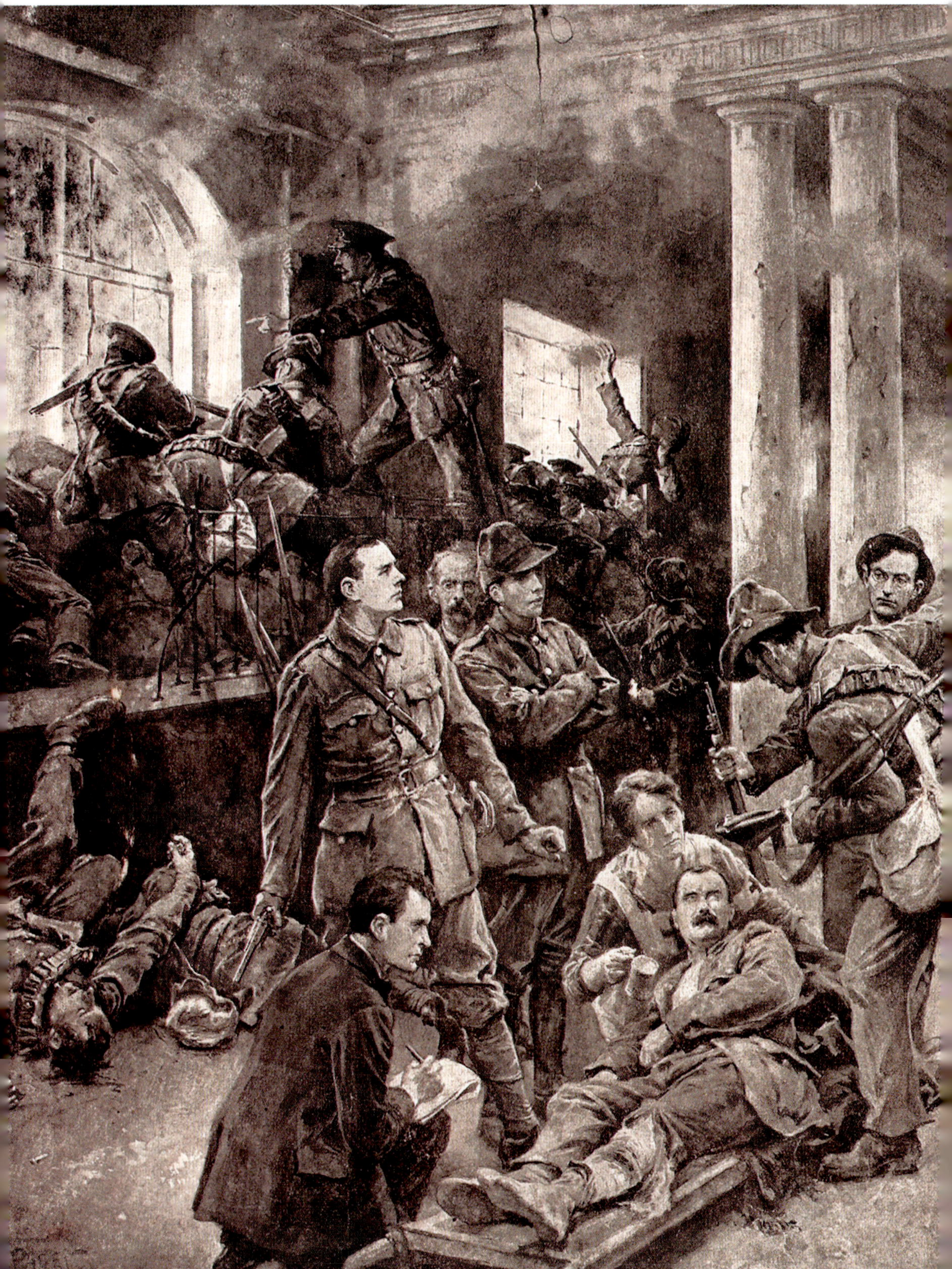

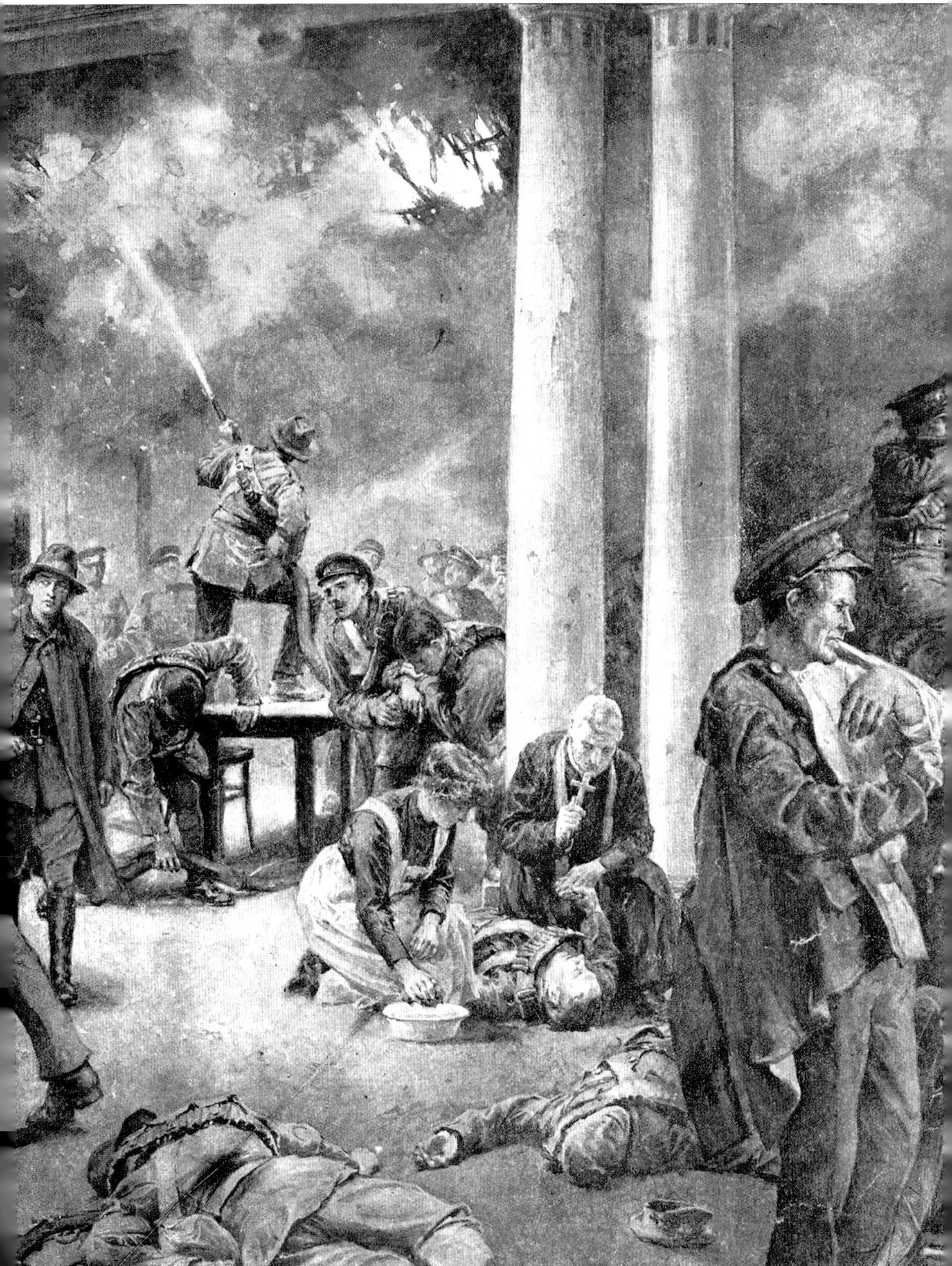

Left: a dramatic painting of the action in the GPO.

By Friday evening the situation in the burning GPO was desperate. Shelling continued and parts of the roof were falling in. Connolly (who on Thursday had been wounded in the ankle by shrapnel), decided with Pearse that the GPO was no longer tenable and they began to plan an evacuation. At around 6 pm, a party of wounded men, accompanied by most of the women, crawled through tunnelled walls to the adjacent Coliseum picture theatre. After sheltering there from heavy rifle fire, they eventually reached Jervis Street Hospital, where they were taken into British military custody.

Pearse decided to move his HQ to the Parnell Street premises (left) of Williams & Woods, confectioners.

The O'Rahilly (right) was assigned to lead an advance party down Moore Street to push through to the new location. First he would have to attack a British barricade at the junction with Parnell Street, to the north.

O'Rahilly, with a party of about 30 men, set out up Moore Street. They split into two sections – one at either side of the street. The guns opened up and O'Rahilly, was hit but bravely continued along the street. Charging against machine-gun and rifle fire – devastating when channelled down a street – there was no escape: he was mortally wounded just by Sackville Lane. As he lay dying in a doorway, he wrote a note to his wife: 'I was shot leading a rush...I got more than one bullet I think...Tons & tons of love...It was a good fight anyhow'.

Right: taken after the action – the British barricade at the top of Moore Street where it meets Parnell Street (see map overleaf).

Irish Rebellion, May, 1916.
Holding a Dublin street against the Rebels.

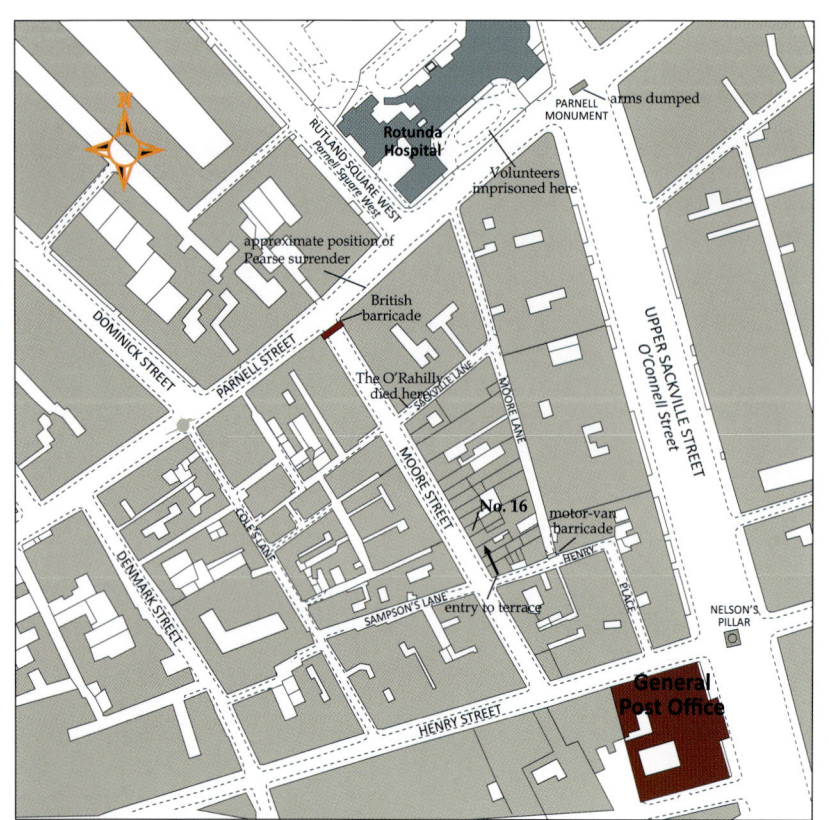

Left: map of the GPO and Moore Street, the 'Via Dolorosa' of the 1916 Rising.

The GPO, by now totally untenable, was abandoned. The main party, including the wounded (with James Connolly on a stretcher) had entered Henry Place. They had to drag a motor van to provide shelter from heavy fire at the Moore Lane intersection. They managed to force their way through the gable of the end of the terrace at the intersection of Henry Place with Moore Street.

Below: Moore Lane, looking south from Parnell Street, with Henry Place at the end.

The Volunteers broke through walls of the terrace of shops on Moore Street. James Connolly was put to bed in a back room of a premises (No. 16 – then Plunket's, poulterers, right) in the middle of the terrace. The members of the Provisional Government held a council of war here, and this unprepossessing location became the final de facto headquarters of the Irish Republic, proclaimed several days before.

As bullets continued to fly along Moore Street, a civilian emerged from a house, carrying a white flag. He was shot by a British volley. Other civilians also lay dead on the street.

One option mooted for the besieged party was to escape west to Capel Street and then head to the Four Courts. Pearse discussed this with the other leaders. However, they decided that, to avoid slaughter among civilians and supporters, they would have to treat with the British.

Right: a record – headed 'HQ Moore St' – of the decision of the Provisional Government to negotiate. It was written by Pearse on rough cardboard, all that was available, and probably taken from a picture frame.

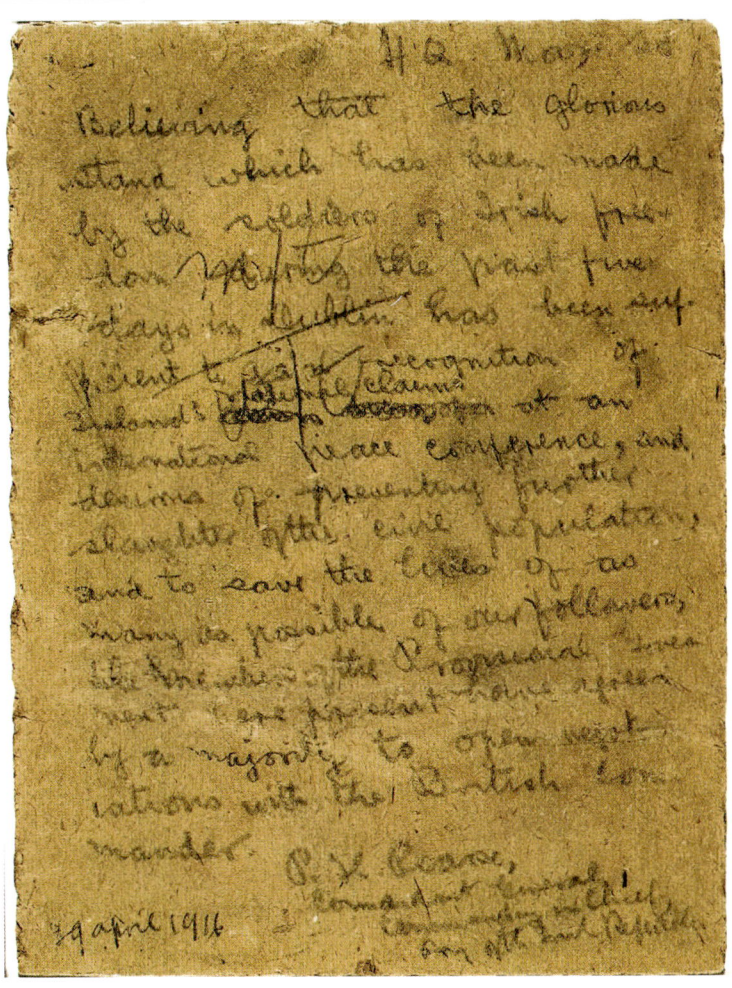

91

About 12:45 pm on Saturday, Cumann na mBan member Elizabeth O'Farrell, carrying a white flag, walked from the Moore Street HQ to the British barricade. She met Brigadier-General Lowe who said that he would only accept unconditional surrender. She returned with the news.

At around 2:30 pm Commandant-General Pearse returned with O'Farrell. He met with Lowe on Parnell Street and surrendered, handing over his sword and pistol.

Left: the defining 1916 photograph, taken by a British officer just after the surrender. O'Farrell had deliberately kept behind Pearse. This photograph was used in the 'Daily Sketch' (below left). O'Farrell's feet and skirts were painted out, most likely as a quick tidy up of a poor-quality image. Despite a legend to the contrary, this is the only image where she was airbrushed out.

Below: Plaque to Elizabeth O'Farrell at Holles Street Hospital, where she later worked.

In accordance with the surrender arrangements, the Volunteers marched out towards Sackville Street and laid down their arms at the Parnell Monument. They were then ordered to the forecourt of the nearby Rotunda Hospital (right). More arrived from other garrisons. By 10:30 pm on Saturday around 400 were assembled there. A British officer (Captain Lea-Wilson) abused the prisoners, attacking Tom Clarke and Seán MacDermott in particular. On Sunday morning all were marched to Richmond Barracks.

Below: prisoners at Bachelors Walk en route to Richmond Barracks.

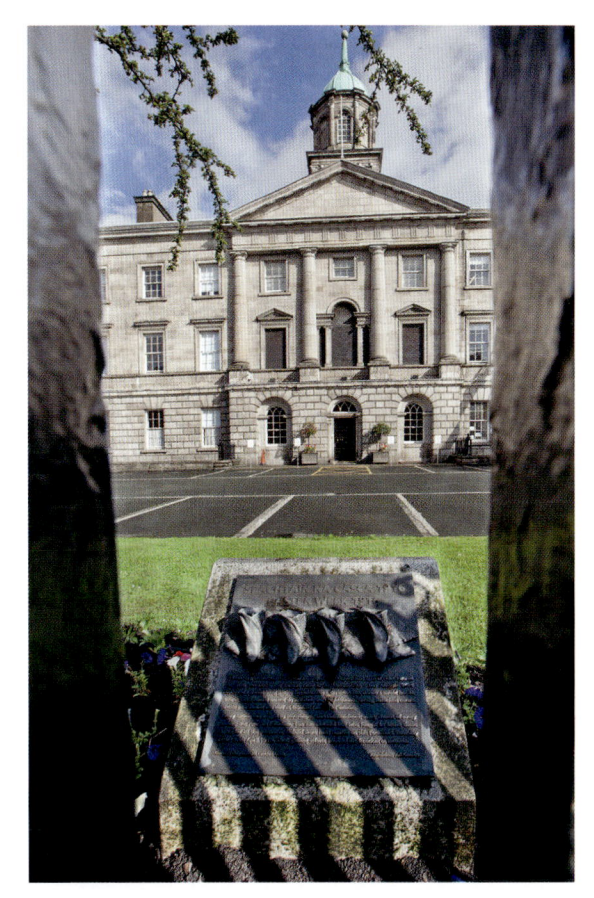

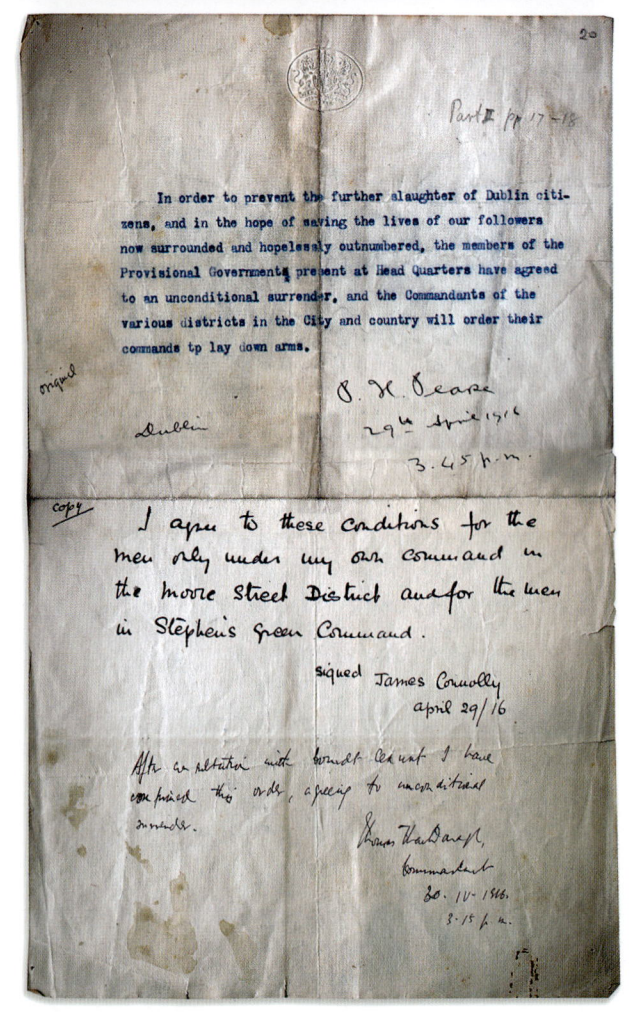

After the surrender James Connolly (wounded with a shattered shin bone) was carried on a stretcher to Dublin Castle. This photograph (above) was taken at the corner of Sackville and Parnell Streets. It shows a person on a stretcher (almost certainly Connolly), attended by Volunteers and guarded by British soldiers.

Patrick Pearse was driven to meet General Maxwell at the Parkgate Street HQ, where he signed the surrender order, (left). An officer brought the document to James Connolly at the Red Cross hospital in Dublin Castle. As Connolly was injured, he dictated his agreement and then signed it. The following day Commandant MacDonagh also signed.

The indefatigably brave O'Farrell, having delivered the surrender note to the Four Courts, spent the night in military custody in the National Bank (at the corner of Sackville and Parnell Streets, in the background of the photograph on the left). On Sunday, she went to other outposts with the surrender note. There was little enthusiasm for surrender in Jacob's. As depicted (right) in their frustration, many Volunteers destroyed their weapons. Commandant MacDonagh was then driven, along with two Capuchin priests, to meet Éamonn Ceannt at the SDU and inform him of the surrender order.

"WHEN THE FLAG CAME DOWN AT EASTER."

The garrison at the College of Surgeons, under the command of Michael Mallin and Countess Markievicz, surrendered to a British officer. Right: Mallin and Markievicz under guard at Richmond Barracks.

Most of those captured were brought to Richmond Barracks. They were held in the gymnasium (left).

Members of the DMP 'G' Division peered through this window of the partition at the back (below left) scrutinising and selecting suspects down below in the body of the gymnasium hall. Those suspected of being in senior roles were held in the barracks, pending trial.

Below: active in picking out prisoners were Detective Sergeant Patrick Smyth (facing camera) and Detective Daniel Hoey, (back to camera, who is reported as being one of those who identified Seán MacDermott). Both were shot by Michael Collins' Squad in 1919.

Right: with martial law in force, the Commander-in-chief, General Sir John Maxwell, was in full control. Having spent much of his career on campaign in the colonies, he now had to deal with this rebellious semi-colony. He set up a regime of punishment, untrammelled (at least initially) by any effective political control or nuanced consideration of the impact on opinion across Ireland. To deter future insurgency, his priority was to punish the rebel leaders quickly, both for association with the German enemy and for the loss of life and damage to property.

Field general courts martial were established at Richmond Barracks. For the British it afforded a simplified wartime method, quicker and with a more predictable outcome. There was no legal representation for the accused and no right of appeal. The trials were held in camera.

Right: en route by prison van to the quays. In the days and weeks that followed, the bulk of the prisoners — those not selected for trial — were sent to be interned in Britain.

Above: soldiers mill and officers confer outside the courts martial room at Richmond Barracks, as Michael O'Hanrahan is escorted to his trial on 3 May.

The first trials were held on 2 May – those of Patrick Pearse, Thomas Clarke and Thomas MacDonagh. All three, signatories of the Proclamation, were sentenced to death.

Left: in captivity at Richmond Barracks. Centre, in Volunteer uniform, Joseph Plunkett's two brothers, George and Jack.

After Éamon de Valera and his 3rd Battalion had surrendered on Sunday, they were initially held at the RDS showgrounds in Ballsbridge. Above: de Valera (arrow) leads his men to captivity.

De Valera (right, under escort) was lucky. He had missed the initial screening and the first wave of executions (which included the other Dublin commandants). General Maxwell, under pressure from Prime Minister Asquith to curtail executions, commuted de Valera's death sentence.

Countess Markievicz (left, escorted by a wardress) was sentenced to death on 4 May, with a recommendation that mercy be shown 'solely and only on account of her sex'. Maxwell, having been instructed by Asquith that there should be no female executions, commuted the sentence to penal servitude for life.

Left: under intertwined serpents, the main entrance to Kilmainham Gaol, Ireland's 'Bastille'. Kilmainham had ceased to be a convict prison in 1910. Subsequently it functioned as a military jail. The condemned men of 1916 were brought here for execution. Conditions were primitive – there was scarcely any furniture for prisoners, only sacks on the floor, and lighting was by candle-light or gas-flame.

Right: Tom Clarke's cell. Clarke, eldest of the leaders, was a veteran Fenian and the IRB éminence grise of the Rising. On the eve of his execution, he fatalistically told his wife that he was relieved to be executed, as he dreaded a return to prison.

Hours before he was executed, Joseph Plunkett married his fiancée, Grace Gifford (below). At around 11 pm, with soldiers as witnesses and by the light of a single candle, they married in the chapel at Kilmainham (right). When she returned to the prison at around 2 am, the couple were allowed 10 minutes together in a cell full of soldiers. Plunkett was then shot at dawn.

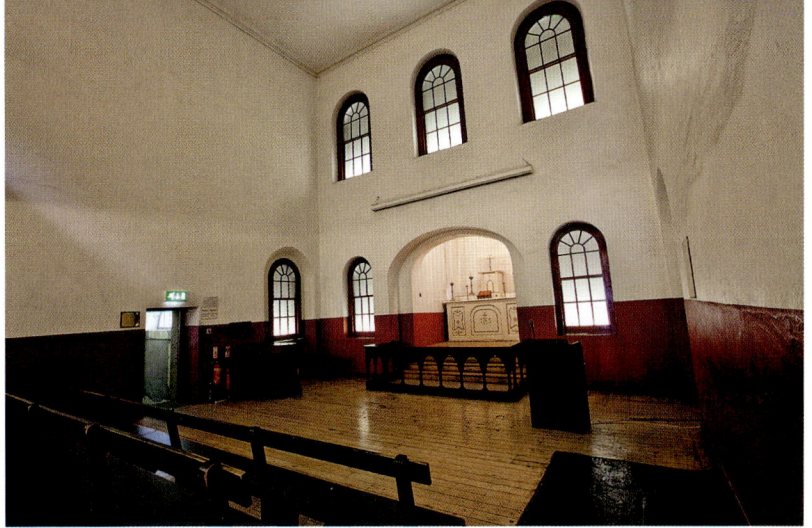

Left: executions were gruesomely simple (depiction, left). An officer had previously inserted a blank in a random rifle of one of a 12-man squad, who were marched into the Stonebreakers' Yard. Along with a priest, the blindfolded and bound prisoner was escorted to the yard. The order rang out: 'Ready, Present, Fire!' The soldiers were then marched away.

Left: a grim place of execution – the Stonebreakers' Yard.

All the executed leaders met their deaths bravely. Those executed in rapid succession at the beginning of May were (right): on 3 May – Patrick Pearse, Thomas Clarke and Thomas MacDonagh; on 4 May – Joseph Plunkett, Edward Daly, Michael O'Hanrahan and William Pearse; on 5 May – John MacBride; on 8 May – Éamonn Ceannt, Michael Mallin, Seán Heuston and Con Colbert.

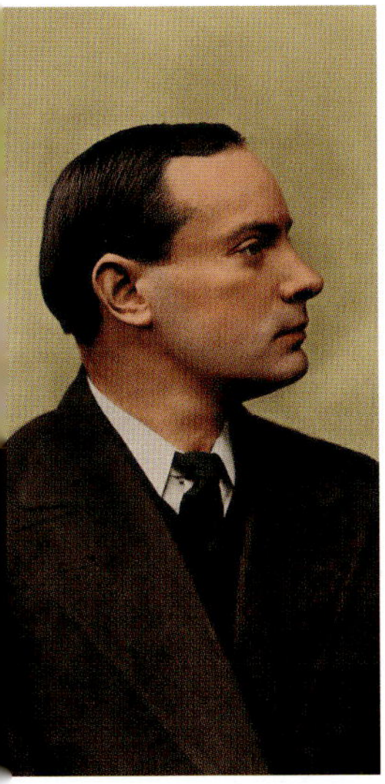
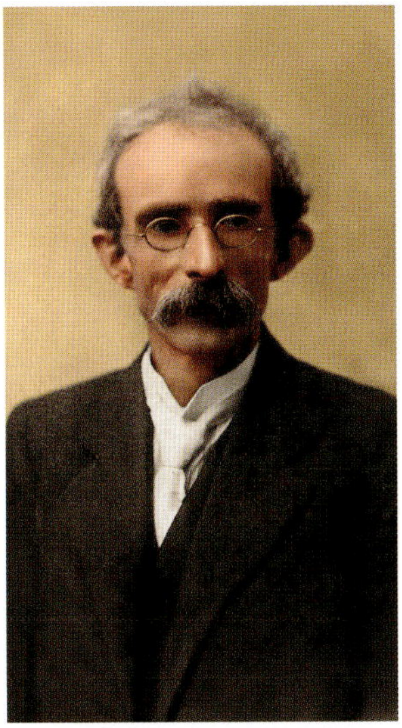
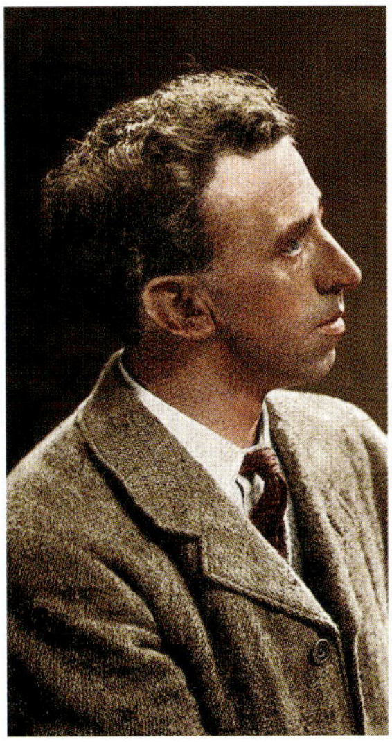
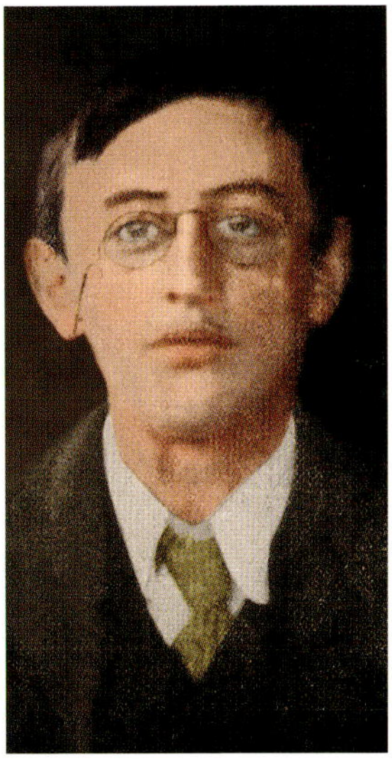
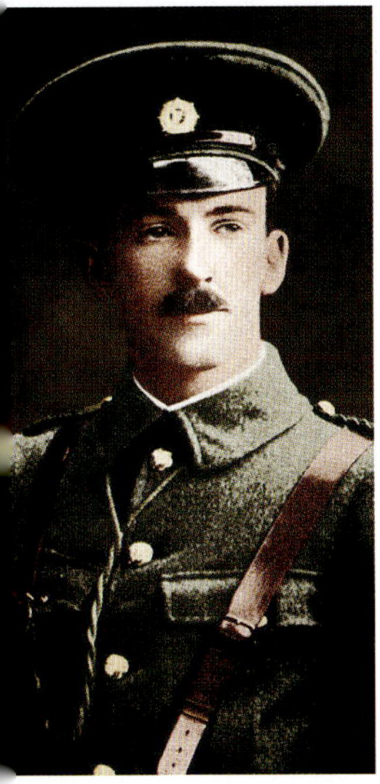
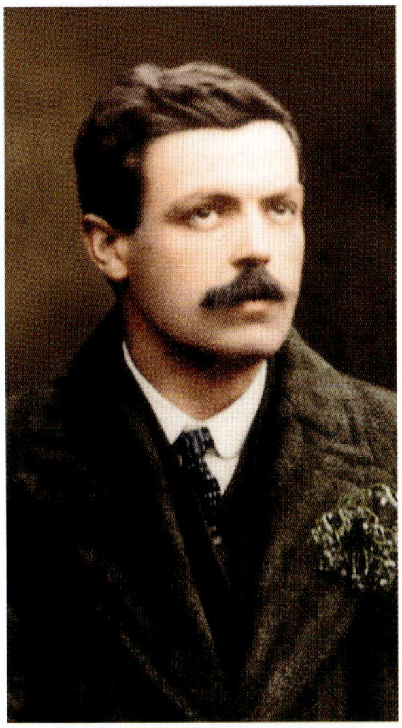
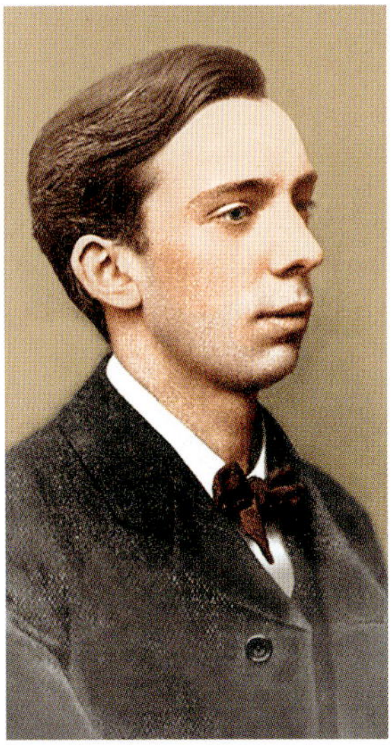
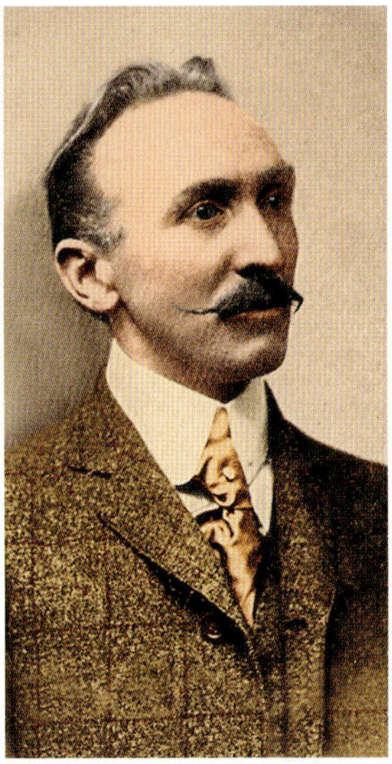
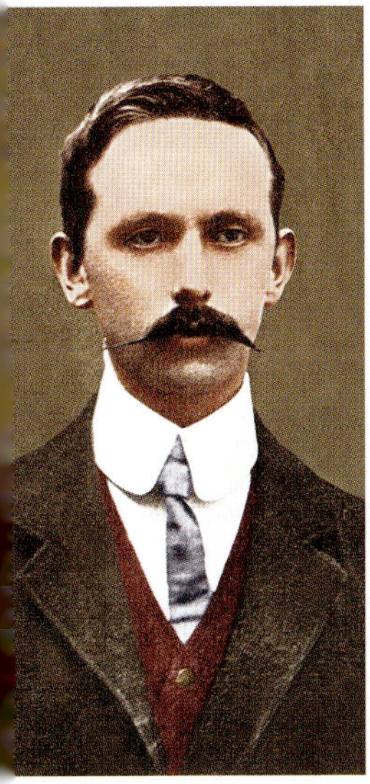
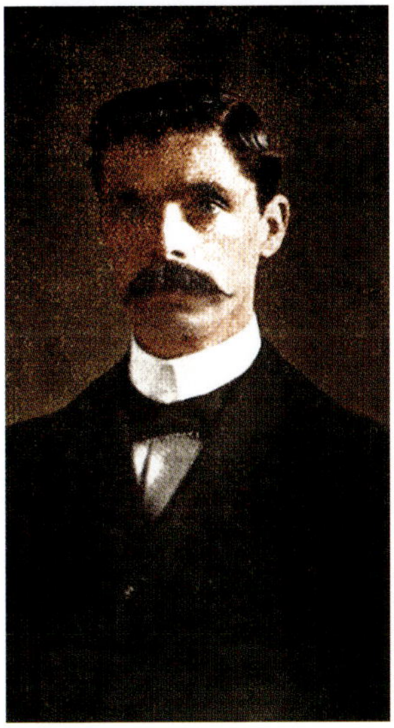
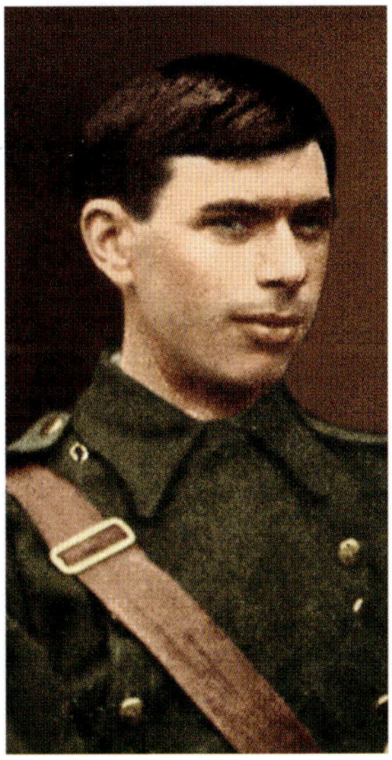
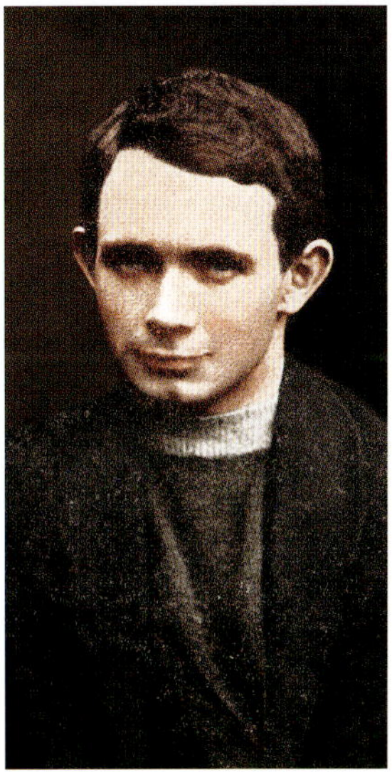

Irish Rebellion, May, 1916.
Arrest of Edmund Kent, at 4 a.m.
He was subsequently shot.

Above: Thomas Kent. As part of a countrywide roundup, on 2 May a party of RIC arrived after daybreak at the Kent farmhouse in Co. Cork to arrest Thomas and his brothers, prominent Republicans. In an exchange of fire, a Head Constable was killed and one of the Kents was mortally wounded. Thomas (the postcard, left, inaccurately refers to 'Edmund') and another brother, William, were arrested. Both were court-martialled in Cork on 4 May. Thomas was sentenced to death and shot on 9 May.

Left: on 12 May, Prime Minister Asquith (centre) made an impromptu visit to Ireland, arriving scarcely after the last volleys had rung out in Kilmainham. He visited the prisoners in Richmond Barracks and promised them 'the best food possible'.

James Connolly (far right) and Seán MacDermott (near right) were executed on 12 May. MacDermott, despite being afflicted by polio in 1911, was the most dynamic of all. Together with Clarke, he had revitalised the IRB. One historian called him the 'mainspring' of the planning and implementation of the Rising.

At midnight on 11 May, Lillie Connolly had been brought to see her husband. As she realised that the end was imminent, Connolly requested her not to cry. He added 'hasn't it been a full life and isn't this a good end?'

Connolly's ghastly form of execution caused outrage. Right: his death is colourfully depicted in this New York poster of October 1916.

The wounded Connolly was conveyed by ambulance to Kilmainham. As dawn broke, he was placed on a kitchen chair (rough sketch by the presiding British officer, below), and shot.

105

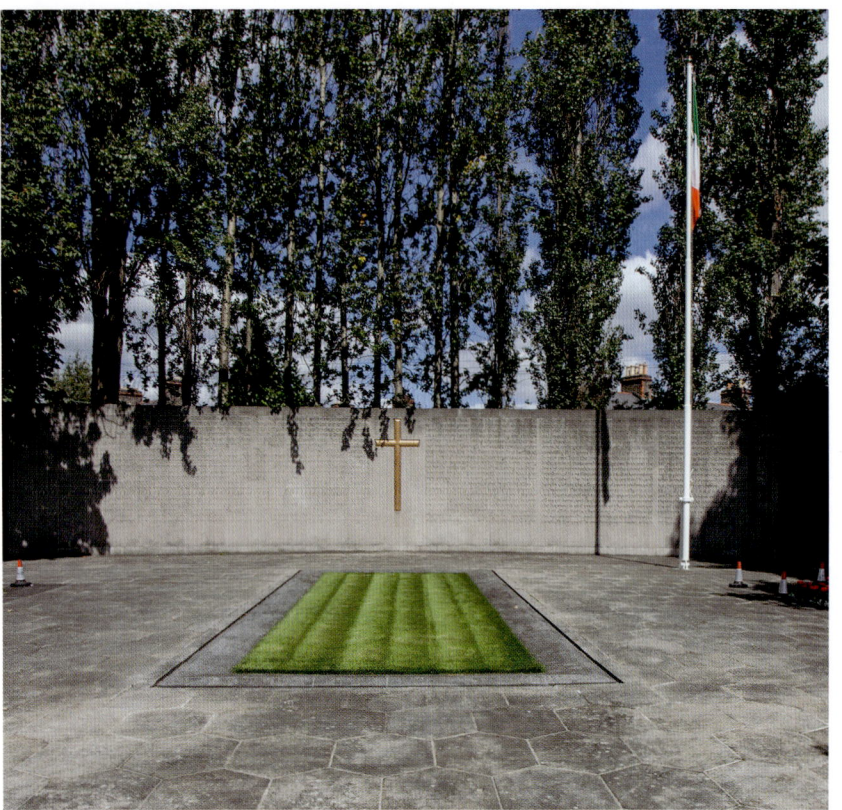

Left: the most obscure location possible was chosen to bury the executed 'ringleaders'. The bodies were interred without coffins in quicklime. They were placed in a pit dug at the rear of a yard at Arbour Hill Detention Barracks in Dublin. The graves are now a central place of national commemoration.

Left: reflecting the clarity of the inspirational Proclamation, its words are chiselled in clear detail on the boundary wall at Arbour Hill.

Left: the names of the executed leaders are set out in the sequence in which they were buried.

Right: the 'New York Times' of 21 May reports on the situation in Dublin in the aftermath of the rising by the 'Sinn Féin Revolutionists'.

As the rising ended, Dubliners took stock of their shattered city centre. The military had single-mindedly shelled insurgent positions using the 18-pounders. The shrapnel shells had caused fires to start in the tinder box that was Sackville Street. A massive conflagration resulted which destroyed the central area.

Right: a map, prepared by the head of the Dublin Fire Brigade, shows the damage in central Dublin.

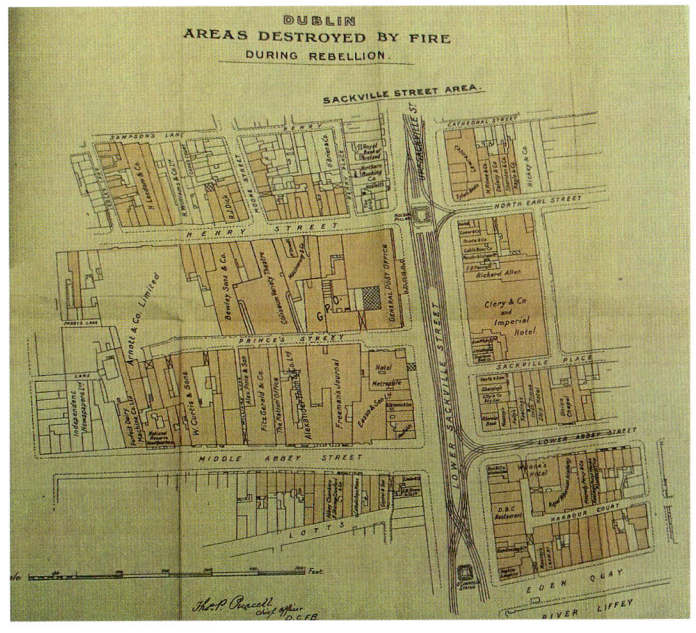

Left: ruin all around in Dublin. This was not one of the Belgian cities that had been flattened in the ongoing 'Great War'. This devastation was in one of the principal cities of the supposedly 'United' Kingdom.

Left: on the other side of Lower Sackville Street, opposite the GPO, the shell of the Imperial Hotel.

For days after the fighting had ceased, dead bodies were being found amidst the rubble. Below: a sanitary notice issued in the aftermath.

PREVENTION OF EPIDEMIC.

Persons discovering dead bodies should inform the Police or the Chief Medical Officer of Health, Municipal Buildings, Castle Street, immediately.

Above: looking east up Henry Street towards Nelson's Pillar. The buildings on both sides of the street were destroyed. The GPO and buildings leading up to it are on the right; buildings at the junction with Moore Street are to the left.

Right: the GPO in ruins. Miraculously, the portico was mostly intact, but the rest of the huge complex was a burnt-out shell. The building had just been extensively – and expensively – modernised a short time before Easter 1916.

Above: lorries, carts and drays amidst the devastation on Eden Quay. In central Dublin building contractors began to clear away the rubble.

Left: a view of the junction of Lower Abbey and Sackville Streets. The distinctive polychromatic (and now skeletal) frontage of the DBC Luncheon Rooms, is in the middle right. Reis's premises at the left-hand corner has disappeared into rubble. Its top floor had housed the Irish School of Wireless; it was taken over by the Volunteers, who broadcast from there.

Above: with ruins in the background, a prisoner is escorted across O'Connell Bridge.

Someone had to be blamed. Right: the 'Daily Sketch' announces the resignation of Augustine Birrell, the Chief Secretary in early May. A 'Royal Commission on the Rebellion in Ireland' began hearings on 18 May. Among its conclusions on the causes of the rebellion were: tolerance of militias, poor intelligence, and a dysfunctional system of government in Ireland.

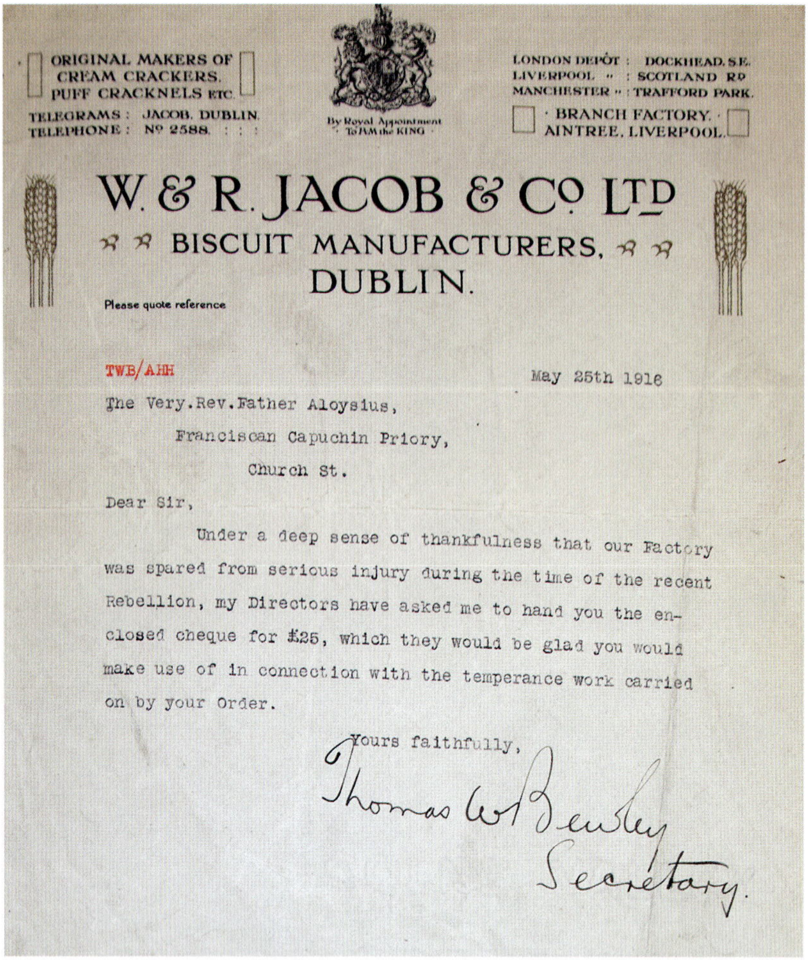

> ORIGINAL MAKERS OF CREAM CRACKERS. PUFF CRACKNELS ETC.
> TELEGRAMS: JACOB, DUBLIN.
> TELEPHONE: Nº 2588.
>
> By Royal Appointment To H.M. the KING
>
> LONDON DEPÔT: DOCKHEAD. S.E.
> LIVERPOOL ": SCOTLAND Rᴅ
> MANCHESTER ": TRAFFORD PARK.
> BRANCH FACTORY.
> AINTREE, LIVERPOOL.
>
> # W. & R. JACOB & Cᴼ LTᴅ
> ## BISCUIT MANUFACTURERS, DUBLIN.
>
> Please quote reference
>
> TWB/AHH
>
> May 25th 1916
>
> The Very. Rev. Father Aloysius,
>   Franciscan Capuchin Priory,
>   Church St.
>
> Dear Sir,
>
>   Under a deep sense of thankfulness that our Factory was spared from serious injury during the time of the recent Rebellion, my Directors have asked me to hand you the enclosed cheque for £25, which they would be glad you would make use of in connection with the temperance work carried on by your Order.
>
>   Yours faithfully,
>
>   Thomas W Bewley
>   Secretary.

Left: in the aftermath of the Rising, W & R Jacob sent a cheque for £25 to the Capuchin Father Aloysius (who had assisted in negotiations of surrender at their premises) in appreciation of the fact that 'our Factory was spared from serious injury during... the recent rebellion'. Aloysius thanked them and returned the cheque, writing that 'any services that I may have rendered... were such as my duty as a Priest... (required)'.

Starting on Easter Monday, Dublin Fire Brigade (left, members in action) struggled manfully all week to extinguish fires.

Above: as the GPO was out of action, 'separation women' (wives of Irishmen serving in the British Army) had to queue for their separation allowance at the Aungier Street post office. Soldiers keep order at the scene.

Just after the surrender at Jacob's, a burst from a British machine gun shattered the window of Marsh's Library, damaging books. One entered the spine of this 1649 French book (right), ripping and distorting it.

113

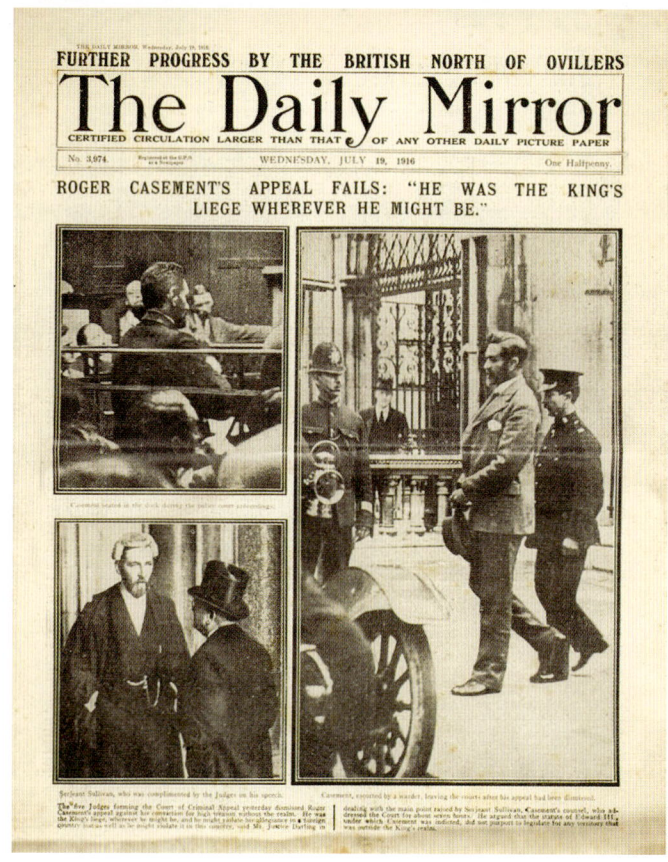

Above: painting of Casement's appearance at the Court of Criminal Appeal, London on 17 July 1916, in an appeal against his sentence.

Left: the 'Daily Mirror' announces the failure of the appeal.

The trial for treason of Sir Roger Casement, has been described as an elaborate show trial. He had been found guilty on 29 June: 'Your crime was that of assisting the King's enemies...' He was sentenced to death.

Casement was hanged at Pentonville Prison on 3 August. In 1965, his remains were exhumed, repatriated, and reburied with full military honours at Glasnevin.

Chapter 3
War of Independence

After the suppression of the Rising in Easter of 1916, it appeared that the British could return to concentrate on winning the 'Great' War. However, the execution of the rebel leaders led to a rise in sympathy for the cause of independence. Immediately after the Rising over 2,500 Republicans had been arrested and shipped to various prisons in Britain. Later most were transferred to the bleak Frongoch camp, a former prisoner of war camp in North Wales. Frongoch and other locations became a university of revolution – there was time to reflect and plan afresh for a redoubled struggle for independence. As the rebels were released from detention in Britain they joined Sinn Féin, which then won a wave of by-elections. Under severe pressure from a German assault, the British miscalculated and proclaimed conscription in Ireland. This generated universal opposition. The Irish Volunteers re-organised in a new purposeful and practical direction. An 'Irish Convention' assembled all shades of opinion, save Sinn Féin,

to discuss the governance of Ireland. A mild proposal for an agreed Home Rule administration for all of Ireland faltered under opposition from a Catholic bishop, and the convention petered out. As they were winning the war the British did not proceed with conscription but the damage was done. Senior Sinn Féin leaders were arrested under the 'German Plot', leaving Michael Collins and others to pursue a more militant course. As the war ended, a long-deferred General Election was held. In Ireland, Sinn Féin gained a commanding 73 seats, resoundingly eclipsing the Irish Parliamentary Party's mere six seats. The Unionists took 26 seats. The First Dáil Éireann, held in January 1919, ratified the Irish Republic, proclaimed in Easter 1916. It also sought recognition of Ireland at the Paris Peace Conference, but the delegation sent there was shunned. An ambush by Volunteers at Soloheadbeg, coincidentally on the same day as the First Dáil, resulted in two RIC deaths. This caused disquiet in senior Republican circles, but in reality the ambush marked the start of a ruthless phase of the war for independence. Several prison escapes by Republicans ensued, particularly that of Éamon de Valera from Lincoln Gaol. Reflecting the new purposeful struggle, Michael Collins established the 'Squad' whose mission was to eliminate spies, the scourge of previous Irish independence movements. The DMP 'G' Division, effective gatherers of intelligence on Dublin Republicans, were neutralised. Across the country, the effectiveness of the RIC, eyes and ears of the British grasp on Ireland, was diminished as they were boycotted. They were withdrawn from smaller, more vulnerable barracks in the face of increased attacks. As 1919 ended, an ambitious (but failed) attempt to assassinate the Viceroy, Lord French, in Dublin shocked the British authorities.

As the IRA assailed the RIC, a wave of new recruits (mostly ex-servicemen), soon known as 'Black and Tans', was recruited. A paramilitary force of ex-officers, the Auxiliary Division, was also established and assigned to the 'hottest' areas. Their brutal approach generated fear and incurred the hatred of the local population. A hunger strike by prisoners in Mountjoy Gaol in Dublin ended with a botched release by the authorities. The refusal by railwaymen to transport Crown forces lasted until the end of 1920. March 1920 saw the Lord Mayor of Cork assassinated by masked men – the RIC Inspector accused of instigating this was killed in Lisburn, sparking sectarian riots. By mid-1920, the IRA switched to ambushes of mobile patrols. Guerrilla warfare has been called the method of the weak versus the strong. The Boers had demonstrated the value of this decades before, as did the Volunteers' action at Ashbourne in 1916. Over the course of the conflict, the IRA adopted guerrilla warfare in an ad hoc way, responding to circumstances. Units across the country empirically crafted their tactics to suit the local situation. A major development was the setting up of flying columns from late summer 1920. Generally operating full-time in groups of around 25, they had more weapons than other units and proved very effective.

They had local knowledge and operated flexibly, enjoying much independence from Dublin GHQ. The Lord Mayor of Cork, Terence MacSwiney, went on hunger strike after being arrested. His death sparked a wave of sympathy. Kevin Barry, a young Volunteer, was executed in November amidst mass protests. Later that month, on 'Bloody Sunday', the IRA assassinated British spies in central Dublin. November ended with an ambush in Kilmichael where 17 Auxiliaries were killed. In December, Cork city centre was burned by Auxiliaries, causing widespread damage.

As 1920 ended, the war had reached a new intensity. The number of casualties among the Crown forces for that year had spiralled – a total of 231 were killed (178 police and 53 military). There had been many reprisals on towns and villages across Ireland in 1920, but in January 1921 at Midleton the first 'official' reprisal occurred: it was allowed for under martial law, recently declared in Munster. In the following months, official reprisals across the province became commonplace. As the British increased their forces and roamed the country, IRA ambushes and raids escalated. Both sides improved their tactics. These included the IRA gaining mastery of road mines. The British Army developed cross-country sweeps; in late March 1921, the RAF was empowered to use machine guns and drop bombs.

On 25 May 1921 Volunteers of the Dublin Brigade mustered to attack the Custom House. The building was set on fire. This, the biggest IRA operation in the war, resulted in the death of four Volunteers (another died later of wounds). Four civilians were also killed. The capture of over a hundred experienced Volunteers was also a blow. However this must be seen against Dublin Brigade's nominal strength of 4,500. The IRA deliberately intensified their Dublin activities in the aftermath. Despite the temporary loss of Gandon's masterpiece, the objective of destroying this vital administrative centre was achieved, another big step in making Ireland ungovernable. This 'spectacular' added to the pressure on the British to begin negotiations. A 'Government of Ireland' bill enacted in the British Parliament established partition on the island of Ireland, entailing 'Northern' and 'Southern' parliaments. In an election in May, Sinn Féin, unopposed, won practically all the seats in the 'South'. Unionists won a majority in the 'North' and King George V opened the Northern Parliament in Belfast in June. Reflecting a mood for conciliation, the King made a speech which asked for all Irishmen 'to pause... to forgive and forget'. The British Government had been embarrassed by a spate of reports about the situation in Ireland and the atrocities of the Crown forces, and ended a period of confused direction of the war by inviting Éamon de Valera to meet Lloyd George for talks in London. General Macready (Commander-in-Chief, Ireland) met de Valera at the Mansion House in Dublin to discuss terms. A truce was agreed, coming into force on 11 July 1921. Under its terms, the British ended military manoeuvres, raids and searches. The IRA were to cease attacks on Crown forces.

Concentration Camp, Frongoch, Bala.

Only a year ago

A Spack at Frongoch, just before bed.

*Above: Frongoch camp. Immediately after the Rising over 2,500 Republicans had been arrested and shipped to various prisons in Britain. Later most were transferred to the bleak Frongoch camp – a former POW camp in North Wales. Frongoch and other locations became a university of revolution – there was time to reflect and plan afresh a redoubled struggle for independence.
Left: life in a hut at North Frongoch.*

With the rebels defeated, Britain could now concentrate on fighting Germany and its allies. Nervousness about the loyalty of Irish regiments in the army meant a positive spin was strongly promoted. Above: the 'Illustrated London News' of June 1916 depicts the Munster Fusiliers responding to German taunts about the Rising. They supposedly sang 'Rule Britannia' and charged the German trenches.

Right: the view was different across the Atlantic. This German-American weekly of May 1916 depicts a heroic Pearse greeting George Washington, with the message: 'We fought the same foe and for the same reason'. The British were rightly uneasy about the US reaction to the Rising.

THE BIRTH OF THE IRISH REPUBLIC - 1916.

The broad spread of Irish public opinion had not initially supported this rebellion by a group of advanced nationalists. However, after the May executions, sympathy grew, leading to a shift in favour of the insurgents and their ideals.

Left: the dream of 1916 and Irish freedom entered the national consciousness. In this poster the Easter Rising is portrayed in a semi-mystical setting.

Right: magical realism? A heroic Volunteer tramples on a Union Jack, while brandishing a tricolour in front of the GPO.

Right: in June 1916, the 'Catholic Bulletin' commenced a series of articles on the lives of the participants in the Rising. The British authorities were outraged and considered censoring the journal. It was a straw in the wind – this influential and respectable journal was sympathetic to the aims of the 1916 rebels. It reflected the groundswell of Irish public opinion that led to the foundation of the revived and more militant Sinn Féin in October 1917.

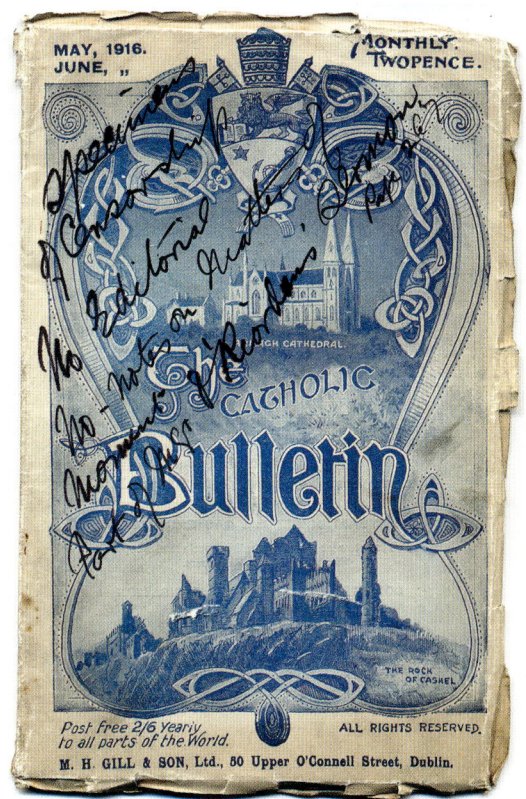

THE GOLDEN MOMENT.

Erin (to Mr. Redmond and Sir Edward Carson). "COME, MY FRIENDS, YOU'RE BOTH IRISHMEN; WHY NOT BURY THE HATCHET——IN THE VITALS OF THE COMMON ENEMY?"

J'ai vu... 2ᵉ année - N°77 6 Mai 1916
LA RÉVOLTE EN IRLANDE
LE GÉNÉRAL SIR JOHN MAXWELL QUI A RÉPRIMÉ L'ÉMEUTE.

MOST REV. DR. O'DWYER
Photo (Late Lord-Bishop of Limerick). LAFAYETTE

At the end of May 1916, Lloyd George was tasked by Asquith to resolve the Irish question. He met the Unionists and the Irish Parliamentary Party (IPP). He proposed implementation of the 1914 Home Rule Bill, with exclusion of six northern counties. Lloyd George gave the impression to the IPP that the exclusion was temporary. However, he assured Unionists that the exclusion was permanent. When this became apparent to the IPP, the negotiations collapsed.
Left: Punch's view of the golden opportunity.

With martial law declared, General Maxwell (below, far left) was now effectively ruler of Ireland. On 6 May 1916, he wrote to Bishop O'Dwyer of Limerick (near left) asking him to restrain two nationalist priests. This rebounded spectacularly; the bishop's reply to Maxwell attracted widespread support. It referred to recent events as being 'cruel and oppressive', and went on: 'You took care that no plea for mercy should interpose on behalf of the poor young fellows who surrendered to you in Dublin...Personally, I regard your action with horror, and I believe that it has outraged the conscience of the country.'

Above: Michael Collins (arrow) at Stafford Detention Barracks. His energy and organising skills came to the fore when he was transferred to Frongoch. He reflected on the Rising, calling it bungled and lacking organisation.

In December 1916 there was a general amnesty. Those from Frongoch were released, arriving in Dublin on Christmas Eve. The last batch of prisoners was released in June 1917. Right: the later releases were greeted by large crowds, as seen here at Westland Row Station.

IRISH REBELLION, MAY, 1916.

GEORGE NOBLE COUNT PLUNKETT, F.S.A.
(Father of Joseph Plunkett, who was Executed, and of George and John Plunkett, Sentenced to Penal Servitude). Arrested May 1st, 1916, and detained in Richmond Barracks till June 5th, and now Deported to Oxford.

Sinn Féin had been a minority 'moderate' separatist grouping and had not supported the 1916 Rising. Nevertheless, mistakenly, the British press dubbed the rebels 'Sinn Féiners'. As the prisoners came home they drifted into Sinn Féin and it began to regroup. With this new influx, it began to embody a more militant nationalism.

The IPP MP for North Roscommon died, which led to a by-election on 3 February 1917. George Noble Plunkett (left), father of the executed leader, Joseph Plunkett, stood for Sinn Féin and won by a large margin.

The death of the IPP member for South Longford, an old Fenian in his late seventies, led to another by-election in May 1917. Joseph McGuinness (left), a veteran of the Four Courts garrison and convicted prisoner in Lewes Prison, was proposed. A well-oiled Sinn Féin election machine campaigned powerfully, eliciting sympathy for the dead of Easter Week, seizing the opportunity to force England 'to open the dungeon doors' and piling opprobrium on the IPP for their role in recruiting for the British Army. McGuinness won by a narrow margin.

Above: Around 2,000 people met at Beresford Place on 10 June 1917 to protest about the detention of those still imprisoned in Lewes Jail. Right: the DMP declared the meeting illegal and the speakers Cathal Brugha (right) and Count Plunkett (far right) were arrested. A scuffle ensued and there was an attempt to rescue the two men. Inspector John Mills was struck with a hurley by a member of Na Fianna Éireann. Mills died, the first Crown forces' fatality since the Easter Rising.

The next by-election, that in East Clare, was due to the death of Major William Redmond MP (John's brother) in France in June 1917 (near left).

Éamon de Valera, Commandant at Boland's Bakery, was nominated as the Sinn Féin candidate for East Clare. The 'Road to Freedom' was a stirring call in a Sinn Féin election pamphlet (far left).

De Valera secured 71% of the vote. He speaks on the Ennis courthouse steps (below), after his decisive win.

Sinn Féin selected 1916 veteran, William T. Cosgrave (just released from jail), for the next by-election, for Kilkenny City. The 'felon' branding (right) was proving to be a powerful vote winner.

Sinn Féin was on a roll. It mounted a strong campaign and on 10 August, Cosgrave won twice as many votes as his IPP opponent. Right: Cosgrave (hatless) makes a speech from the balcony of Kilkenny Courthouse after being elected. His fellow MP, Éamon de Valera (wearing glasses), looks on.

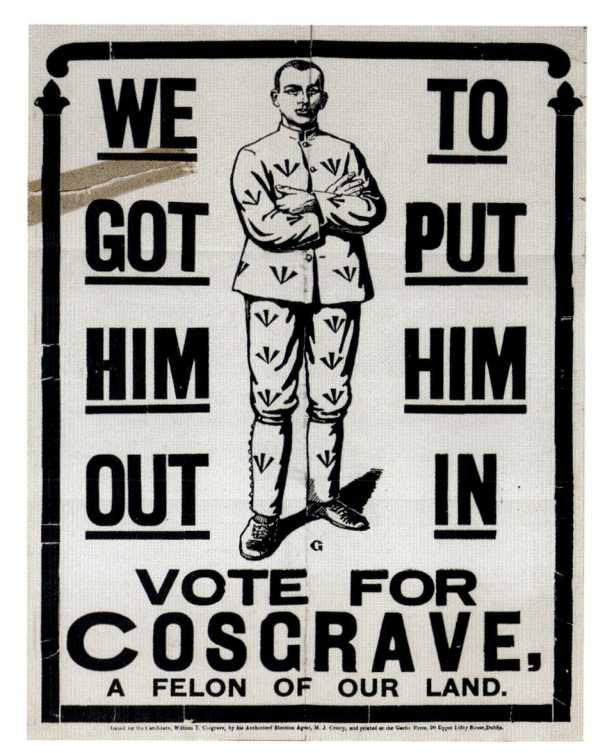

In May 1917, Lloyd George (left), Prime Minister since December 1916, proposed a forum to discuss how Ireland might try 'hammering out an instrument of government for her own people'. The Irish Convention was convened in July 1917. Participants included the Unionists, the Catholic hierarchy and the IPP. Significantly, Sinn Féin declined to attend.

Over the months, amidst the debates, extensive efforts were made to promote agreement. Intriguingly, a form of mild 32-county Home Rule gained fleeting acceptance by the Unionists but foundered on opposition by the Catholic Bishop O'Donnell.

John Redmond's death on 6 March 1918 and the conscription crisis were some of many setbacks for the convention, which ended in an impasse. In its report, a majority recommended Home Rule, with special provisions for Unionists. However, the Unionists inserted their dissenting minority report.

Left: the Irish Convention meets in Regent House, Trinity College.

Above: in a replay of the O'Donovan Rossa funeral, vast crowds attend Thomas Ashe's in Dublin. This 1916 veteran (right), convicted for sedition, went on hunger strike, dying on 25 September 1917.

Michael Collins gave a brief graveside oration: 'Nothing additional remains to be said. That volley which we have just heard is the only speech which it is proper to make above the grave of a dead Fenian'.

THOMAS ASHE,
BORN AT
LISPOLE, Co KERRY, 1882.
Teacher of Corduff National School, prior to April, 1916; Leader of North Co. Dublin Volunteers in Rising, winning the battle of Ashbourne; sentenced to death (commuted to Penal Servitude for life); and released under Amnesty, June 1917.

18 · VIII · '17

Re-arrested for speech made in Co. Longford, and sentenced to one year's imprisonment. Succumbed to prison treatment and forcible feeding in Mountjoy Prison, and

DIED
25TH SEPTEMBER, 1917.

Go nDeunfaid Dia Trocaire ar a h-anam.

On 25 October 1917, the Sinn Féin annual convention was held at the Mansion House in Dublin. Éamon de Valera was elected President. This was immediately followed by an Irish Volunteers' convention in Drumcondra. Demonstrating the close links and interchangeability between the two organisations, de Valera was also elected President of the Irish Volunteers.

Left: monument to Irish Volunteers at Phibsboro, Dublin.

At the Volunteers' convention, Michael Collins (left), was selected as director of organisation and Richard Mulcahy was made director of training. In March 1918 the Volunteers' GHQ was set up. Collins was appointed Adjutant-General and Mulcahy became Chief of Staff.

Right: a cyclist company of the Volunteers parade in Co. Kildare in June 1918. All over Ireland, with new vigour, the Volunteers recruited, organised, drilled and trained.

Early armed actions by the Irish Volunteers, post-Rising in 1918:

Two Donegal men from the Rosses, deserters from the British Army, were being conveyed under armed escort, on 4 January 1918, by train from Burtonport to Derry and Ebrington Barracks there. They were rescued by local Volunteers at Kincasslagh Road.

On 17 March Volunteers raided the RIC barracks at Eyeries, Co. Cork, and seized five carbines (memorial plaque, right).

Gortatlea RIC barracks in Kerry was seized by Volunteers on the night of 13 April. An RIC patrol returned and fired into the barracks. Two Volunteers died as a result.

Right: the isolated terrain at Béal a' Ghleanna, West Cork. On 7 July, a group of Volunteers ambushed two RIC policemen, one of whom was injured. The Volunteers escaped with Lee Metford carbines and ammunition.

131

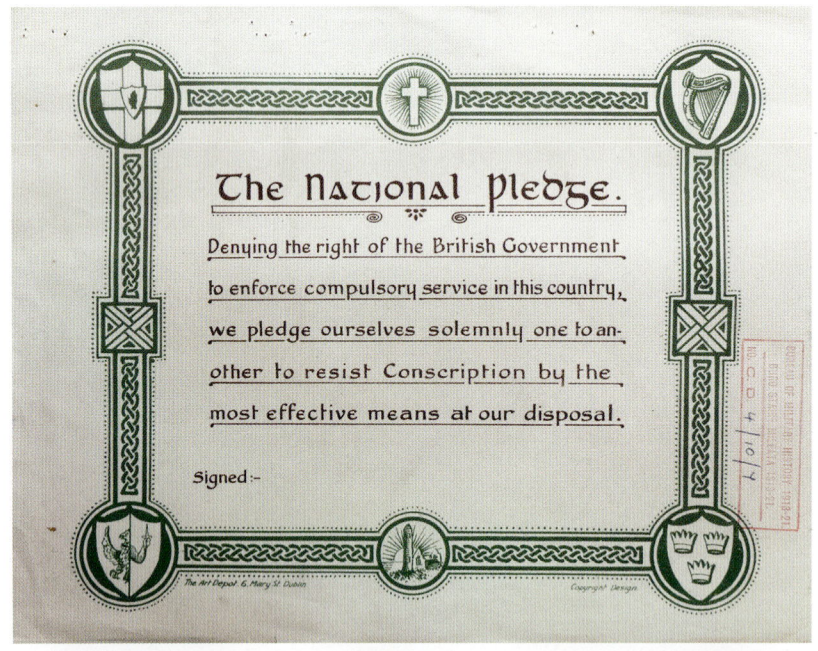

Left: a cartoon showing the 'first Irish conscript'.

Irish recruitment into the British Army for the war was a constant preoccupation for the British. In early March 1918, peace between Germany and Bolshevik Russia allowed the Germans to transfer around 50 divisions from the Eastern to the Western Front. The Germans initiated a series of attacks and made deep incursions through Allied lines.

Facing a dangerous shortage of troops, Lloyd George announced on 9 April that he intended to extend conscription to Ireland.

On Sunday 21 April the pledge against conscription was declaimed at the doors of Catholic churches across Ireland. Two million people signed the pledge (left).

Below left: opposition was almost universal. Sinn Féin, the IPP, Labour, trade unions and others met on 18 April 1918 in the Mansion House to plan resistance to conscription.

In the event, it was postponed to June and then to October – and by then the war had been won. The botched attempt to introduce conscription was a huge miscalculation, by the British – it helped radicalise public opinion in Ireland.

ARRESTED IN IRELAND: THE COUNTESS MARKIEVICZ.

A NOVELIST SINN FEINER ARRESTED: MR. DARRELL FIGGIS.

A SINN FEINER ARRESTED IN IRELAND: MR. JOSEPH McGUINNESS, M.P.

A PROMINENT SINN FEINER ARRESTED IN DUBLIN: COUNT PLUNKETT, M.P.

THE SINN FEIN LEADER ARRESTED AT GREYSTONES: MR. EDMUND DE VALERA, M.P.

ONE OF THE ARRESTED SINN FEINERS: MR. JOHN McGARRY.

SON-IN-LAW OF COUNT PLUNKETT: DR. THOMAS DILLON, ARRESTED.

THE TREASURER OF THE SINN FEIN MOVEMENT ARRESTED: MR. WILLIAM COSGRAVE.

Dublin Castle decided that Sinn Féin had plotted with the Germans. Lack of any hard evidence did not stop a round-up of prominent Sinn Féiners (some pictured above) starting on 17 May 1918. In an ominous portent for the British, the more radical cadre, such as Michael Collins, Richard Mulcahy and Harry Boland, were still free.

Field Marshal Lord French (right) had been appointed Lord Lieutenant, arriving in Dublin on 11 May 1918. The intention was that he would act with a military-style firmness.

133

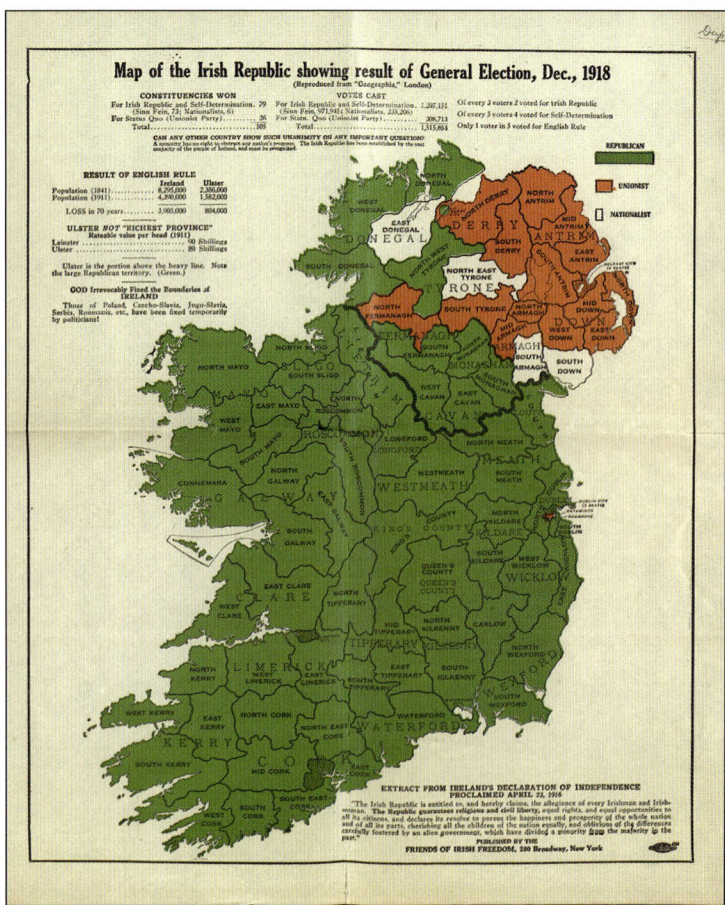

Left: Countess Markievicz campaigns at the Kilkenny by-election in 1917. Over a year later, a general election was in prospect and it was now Sinn Féin's opportunity.

With the war at an end the British Government called a general election for 14 December 1918. The franchise had been extended to include all men over 21 and women over 30, thus practically tripling the Irish electorate. Foreseeing the election, Sinn Féin had selected its candidates by the end of November. The IRB was well represented.

Sinn Féin offered abstentionism, with a hope of obtaining Ireland's sovereign independence at the post-war Peace Conference in Paris. Significantly, Sinn Féin's manifesto committed to using 'any and every means available to render impotent the power of England to hold Ireland in subjection by military force or otherwise'.

Left: overwhelmingly green – the map details the results of the 1918 general election in Ireland. It heralded the end of the IPP, which won only six seats. Unionists won 26 seats and Sinn Féin won by a landslide, gaining 73 seats.

Above: the first meeting of Dáil Éireann, the Mansion House, 21 January 1919. Sinn Féin decided to establish a separate parliament. Unionist and IPP MPs were invited but didn't attend. Seventy-three Sinn Féin deputies had been elected, but only 28 (right) attended as the rest were in detention.

The Dáil ratified the establishment of the Irish Republic and also issued the 'Democratic Programme'.

Left: Seán T O'Kelly, in Paris, with Mr and Mrs Gavan Duffy, May 1919, on their way to see French prime minister Clémenceau. O'Kelly had been delegated to attend the Paris Peace Conference to win support for Ireland's independence. In the event, his efforts were not successful. The victorious powers did not want to irritate their ally, Britain, or consider the desires of a movement that had seemingly allied itself with the Germans in 1916.

Left: the postcard shows Uncle Sam welcoming Ireland to the conference. The reality was radically different.

On 21 January 1919, Tipperary Volunteers, on their own initiative, ambushed a convoy bringing gelignite to a quarry at Soloheadbeg. As the council workers and a cart, followed by two RIC men, approached, the shout went out: 'Hands up!' The constables raised their rifles and were shot dead. The ambushers made off with the cart and gelignite.

Left: 'looks rather like a blacksmith' – a wanted poster for Dan Breen, one of the leaders of the ambush. There was general outrage at the RIC deaths. South Tipperary was declared a Special Military Area.

Right: Christmas postcard sent by Seán McGarry from Lincoln Gaol. A key, made according to the scale shown here, was smuggled in inside a cake – however, the key didn't work.

After much manoeuvring, a working key was made and Éamon de Valera, together with McGarry and Seán Milroy, managed to escape on 3 February 1919. Michael Collins, and Harry Boland, waiting outside, brought them by taxi to safe houses. De Valera eventually reached Dublin.

A Volunteer, Robert Byrne, detained for gun possession in Limerick, was rescued on 6 April 1919 by the IRA. An RIC guard was killed. Byrne died of his wounds and thousands attended his funeral. Panicked, the British declared Limerick a Special Military Area.

In protest, the local Trades Council called a general strike for 13 April. A committee, or 'Soviet' (workers' council) as it became known, managed the city in a peaceful and skilful manner, while the military were boycotted. The strike ended two weeks later.

Right: in response to a shortage of money, the strikers printed their own.

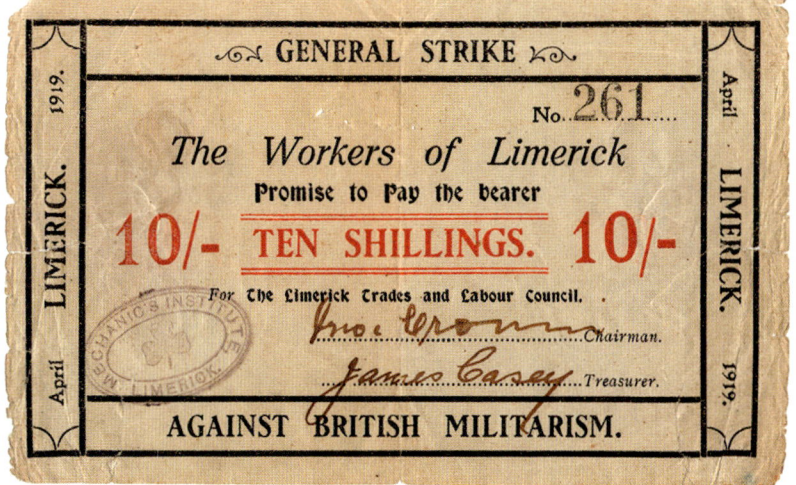

Left: Boland, Collins and de Valera in jovial mood outside the Mansion House.

Dáil Éireann sat in private session at the Mansion House on 1 April 1919. There was a fuller attendance as the 'German Plot' arrestees had been released. De Valera was elected President of the Council of Ministers; ministers included Collins in Finance and Cathal Brugha in Defence. On 10 April the Dáil authorised a bond sale of £500,000, as well as a boycott of the police. With his customary vigour and thoroughness, the new Finance Minister set to organising the sale of bonds.

Left: Collins issued bond certificates (here, to Patrick Pearse's mother) at St Enda's School. It was masterful propaganda – Collins arranged for the ceremony to be filmed; in attendance was Republican 'royalty' including the widows of the 1916 leaders.

Right: Seán Hogan, one of the Soloheadbeg Volunteers, had been captured by the RIC and was being escorted to prison in Cork on 13 May 1919. His comrades, including Dan Breen and Seán Treacy, stormed Hogan's carriage on the Cork train as it stopped at Knocklong. After a gunfight, Hogan was rescued, Breen and Treacy were injured and two RIC men were killed.

Michael Collins was appointed IRA Director of Intelligence in January 1919, and began to develop an extensive intelligence network. He realised that British control was founded on its spy network: while soldiers were replaceable, spies with their knowledge were not – and he now planned to eliminate these.

Right: the initial members of the 'Squad'. From left: Mick McDonnell, Tom Keogh, Vinnie Byrne, Paddy O'Daly and Jim Slattery. This group of tough young men had been selected from the IRA Dublin Brigade. Collins reminded them that previous Irish independence movements had not had an intelligence system which dealt with spies and informers; this was now going to be rectified.

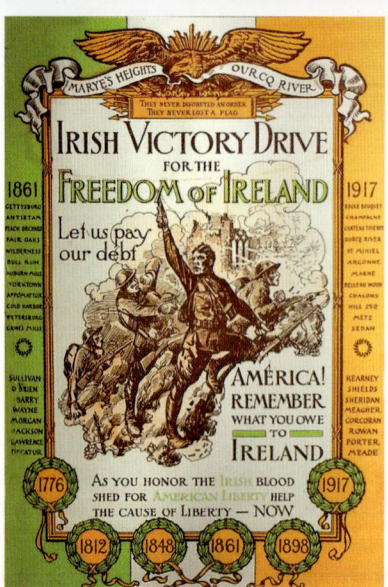

As the hopes of Irish success at the Peace Conference evaporated, Éamon de Valera took the view that salvation lay in harnessing American support. He set off as a stowaway in a cargo ship and arrived in New York, the city of his birth, on 11 June 1919.

As 'President of the Irish Republic' he embarked on holding a series of mass meetings across the United States making the cause for Irish independence. He launched a bond drive with a $5 million target.

Left: there was much coverage in the American press when de Valera visited the Chippewa reservation in Wisconsin. He sympathised with the native Americans ('we are making a similar fight'), and was made a chief,

Left: 'As you honour the Irish blood shed for American Liberty, help the cause of Liberty – now'. A Friends of Irish Freedom Victory Drive leaflet of 1919. It cleverly links the bravery of the Irish-American 69th Regiment during previous actions, including WWI, with the struggle for Ireland's freedom.

Right: Liam Lynch, Officer Commanding (OC), No. 2 Cork Brigade, IRA and one of the outstanding commanders of the War of Independence.

On Sunday, 7 September 1919, it was the turn of the British military to be attacked – a first in the developing conflict. Volunteers, led by Liam Lynch and armed with just six revolvers, intercepted a party of soldiers who were marching to attend service at the Wesleyan Chapel in Fermoy. Lynch called on the soldiers to surrender – one of them swung his rifle and was shot dead. The attackers made off with a haul of rifles. In a foretaste of things to come, soldiers later emerged from the barracks, and looted shops in the town.

Right: the Wesleyan Chapel, Fermoy.

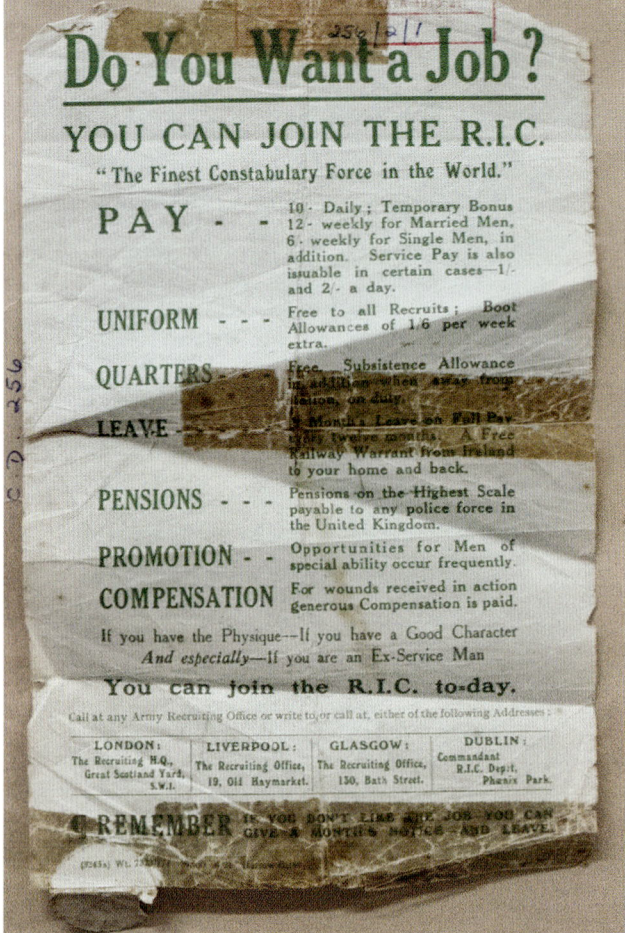

Left: a newspaper photograph of an RIC man posing for the camera. The caption notes that 'revolvers and hand-grenades are the new weapons of the RIC against assassination'.

The RIC had been the eyes and ears of British rule in Ireland. As well as enduring a boycott, the force was to bear the brunt of the increase in violence as the months rolled on. At the end of 1919 the RIC was withdrawn from small isolated barracks.

The British Cabinet considered that Ireland was being afflicted by a criminal conspiracy, not a war. Thus the foremost necessity was to use the police, rather than the army, to defeat what they saw as the Sinn Féin 'murder gang'. In November 1919 approval was given to greatly enlarge the RIC and recruit ex-soldiers.

Left: a recruitment flier. By year's end, recruiting for the RIC had begun in Britain. At a time of high unemployment, ex-servicemen were being invited to join the 'Finest Constabulary Force in the World' with an attractive pay of ten shillings a day.

Right: the Sinn Féin headquarters at 6 Harcourt Street, was raided by the DMP and the military in September 1919.

SINN FEIN HEADQUARTERS RAIDED.

Irish Independent 13 Sept 1919

Military, uniformed police and detectives co-operated in a raid on Sinn Fein headquarters at No. 6 Harcourt St. yesterday. The photograph shows scene outside the premises.

Literature and documents found on the premises were seized and carried away in the military motor.

Messrs. Ernest Blythe, M.P., and P. O'Keefe, M.P., were taken into custody. This photograph shows Mr. O'Keefe in custody and in the upper picture Mr. Blythe, under arrest, is facing the camera.
"Irish Independent" Photos.

On 26 November 1919, Dublin Castle proscribed Sinn Féin and allied organisations: the Irish Volunteers, Cumann na mBan, and, for good measure, the Gaelic League (mistaken for the Gaelic Athletic Association). Dáil Éireann had already been banned in September.

Left: a close call – a bullet hole in the Viceroy's car.

On 19 December 1919, the Viceroy, Lord French, was returning by train from his country house in Co. Roscommon. Volunteers (including Seán Treacy and Dan Breen), led by Mick McDonnell, lay in wait to assassinate him as he travelled in a convoy from Ashtown station to the Viceregal Lodge. The plan was that a cart would be pushed onto the road near Kelly's public house at Ashtown Cross, after the first car (assumed to be just an escort) passed by. As planned, they attacked the second car, but French was actually in the first car. A furious gunfight ensued. Volunteer Martin Savage was killed. Dan Breen and several RIC men were wounded.

Left: map of the Ashtown ambush.

Right: against a background of uproar by British unions and threatened direct action (strikes), Punch suggests Lloyd George should try direct action in Ireland.

Towards the end of the year there was an element of gloom in the British Cabinet. There was continuing bad news from Ireland (including the shocking news of the attack on Lord French). Many new initiatives were discussed and begun, including reinforcement of the police.

The 'Home Rule' Act of 1914 had provided for all-Ireland Home Rule. Suspended during the war, it was due to come into force. However, in October 1919, in what was presented as 'a fresh attempt to solve the Irish problem' Lloyd George established a cabinet committee to draft a new bill as a replacement. It was chaired by Walter Long (right, with his committee), former leader of the Unionists, The resulting 'Government of Ireland' bill was introduced in December 1919. It was direct action of a most astringent kind. This new attempt at Home Rule was totally partitionist, proposing an Ireland divided into 'Northern Ireland' and 'Southern Ireland'.

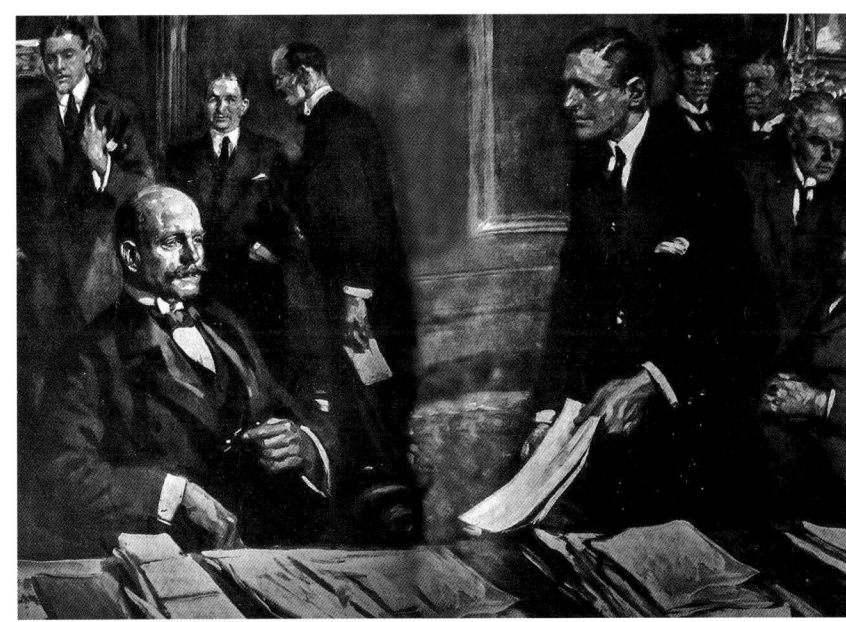

THE SOLUTION.

MR. LLOYD GEORGE. "'DIRECT ACTION'? BY JOVE, THAT'S AN IDEA!"

Left: the harp surmounted by the British crown – RIC ceremonial parade helmet.

Throughout the first half of 1920, there was a wave of IRA attacks on RIC barracks. As a result the RIC was forced to move from its previous traditional police role towards a more paramilitary character.

While the RIC was under assault across the country, in Dublin the DMP was also suffering. In particular, the 'G' (Detective) Division was losing its effectiveness due to severe pressure from Collins' 'Squad'. The most high-profile victim was WC Forbes Redmond, who had been brought from the north and appointed Assistant Commissioner to reorganise the 'G' Division. As he was heading to his hotel on 21 January 1920, Redmond was killed on Harcourt Street by Paddy O'Daly with a single shot to the head: the IRA knew he was wearing a bullet-proof waistcoat. One estimate is that a total of nine DMP members were killed by the Squad during the War of Independence.

Left: 'Punch' cartoon articulating British sympathy for the RIC, now reeling under IRA attacks.

HOMAGE FROM THE BRAVE.

"Old Contemptible" (*to Member of the Royal Irish Constabulary*). "WELL, MATE, I HAD TO STICK IT AGAINST A PRETTY DIRTY FIGHTER, BUT THANK GOD I NEVER HAD A JOB QUITE LIKE YOURS."

Above: a Lee Metford bolt-action carbine. These had been issued to the RIC in 1904.

The new RIC recruitment drive of British ex-servicemen gained pace over the first half of 1920. There was a shortage of RIC dark green cloth – so the recruits were temporarily clad in a mix of military khaki and RIC uniform, but with an RIC hat (an explanation of the uniform, right). Soon they earned the soubriquet 'Black and Tans'. Later in 1920 all the new constables received full RIC uniforms. The original idea was to recruit an RIC special reserve of temporary constables, but in the event the new recruits were assigned to RIC barracks as ordinary constables. They soon gained a reputation for indiscipline.

By mid-1920 British policewomen arrived to serve as searchers. Right: a 'lady police searcher' sits amidst Auxiliaries at Killaloe.

147

Left: Tomás Mac Curtain, elected since January 1920 as Sinn Féin Lord Mayor of Cork. He was a Frongoch veteran and OC of Cork No. 1 Brigade.

Early in the morning of 20 March 1920, a group of men with blackened faces burst into his house at Blackpool, a northern suburb of Cork. Two raced upstairs and shot Mac Curtain dead in front of his wife. There was widespread outrage and Mac Curtain's funeral was called the most impressive ever seen in Cork.

On 17 April the coroner's jury (below left, the verdict being handed over) issued the unanimous verdict that 'the murder was...carried out by the RIC, officially directed by the British Government'. They returned a verdict of wilful murder against Lloyd George, Lord French, the head of the RIC, and two RIC Inspectors including District Inspector Oswald Swanzy, who was immediately transferred to Lisburn. Collins sent a team from Cork to work with the Northern IRA. On 22 August, they shot Swanzy in Lisburn. Sectarian riots broke out and over a thousand Catholics had to flee.

Alan Bell, a former Resident Magistrate, was a member of a secret intelligence committee in Dublin Castle. He was engaged in efficiently and forensically conducting an enquiry into the location of Sinn Féin funds. However, he was dicing with danger as, unlike other Ministers of Finance, Michael Collins had an assassination squad at his disposal.

On 26 March 1920 Bell was taken off a tram at Ballsbridge, and shot. Right: Bell's grave at Deansgrange Cemetery.

Below: the location at Merrion Road, Ballsbridge, where Alan Bell was shot. Below, inset, a photograph of the scene after the shooting. Right inset: Mick McDonnell, one of the Squad who shot him.

NOTICE.

All persons committed to prison are informed that they will not be able by wilful injury to their bodily health caused by refusal of food or in any other way, to procure their release before their discharge in due course of law.

Police and military carried out mass round-ups of 'Sinn Féiners' in early 1920. On 5 April 1920 Republican prisoners in Mountjoy Gaol went on hunger strike, demanding prisoner-of-war status.

Left: warning notice given to the prisoners.

Mass demonstrations ensued. Middle left: protest outside Mountjoy. A general strike began on 13 April.

On 14 April, in an embarrassing volte-face, the authorities decided to release the hunger strikers. In the confusion, both internees and convicted prisoners were released.

Below: soldiers and tanks hold back the crowds outside Mountjoy.

The new masters of Ireland: perceiving the Irish administration to be dysfunctional, a new team was put in place in early 1920.

Right: General Sir Nevil Macready, appointed Commander-in-Chief of the army in Ireland.

Below near right: the new administrators pose at Dublin Castle. Below far right: Major-General Sir Henry Tudor became police supremo, bringing a pugnacious approach to crushing the 'outrages'.

Below: Sir Hamar Greenwood, appointed Chief Secretary in April 1920. Lord Oranmore noted in his journal: 'a Canadian bagman and a windbag at that'.

IRISH ENGINE DRIVER—
"STEAM IS OFF, BLACK AND TAN. NOTHIN' DOIN'."

In mid-May 1920, Dublin dockers refused to handle a military cargo. Troops had to intervene and operate the dockside crane (above, soldiers guard a ship). The Irish Transport and General Workers' Union applied the embargo to all members and the action spread to other ports and the railways – it became known as the 'Munitions Crisis'.

Left: the postcard summarises the situation.

No train which carried munitions or armed troops or police would be worked. The railway companies responded by suspending or dismissing the employees concerned. The railways came to a standstill in many parts of the country. The British military had to resort to the roads to transport men and supplies.

With lost wages and dismissals growing, the railwaymen returned to work in December 1920.

Left: the extensive Irish railway network had reached its peak by the early twentieth century.

The 'Munitions Crisis' of 1920 resulted in the Crown forces having to travel exclusively by road rather than rail. In the light of an increasing frequency of attacks, vehicles were 'up-armoured'. Where 25mm armoured plate (adequate for machine-gun fire) was used, the vehicles were called 'tactical lorries' and those with 12mm plate (adequate for small-arms fire) were called 'protected lorries' – the latter mainly used in urban situations.
Above right: Sir Hamar Greenwood examines the new armour on a truck at Beggar's Bush Barracks.

Several vehicle types were used to transport military and police. The most ubiquitous was a kind of rugged light truck, known as a 'Crossley tender'. Another armoured personnel carrier used was the Lancia (middle right). An angled armoured front enclosed the driver. A sloped mesh wire was erected on top to repel grenades, with a space beneath to allow firing through.

Right: an RIC Transport Division vehicle yard.

Above: in a not-so-subtle demonstration of might, soldiers use a heavy Mark V tank to punch in the door of a premises in Capel Street, Dublin, during a large sweep in January 1921.

A tank was a visible manifestation of military might, thought appropriate for Ireland at that time. By late 1919 a variety of tanks had been assigned around the country.

Left: 'Preserving the Peace in Disordered Dublin'. This edition of the 'Graphic' in February 1920, presents the Mark A Whippet tank as an instrument of peace.

154

Above: don't scare the horses. Mark A Whippet tanks on patrol along a misty Co. Clare road in November 1919. The Whippets were scouting vehicles, much lighter and faster than the Mark Vs.

Right: three Mark V tanks being transported by rail in Ireland.

In 1914, the Russian Army had ordered twin-turret armoured cars from the Austin Motor Company. When the revolution intervened, a batch which couldn't be sent to Russia was purchased by the British Army. Some of these were sent to Ireland in 1919.

Left: an Austin armoured car, armed with Hotchkiss .303 machine guns, in front of the RIC barracks at Ennis, Co. Clare in November 1919.

Left: a Peerless armoured car. From July 1920, Austin armoured cars were replaced by these models, where an Austin twin-turret body had been placed on a Peerless lorry chassis.

Weighing over seven tonnes, the Peerless was difficult to manoeuvre. It had solid rubber tyres and could not easily travel on the many poorly surfaced Irish country roads. Liable to bog down on softer ground, it was better suited to more well-paved urban roads.

On the night of 27 May, Kilmallock barracks was attacked. Thirty Volunteers led the assault. After a fierce exchange of fire and with the barracks in flames, the RIC withdrew to a rear building, leaving behind two dead – a Volunteer also died. Right: Mick O'Dea's painting 'The Defenders', showing the RIC survivors at Kilmallock.

On 19 June 1920, Lieutenant-Colonel Smyth (near right, accompanied by Major-General Tudor, far right), arrived at Listowel barracks where the RIC had mutinied. Smyth told the men that there was going to be a ruthless campaign and that 'no policemen will get into trouble for shooting any man'. Constable Jeremiah Mee replied: 'To hell with you, you murderer'. The RIC men there resigned afterwards. Smyth was shot the following month by the IRA in Cork. His killing sparked sectarian riots in the North.

Percival Lea-Wilson (right) was RIC District Inspector for North Wexford. Remembered for brutal behaviour in 1916 (page 93), he was also noted as being too zealous in discharging his duties. Collins sent Squad members to Gorey, Co. Wexford, and they shot him on 15 June 1920.

On 26 June, Brigadier-General Lucas, fishing on the river Blackwater, was kidnapped by the IRA. Lucas (left, with his captors), was held in Limerick and Clare, and well treated – reflecting the level of humanity still prevailing in mid-1920. On 30 July, he escaped, possibly facilitated by his captors.

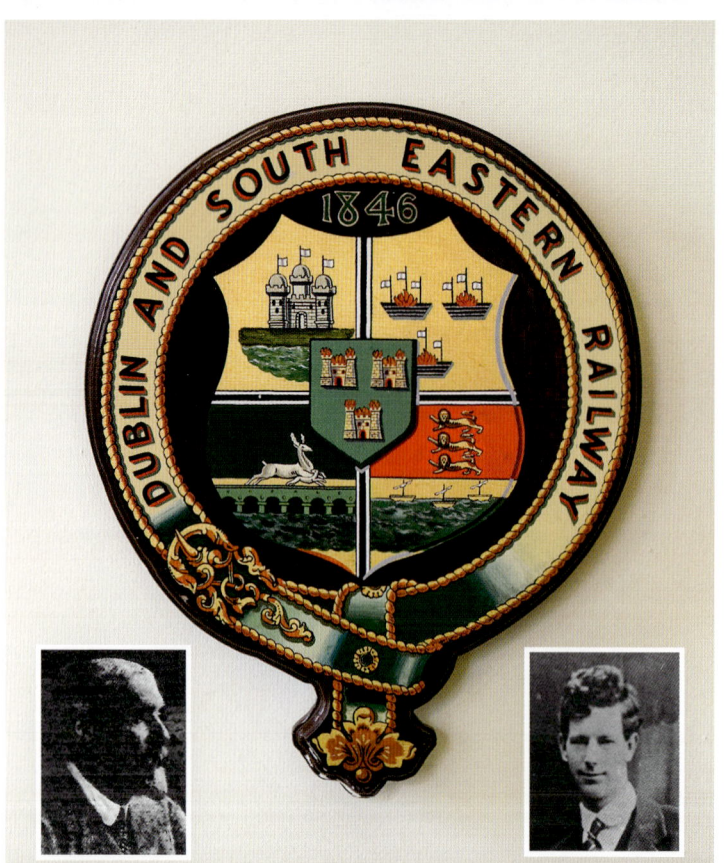

Left: the Dublin and South Eastern Railway (D&SER) insignia.

On 30 July 1920 Squad members entered the D&SER Headquarters at Westland Row (now Pearse) Station. They burst into the boardroom and shot Frank Brooke, director, (inset, far left). Jim Slattery later recounted that Paddy O'Daly (inset, near left) asked him as they descended the stairs: 'Are you sure we got him?' Slattery went back and shot him again. Brooke (a cousin of Basil Brooke, future NI Prime Minister), was a confidential advisor to Lord French and a Privy Councillor.

Right: a December 1920 postcard, with a jolly and multi-coloured line-up of the different branches of the RIC.

As the conflict escalated, Major-General Tudor, the Police supremo, pushed through a proposal for a counter-insurgency force with experienced ex-officers for the new Auxiliary Division of the RIC (ADRIC) on a six- and twelve-month (extendable) contract. Recruiting began in July 1920.

In the rushed recruitment, some Auxiliaries wore khaki (as happened with the ongoing recruitment of ex-servicemen to the RIC). Shortly afterwards their uniform was standardised to a dark-green RIC one, like this replica (right). The leather gaiters were phased out.

Below: an advertisement seeking ex-officers. The pay, at £1 per day, was double what the ex-servicemen recruited earlier for the RIC were receiving.

THE NEW R.I.C.

in—The Corps d'élite
for Ex-Officers.
IN the Auxiliary Division of the
Royal Irish Constabulary. Ex-Officers
with first-class record are eligible.
urage, Discretion, Tact and Judgment
uired. The pay is £1 per day and
wances. Uniform supplied. Generous
leave with pay. Apply now to
R.I.C.
ECRUITING OFFICES,
eat Scotland Yard, London, W.
particulars will be sent by post if you wish.

159

Above: Auxiliaries patrol by Amiens Street (now Connolly) Station. The ADRIC were assigned the arms and transport needed for counter-insurgency and were posted mostly in the 'hottest' areas, which included Dublin and the southwestern counties. They formed 21 companies, each with a nominal strength of 100. By the time of the Truce in July 1921, only 2,264 men had served. This relatively small force, over the course of just one year's operation, gained a fearsome reputation.

Left: a joint patrol by 'I' Company with the army in Co. Monaghan.

Right: happier times. Terence MacSwiney, Lord Mayor of Cork, visiting the Capuchin College at Rochestown.

MacSwiney was a Teachta Dála (TD, Dáil deputy), poet and playwright, as well as OC of the Cork No. 1 Brigade. On 12 August 1920, he was meeting IRA officers in the City Hall when Crown forces raided and detained them. MacSwiney immediately began a hunger strike. Tried by court martial for sedition, he was sentenced to two years imprisonment and sent to Brixton Gaol.

Right: 'Le martyr irlandais' – MacSwiney's hunger strike soon gained international attention.

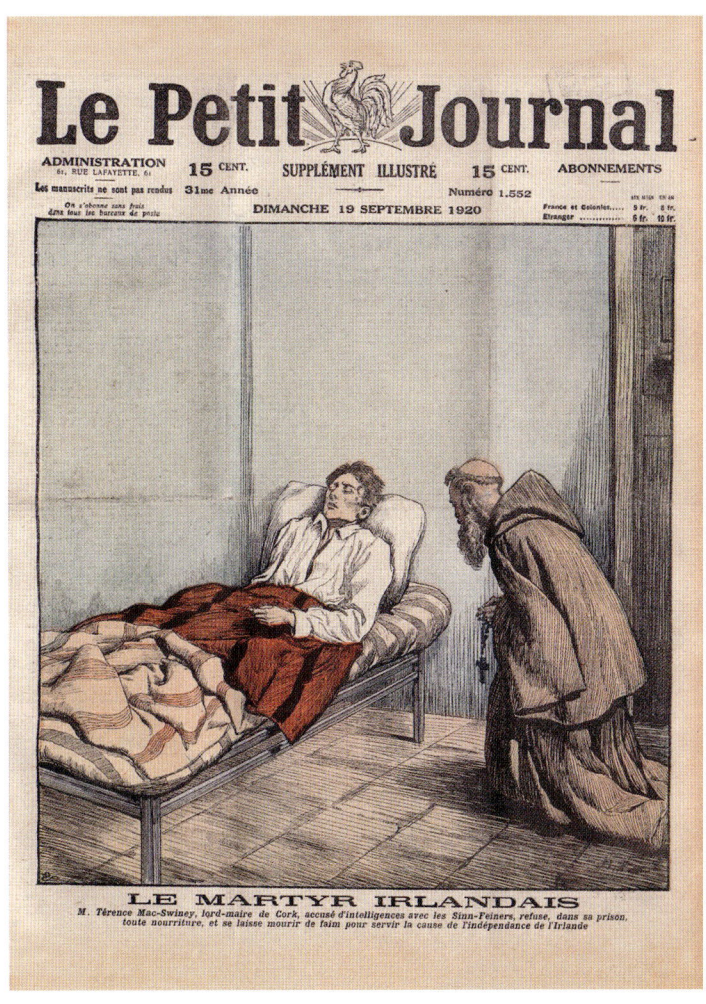

161

Above: the arrival in Cork of MacSwiney's coffin. The authorities had diverted the coffin at Holyhead to Queenstown.

A huge campaign developed worldwide in support of MacSwiney, but Lloyd George stood firm. On 25 October 1920, MacSwiney died after 74 days on hunger strike. His remains laid in state at Southwark Cathedral where 30,000 mourners filed past.

Left: the procession after the Requiem Mass at the cathedral in Cork on 31 October.

Right: the 'Daily Mirror' reports the dramatic events at Brixton Gaol.

There was much international reportage of the death of MacSwiney. Catalonia, in particular, mourned him. There were mass demonstrations in Barcelona, including a march on the British Consulate. In India, he proved an inspiration for both Nehru and Gandhi. A young Vietnamese, now known in history as Ho Chi Minh, then working in Paris, said: 'a nation which has such citizens will never surrender'.

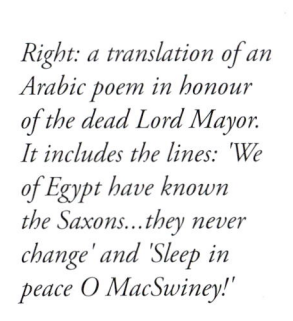

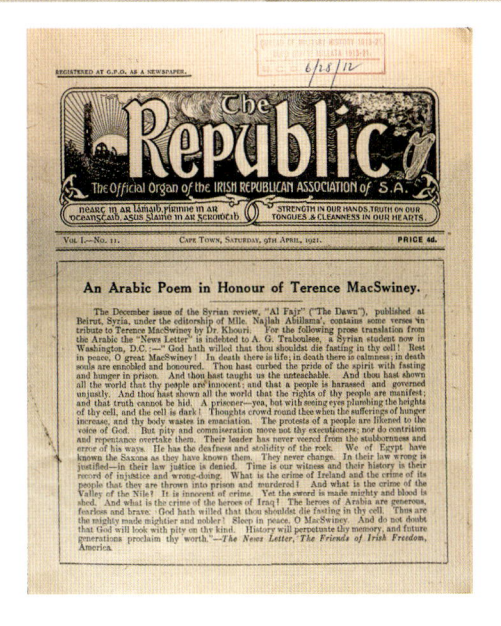

Right: a translation of an Arabic poem in honour of the dead Lord Mayor. It includes the lines: 'We of Egypt have known the Saxons...they never change' and 'Sleep in peace O MacSwiney!'

Left: 'Just a lad of 18 summers'. Kevin Barry in a Belvedere rugby jersey.

On 20 September 1920, Volunteers of the Dublin Brigade intercepted a military bread ration party at Upper Church Street. Instructed to raise their hands and surrender their weapons, the soldiers grabbed their rifles and there was an exchange of fire. The attackers escaped, leaving one soldier dead and two fatally wounded. Kevin Barry, a UCD medical student, was captured. On 20 October, he was court-martialled at Marlborough (now McKee) Barracks. Found guilty of the murder of one of the soldiers, he was sentenced to be hanged.

There was a huge outpouring of sympathy for Barry. *Below: women pray for Barry outside Mountjoy, on 1 November, the day of execution.*

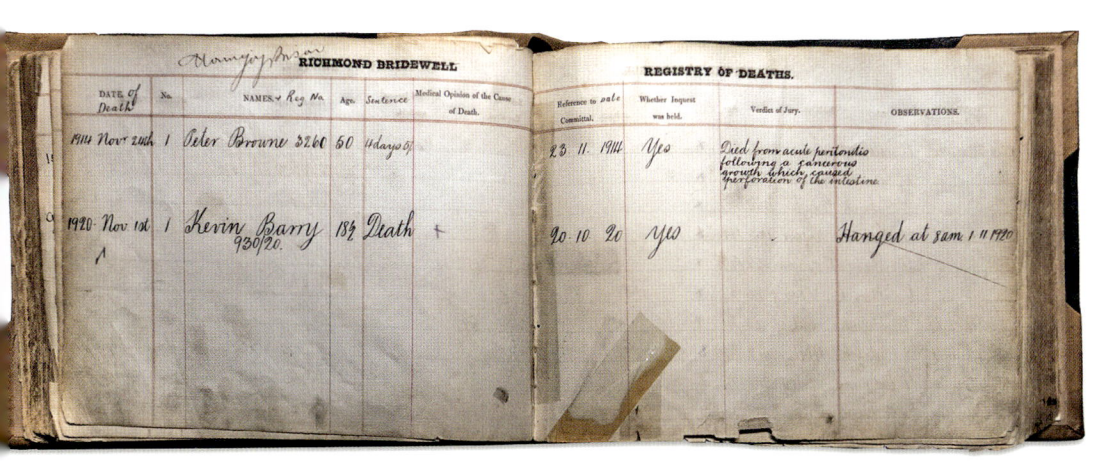

Above: the Mountjoy 'Death Book' recording Barry's death.

As was the custom, an English professional hangman was engaged; John Ellis had also hanged Roger Casement.

Right: the bare execution chamber in the hanghouse at Mountjoy where Barry was hanged (railings now surround the twin trapdoors for safety). The hang rope was suspended from a chain attached to beams on the underside of the roof. The condemned man spent his last night in a nearby cell. In the morning he was escorted to the chamber. The hooded and bound prisoner was placed at a chalk-mark on the trapdoors and the rope was positioned around his neck. The hangman then removed a lock-pin and pushed the lever forward, opening the trapdoors.

Impromptu reprisals by Crown forces became the norm in 1920. Amongst other cities and towns, Limerick, Thurles, Nenagh, Bantry and Fermoy suffered.

Left: the 'Graphic' tells how Trim, Co. Meath was wrecked by Auxiliaries and 'Black and Tans' on 27 September 1920 as a reprisal for a Sinn Fein 'outrage' (an attack on the RIC barracks). The photo shows residents leaving the town, after it was wrecked, helpfully (and justifying the wrecking) pointing out that 'as they depart they take pride in displaying the Sinn Féin colours'.

REFUGEE INHABITANTS OF THE STRICKEN AREA LEAVING THE TOWN TO SEEK SHELTER ELSEWHERE
As they depart they take pride in displaying the Sinn Fein colours.

On 16 August British troops attacked Templemore, Co. Tipperary, after the shooting of an RIC Inspector. Templemore Town Hall (middle left) – a captain and a corporal died from burns as they set it alight.

Left: the Catholic parochial house in the northern town of Lisburn was set alight by a sectarian mob in August 1920. A group poses with children and a Union Jack in front of the ruins.

166

Right: twenty houses were burnt out on Clonard Street, Balbriggan, Co. Dublin.

On 20 September 1920 RIC District Inspector Burke and his brother (a sergeant) were shot dead in a Balbriggan public house. At around 11 pm that night lorries laden with Auxiliaries and RIC from the nearby Gormanston Camp raced into town where they began an orgy of violence.

In a night of terror, the Auxiliaries laid waste to the town. Local businesses and scores of houses were destroyed; public houses were looted and burnt. Two Volunteers were brought to the town barracks, where they were beaten up, bayonetted to death. Their bodies dumped.

Right: 'Il terrore in Irlanda'. 'La Tributa Illustrata' (Rome) depicts the fleeing Balbriggan population.

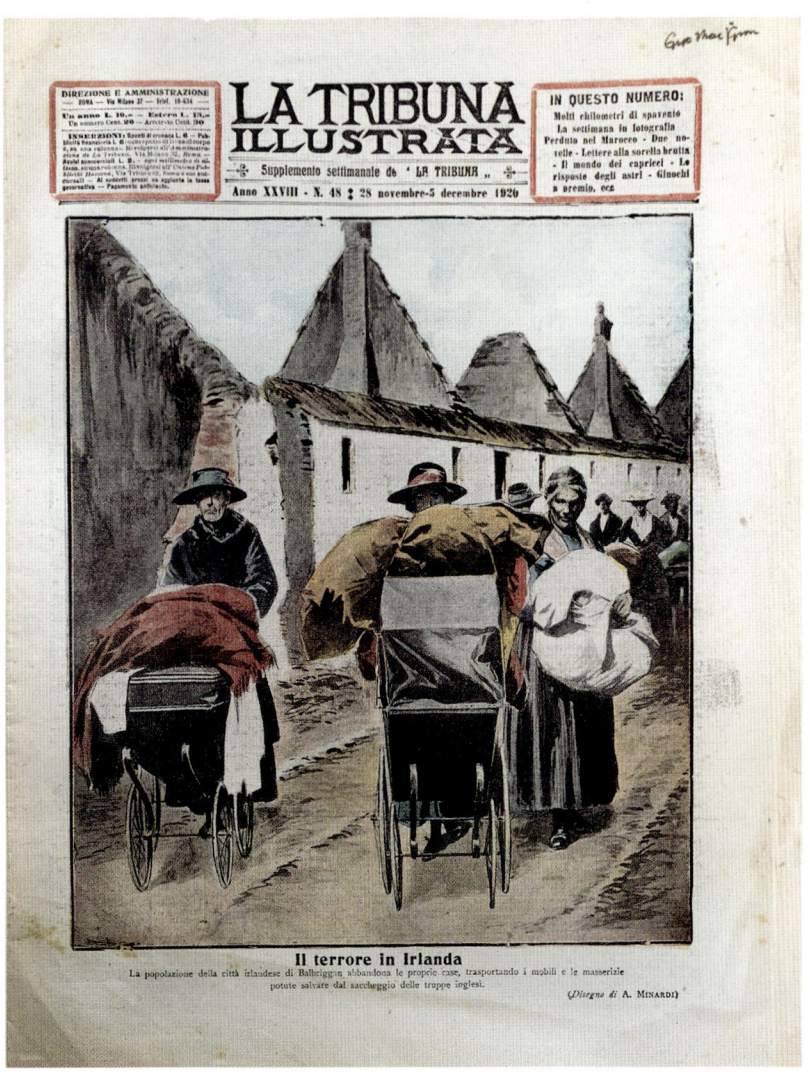

By mid-1920, the IRA had changed tactics – from mainly attacking barracks to mounting ambushes.
In one of these actions, Denis Lacey (above), led an attack at Thomastown, between Cashel and Tipperary town. Six military were killed.

Left: statue of Seán Mac Eoin at Ballinalee, Co. Longford. He and his Volunteers attacked several RIC barracks during the first half of 1920. On 18 August Mac Eoin led an audacious raid on the Longford military barracks, seizing arms and ammunition.

On 22 September the Mid-Clare IRA ambushed a RIC patrol at Rineen (left) between Ennistymon and Milltown Malbay, Co. Clare. Six RIC constables were killed, the heaviest Crown casualties in the conflict up to then. Immediately afterwards, Crown forces sacked nearby towns. Several civilians were murdered.

On 28 September, Volunteers led by Ernie O'Malley (above) and Liam Lynch approached the barracks at Mallow, Co. Cork (memorial, right). Two Volunteers on the civilian staff had related that most of the 17th Lancers garrison regularly left to exercise the horses. O'Malley approached the wicket gate with a fake letter. The Volunteers then forced their way in and overpowered the 15 soldiers within. The sergeant in charge was mortally wounded in the fracas. With a haul of 27 rifles and two Hotchkiss machine guns, the IRA withdrew.

On the night after the attack, troops torched Mallow (right, the aftermath). The Town Hall and other premises were put on fire. Townsfolk ran down the burning main street seeking refuge.

The London 'Times' was moved to report: 'the accounts of arson and destruction by the military at Mallow...must fill English readers with a sense of shame'.

On 12 November 1920, an ADRIC engagement at Ballymacelligot, near Tralee, Co. Kerry, left two men dead. Coincidentally, a press party (with a Captain Pollard) showed up that afternoon.

Left: the 'Illustrated London News' depicts 'the Battle of Tralee'. Three dead lie in the foreground while Auxiliaries take 'Sinn Féiners' prisoner.

However, this was 'fake news'. In an effort to show that they were winning, Dublin Castle press officers — principally Captain Hugh Pollard — reenacted the event using Auxiliaries, some dressed as civilians, at Vico Road, Killiney, Co. Dublin, over 300 km from Tralee. Pathé also filmed the fictional encounter. In the House of Commons on 2 December an MP asked about the faked photograph. 'I know nothing as to the circumstances in which the picture...was taken', was the official reply.

Left: with more tree growth – the scene at Vico Road today.

170

The news-sheet 'Irish Bulletin' (near right), produced from November 1919. It circulated internationally, presenting the Republican view. For journalists, it provided a more reliable source of information than Dublin Castle.

The staff, initially Frank Gallagher and a doughty typist, Kathleen McKenna (far right), had to move frequently from hide-out to hide-out. On 26 March 1921, the office of the Bulletin was raided by Auxiliaries, who seized the equipment.

Castle press officers, (including Pollard) decided to produce fake issues, using the captured equipment. However, the deception was soon discovered.

Right: a fake 'Irish Bulletin' of 30 March 1921. Later, genuine copies (below right) were stamped 'official copy'.

In 1936, Pollard (below) was on the plane that flew to the Canaries which then conveyed General Franco to Spanish Morocco at the start of the Spanish Civil War.

REMOVING THE BLACK BOX WHICH CONTAINED THE NOTORIOUS TYPHOID PLOT PAPERS: SOLDIERS AT A HOUSE IN DUBLIN.

Above: Longwood Avenue, near the South Circular Road.

Left: removing the 'Typhoid Plot papers' at a house in Dublin, according to the 'Illustrated London News'. It is incorrect – the photograph shows a different raid at North Great George's Street. In reality there had been a raid at the house of Michael Hayes at Longwood Avenue on 16 November 1920. The British claimed that details of a 'Typhoid Plot' had been among papers seized in the raid, of the IRA Chief of Staff, Richard Mulcahy, who had been in the house but escaped. It shocked Dublin Castle so much that the documents were sent by plane to London post-haste. Hamar Greenwood (left) read out the captured document in Parliament on 18 November. Joseph Devlin MP responded that this was a concoction by Dublin Castle.

Left: the plot was widely reported in the press.

Sinn Fein Plot to Spread Typhoid Among Troops

By Associated Press.

London, Nov. 18.—Sir Hammar Greenwood, chief secretary for Ireland, said in the house of commons today that during a recent raid in Ireland troops captured a document sent by the commander-in-chief of the Irish republican army to his chief of staff containing a "series of remarkable and horrifying statements regarding the spreading of typhoid among the troops and glanders among the cavalry horses."

Right: the captured document. It muses on spreading glanders amongst British horses, as well as using milk to infect troops with typhoid. It concludes with a hearty 'God bless you all'.

The British were widely disbelieved about the 'Typhoid Plot' – they had form in black propaganda, after all. News about the alleged plot was eclipsed by the shocking events of Bloody Sunday on 21 November 1920 and little was heard about the affair afterwards.

However, the document was genuine. In 1962 Richard Mulcahy recalled that Dr Pat McCartan had sent the 'Typhoid Plot' paper to Michael Collins, who had passed it on to Mulcahy, but that 'this was a joke as far as Mick and myself were concerned'. It was destined for the wastepaper basket when the raid occurred.

McCartan (right) was a doctor from Co. Tyrone, and a member of the First Dáil. In 1919 he was appointed Sinn Féin's representative in the USA. At de Valera's request, in February 1921 he travelled to Russia, to negotiate a treaty with the Soviets, from which nothing materialised.

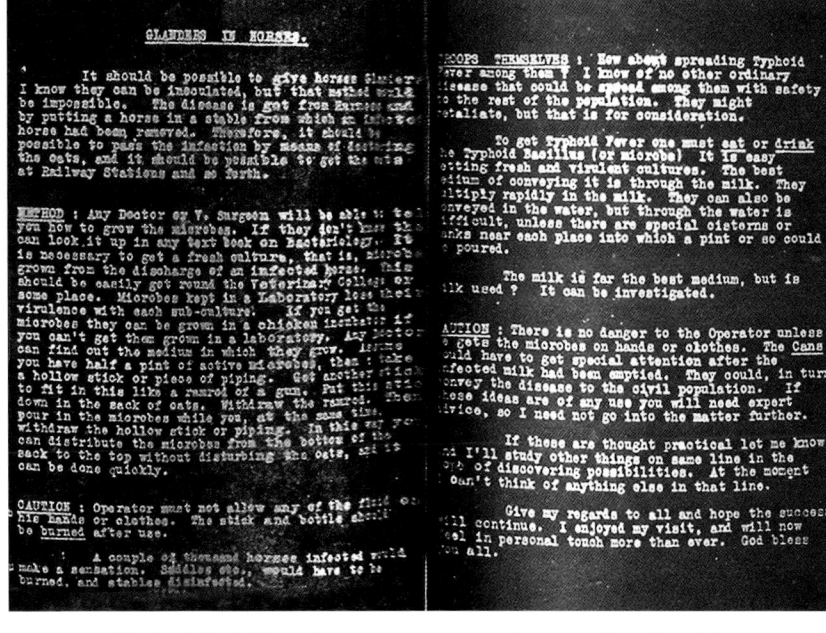

173

Left: Seán Treacy; Major George Osbert Smyth. Seán Treacy and Dan Breen were on the run in Dublin. Early on 12 October 1920, a raiding party burst into their Drumcondra safe house, the home of Professor John Carolan. In the ensuing gunfight Major Smyth and a captain were mortally wounded, as was Carolan. The IRA pair escaped out the back. A wounded Breen was brought to the Mater Hospital.

On 14 October 1920 Seán Treacy headed to a Squad meeting at Talbot Street. However, he was followed. As an armoured car and lorry raced up, Treacy emerged and tried to escape down the street. A plain-clothes agent grappled with Treacy who drew his Parabellum. In an exchange of fire Treacy was killed. The agent was also killed, as were two civilian bystanders.

Left: Auxiliaries hurry towards the scene of the shooting on Talbot Street.

Below: plaque at Talbot Street.

Dublin was flooded with Auxiliaries and British military. Right: a soldier stands on a Kennedy bread van at Summerhill as he removes a Republican flag from a pole.

Right: a page from an IRA intelligence ledger (now in the Military Archives, Dublin), with an original photograph of what in later decades became known as the 'Cairo Gang.' This inaccurate term possibly derives from the Café Cairo (on Grafton Street) or from officer-spies drafted from imperial service in Cairo. In reality, the ledger denotes them as the 'Special Gang', of the 'F' Company, Auxiliaries – it also provides a helpful identification key. The photograph was taken in a lane at Dublin Castle, near the Palace Street gate.

```
         SPECIAL GANG "F" COY. AUX.
   I. Denteith. 2. Fletcher (Irish).
   3. Moore (Irish). 4. Swaffer. 5. Dove.
   6. Appleford (Dead). 7. Gorman. 8.
   Winch. 9. McClaen. IO. Stapley (Leader)
```

MURDER MOST FOUL IN DUBLIN
THE BLACKEST SUNDAY IN IRISH HISTORY

THE MURDERED OFFICERS: 1, CPT. L. PRICE, M.C.; 2, LT. G. BENNETT, late R.A.; 3, MAJ. DOWLING, Gren. Gds.; 4, CADET F. GARNISS; 5, CPT. BAGGALAY

THE ILLUSTRATED LONDON NEWS, DEC. 4, 1920.—923

VICTIMS OF "THE MURDER GANG": OFFICERS KILLED IN DUBLIN.

CAPT. W. F. NEWBERRY, 4TH QUEEN'S (ROYAL WEST SURREY) REGIMENT.
MAJOR C. M. G. DOWLING, GRENADIER GUARDS.
CAPTAIN P. McCORMACK, R.A.V.C.
LIEUTENANT D. L. MacLEAN, LATE RIFLE BRIGADE.
CADET FRANK GARNISS.
LIEUTENANT G. BENNETT, LATE R.A.
CADET C. A. MORRIS, AUXILIARY R.I.C.
LIEUT. H. ANGLISS, D.C.M. INNISKILLING FUSILIERS.
CAPTAIN LEONARD PRICE, M.C. LATE MIDDLESEX REGIMENT.
LIEUTENANT A. AMES, LATE GRENADIER GUARDS.
CAPTAIN G. T. BAGGALLAY (EXTRA REGIMENTALLY EMPLOYED).

On the day following the Sinn Fein murders in Dublin (on Sunday, November 21), Sir Hamar Greenwood, Chief Secretary for Ireland, said in the House of Commons: "I hope that this series of cold-blooded and carefully planned atrocities will bring vividly before the House and the public the cruel reality of the Irish situation. We are fighting an organised band of paid assassins, whose plans, recently discovered, include the destruction of life and property in this country as well as in Ireland.... Now I shall read the details of, I think, one of the most foul tragedies in the history of our Empire. There have been 14 deaths and 6 injured, including 1 assassin, and 3 assassins captured red-handed with arms." We have not space here to give the details referred to, even in outline, nor have we been able to obtain portraits of all the murdered officers. The list of killed included also Capt. Fitzgerald, Mr. T. H. Smith, and Mr. L. Wilde. In earlier published accounts Lieut. Angliss was mentioned incorrectly as Lieut. Mahon. We have just heard of the mistake, too late to alter it on pages already gone to press.

Left and below: 'murder most foul' in Dublin – some of the British officers and cadets killed.

The most violent day of the War of Independence occurred on 21 November 1920, when it truly earned the epithet 'Bloody Sunday'. Thirty people died that day, with several others dying later of their wounds. On that morning, the IRA set out to assassinate suspected British spies. Later that day, the Crown forces fired on the crowd at a football match at Croke Park. That night, also, three men in custody in Dublin Castle were 'shot trying to escape'.

The British had set out to build up their Secret Service and Military Intelligence network in Ireland. It has been estimated that around 60 men, mostly young veteran officers, had been drafted in from Britain and the Empire. Based on reports from a multitude of informants, Michael Collins and senior IRA staff devised a target list. With large backup groups of lookouts and protection in place, the selected hit teams fanned out to strike at the most effective time, 9 am on Sunday 21 November 1920.

Above: an assassination on Bloody Sunday as depicted in the 'Illustrated London News'.

Right: map showing locations of the assassinations. Most of the killings were in the south city centre. The only assassinations north of the Liffey occurred at the Gresham Hotel. Lieutenant Leonard Wilde was registered here as a commercial traveller – he was shot at his bedroom door. A veterinary officer and ex-captain, Patrick MacCormack, was also shot.

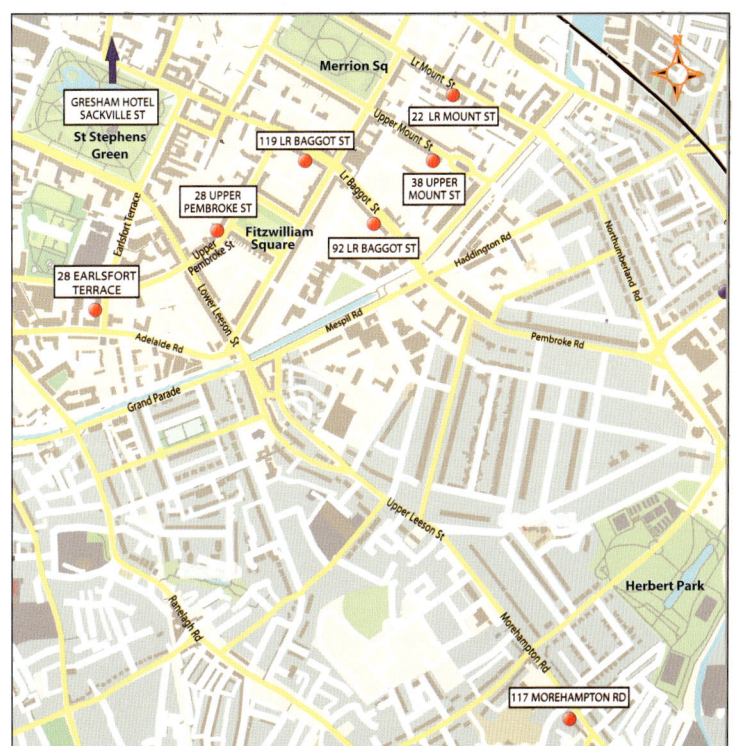

Left: a nest of spies? No. 28 Upper Pembroke Street is a terraced house of three storeys over basement. In 1920, it contained ten flats. Most of the tenants were military officers. The raiders entered via the rear garden (accessible by the side lane) and by the front door. They raced up to a third-floor flat where they shot dead Captain Leonard Price, as well as Major Charles Dowling, both intelligence officers. Senior staff officer Lieutenant-Colonel Hugh Montgomery (a cousin of Bernard Montgomery, the future General) was shot at the entrance to his ground-floor flat. His wife was slightly wounded. Montgomery died of his wounds on 10 December. Three other officers were wounded.

THE LATE CADET MORRIS (CENTRE)

A party of Auxiliaries heard the disturbance at Mount Street. Two were dispatched to Beggar's Bush to get reinforcements. They (including Cadet Morris, left) were seized by the IRA at Northumberland Road and shot.

Left: news of the 'Dublin Day of Terror' flashed around the world.

On 20 November, Dublin Brigade leaders Dick McKee and Peadar Clancy (right) had attended a GHQ meeting with Michael Collins, where the plans for the following day were finalised. In the early hours of the following day, Clancy and McKee were arrested.

They were brought to a guardroom in the Castle (right, Exchange Court). Also there was Conor Clune (not a Volunteer), rounded up at Vaughan's Hotel. Brigadier-General Winter, head of the Secret Service in the Castle, led the interrogation. The authorities later announced that the three had been shot while 'trying to escape'.

It was widely believed that they had been tortured to extort the names of the assassins of earlier that day and summarily shot. There was extensive bruising on the bodies, and many bullet wounds.

The Castle press office staged a reenactment and presented their spin, as relayed in the 'Daily Graphic' (right): the prisoners got hold of grenades supposedly stored there, and thrown them, but they did not detonate. Next they grabbed rifles and fired at their guards who killed them in the 'exchange of fire'.

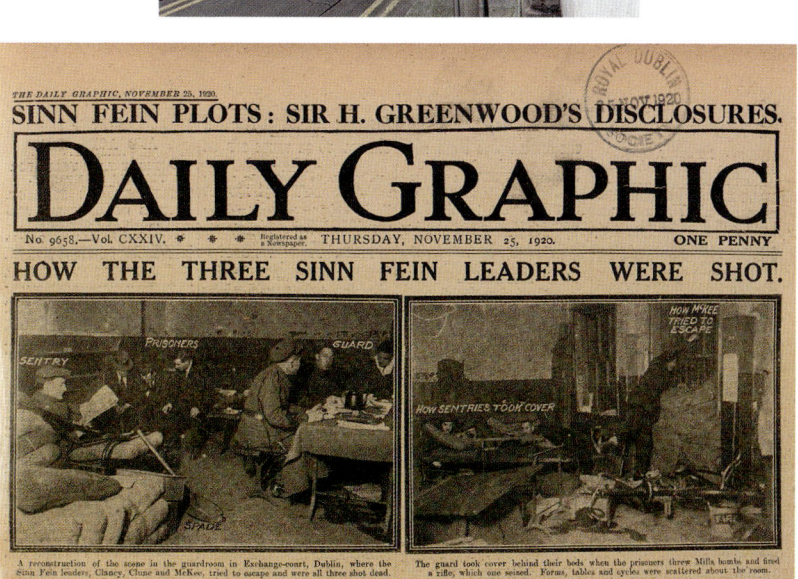

179

Left: Auxiliaries en masse – at a Viceroy's inspection.

Below left: ticket for the Tipperary-Dublin football match at Croke Park on Bloody Sunday.

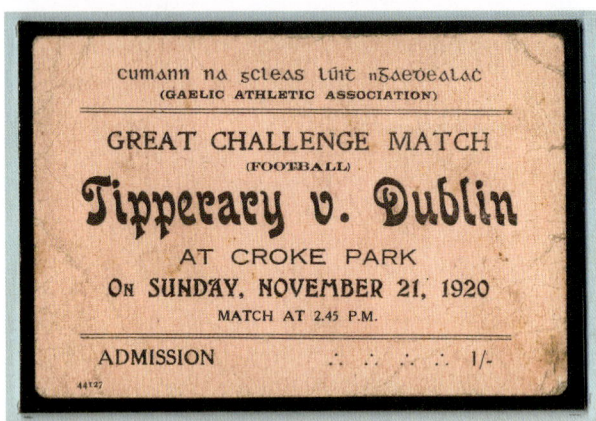

The match, attended by a large crowd, began late, at 3:15 pm. The Crown forces, in a state of high agitation after the morning's events, set out to surround and search the crowd. As a convoy of troops arrived along Clonliffe Road, Auxiliaries approached from the southern (canal) direction. The cadets began firing at ticket sellers (mistaking them for IRA pickets). As these ran away, the Auxiliaries entered the grounds. Fire was directed on the panicked and fleeing crowd. Seven were shot dead, five more died later and two were trampled to death.

Left: relatives of the Croke Park victims at Jervis Street Hospital, where a military enquiry was held.

In the aftermath of Bloody Sunday the British feared more assassinations. Senior officials and officers moved into a crowded Dublin Castle. There was a massive crackdown. In Dublin, there were roadblocks and widespread raids, and a curfew was imposed.

Right: in a raid on Liberty Hall on 24 November, Thomas Johnson, Secretary of the Labour Party (left), was arrested.

Right: bird's-eye view of Ballykinlar Camp.

Over 500 arrests were made in the roundup at the end of November 1920. Ballykinlar Camp in Co. Down was opened to house the internees. By December, Ballykinlar was getting full. The Admiralty was asked to provide vessels to carry prisoners. 'Rebels' were detained over the following months all over Ireland in a wide variety of jails, detention barracks and internment camps.

Right: prisoners set up an internal military-style organisation in Ballykinlar. It extended to developing their own camp tokens in different denominations.

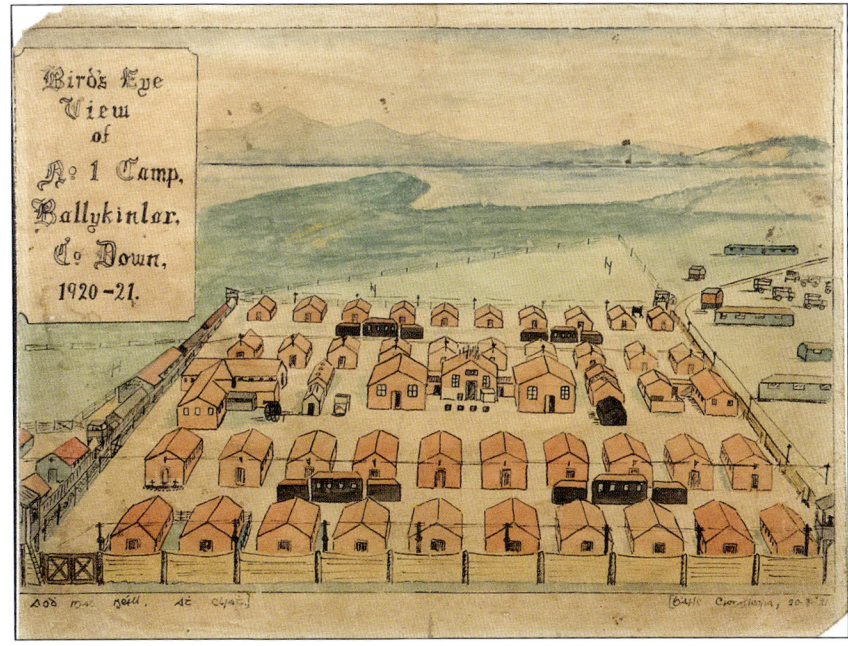

181

Left: a covert photograph taken at Rath internment Camp, the Curragh, 1921, by Joseph Lawless (who had been arrested in December 1920). A Black Watch sergeant is in the centre, an IRA prisoner on the left. Lawless was a veteran of the Ashbourne action in 1916. On his return to Dublin from Frongoch, he had started a cycle business at Parnell Street. This acted as cover for an IRA grenade factory in the basement.

Left: the dream of freedom. A sketch from an 1921 autograph book at Kilmainham Jail, depicting an imaginary escape tunnel.

Right: jovial times. A 'D' Company, Christmas card from December 1920

'D' Auxiliary Company, whose HQ was at Lenaboy Castle, Galway, earned a reputation for brutality. In early November 1920 they shot dead a pregnant woman sitting on her lawn near Gort, as they drove by. On the night of 14 November, Fr Michael Griffin, a curate sympathetic to the Republican cause, was arrested and taken to the 'D' Company HQ. Days later his body was found buried in a bog near Barna.

On 26 November a large force, made up of RIC and 'D' Company Auxiliaries, made a sweep through south Galway. As Patrick and Harry Loughnane (both Volunteers) were threshing at their farm at Shanaglish, they were picked up and arrested. After being tortured they were dragged by ropes attached to the back of a lorry, and brought to an Auxiliaries' base. On 5 December their charred and mutilated bodies were found in a pond near Ardrahan.

Right: in an open coffin, the body of Patrick Loughnane alongside the coffin of his brother, Harry.

Above: looking north, Kilmichael, Co. Cork — site of the ambush.

At around 4 pm on 28 November 1920, 18 Auxiliaries of 'C' Company set out in two Crossley tenders from Macroom Castle for Dunmanway.

Commandant Barry and 40 men of the 3rd West Cork Brigade flying column awaited them. He had established a command post to the east and placed three sections in commanding positions on high ground, on both sides of the road

Left: site of the IRA command post. The marker states unambiguously that 'seventeen terrorist officers of the British forces' died here.

Barry stepped out and threw a Mills bomb into the leading tender, which then came under intense fire. The driver of the second tender, about 150m behind, tried to turn around but got stuck. No. 2 Section opened fire on them. With the cadets in the first tender vanquished, Barry and his men headed west to deal with the second tender. By the end of the action 16 Auxiliaries were dead. Another, Cadet Forde, suffering a head wound, was left for dead, but survived. Another wounded Auxiliary escaped but was captured and shot. Two of the IRA men were killed; another died of his wounds.

Right: map of the Kilmichael ambush.

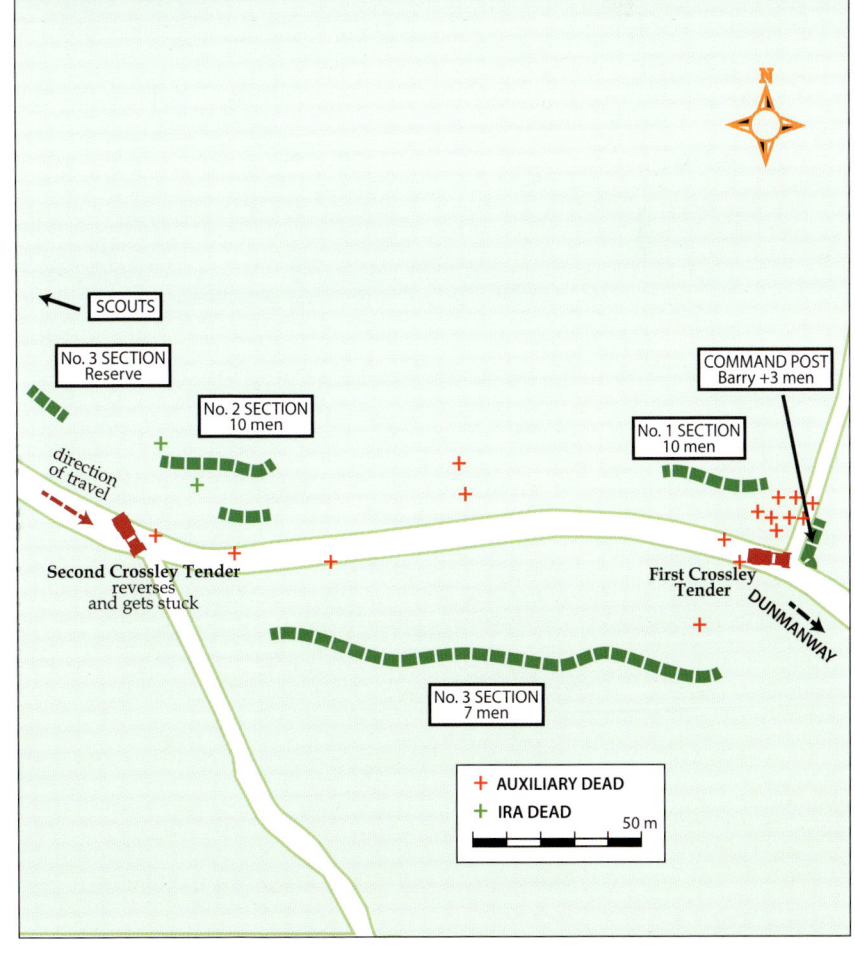

THE ILLUSTRATED LONDON NEWS

No. 4261—VOL. CLVII.   SATURDAY, DECEMBER 18, 1920.   ONE SHILLING.

THE BURNING OF CORK: DEVASTATION IN THE HEART OF THE CITY AFTER A NIGHT OF FIRE.

A new scene in the Irish tragedy was enacted on the night of Saturday, December 11, when fires broke out at several points in the central part of Cork. They were evidently the work of incendiaries, but of what faction it is impossible to say. The City Hall, the Corn Exchange, the Carnegie Free Library, and many important business premises—some three hundred buildings in all—were destroyed. The total damage was estimated at over £3,000,000. On the next day many people left the city, fearing fresh trouble. At the request of a deputation of citizens, General Strickland, the officer commanding the district, posted military patrols in the streets, with orders to shoot looters. On December 14 it was announced that martial law had been proclaimed in the counties of Cork, Tipperary, Kerry, and Limerick. Our illustration shows ruined buildings in Patrick Street, the chief business thoroughfare of Cork.

PHOTOGRAPH BY L.N.A

At around 8 pm on 11 December 1920, six Volunteers of Cork No. 1 Brigade ambushed two tenders at Dillon's Cross. One Auxiliary was killed and 11 wounded.

The Auxiliaries had been on edge – it was less than two weeks since their colleagues had been killed at Kilmichael. The new ambush proved to be the tipping point.

The Auxiliaries immediately headed to the city centre. They began an orgy of burning, drunkenness and looting. Auxiliaries and soldiers roamed along St Patrick Street, Cork's main thoroughfare. Some were uniformed, others in plain clothes. Civilians were beaten up, while others fled. Bombs were thrown in stores. As the streets emptied the burnings began. The Crown forces poured petrol into buildings. (Some 300 gallons of petrol had been taken from the stores at Victoria Barracks.) By 4 am the City Hall was ablaze.

Left: fake news from the 'Illustrated London News'. It ably bends the truth about the devastation of Cork, falsely noting that the fires 'were evidently the work of incendiaries, but of what faction it is impossible to say'.

Right: map of damage. Cork city centre was devastated. There were 20 burned stores on Patrick Street, with 35 wrecked premises in the side streets. Hundreds of residences were destroyed. The City Hall and the Carnegie Library were in ruins. Damage amounted to over €160 million in today's values.

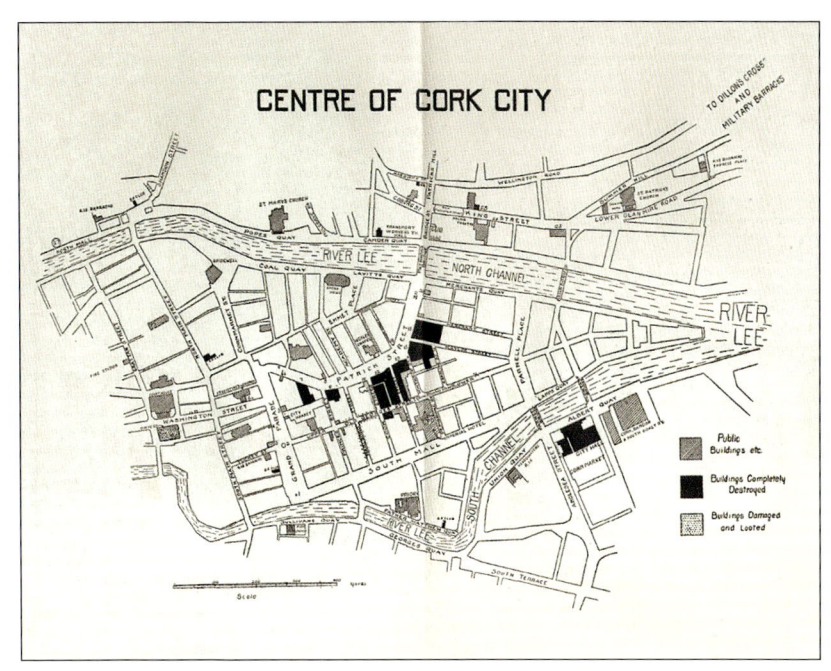

Right: more 'fake news', this time from Italy. 'La Tribuna Illustrata' accepts the official British spin that troops were defending the city. It says that in the '...historic... city – the troops had to... disperse looters'.

La caccia alle jene fra le rovine di Cork

Durante l'incendio di Cork, in Irlanda, — incendio che ha distrutto in breve ora oltre trecento case della storica città nordica — la truppa ha dovuto affrontare e disperdere numerose bande di saccheggiatori che attorno all'immenso braciere depredavano i cadaveri e frugavano fra le rovine che le fiamme avevano abbandonato.

(Disegno di E. Asso)

187

Above: fire brigades from other cities came to Cork's assistance – a steam pump and the Dublin Leyland fire engine pump water from the River Lee.

In the aftermath, two military courts of enquiry, held in sequence, concluded that the Auxiliaries were responsible. The Government refused to publish the report of the second enquiry, by Major-General Strickland.

Left: a cartoon by 'Shemus' shows Lloyd George and Hamar Greenwood shying away from the awkward spectre of truth, as set out in the Strickland Report.

Above: British troops at a bridge blown up by the IRA, near Kinsale, Co. Cork.

Right: Major-General Peter Strickland (Commanding 6th Division), who was based at Victoria Barracks, Cork.

On 27 December 1920, Major-General Strickland proclaimed martial law covering most of Munster – the counties of Cork, Tipperary, Kerry and Limerick.

THE KINDEST CUT OF ALL.

WELSH WIZARD. "I NOW PROCEED TO CUT THIS MAP INTO TWO PARTS AND PLACE THEM IN THE HAT. AFTER A SUITABLE INTERVAL THEY WILL BE FOUND TO HAVE COME TOGETHER OF THEIR OWN ACCORD—(ASIDE)—AT LEAST LET'S HOPE SO; I'VE NEVER DONE THIS TRICK BEFORE."

Right: taking a break during a search for Éamon de Valera on an American ship at Dublin docks. On 23 December 1920, smuggled aboard a ship from Liverpool, he arrived back in Dublin.

Left: a view by Punch in March 1920 of Lloyd George's partition trickery. His decision to procrastinate and give the Unionists what they wanted, still reverberates today.

The 'Government of Ireland Bill' made a slow passage through parliament during 1920. It finally became law on 23 December
With this bill the British Parliament imposed partition on an Ireland divided into the six north-eastern counties ('Northern Ireland') and the remaining 26 counties making up 'Southern Ireland'. Each entity was to have a bicameral parliament with limited powers. A Council of Ireland was to coordinate, with (as a sop to nationalists) the implication that it might evolve into an All-Ireland Parliament in the future.

Right: members of the Dublin Brigade Active Service Unit (full-time Volunteers) pose. This was established at the end of 1920.

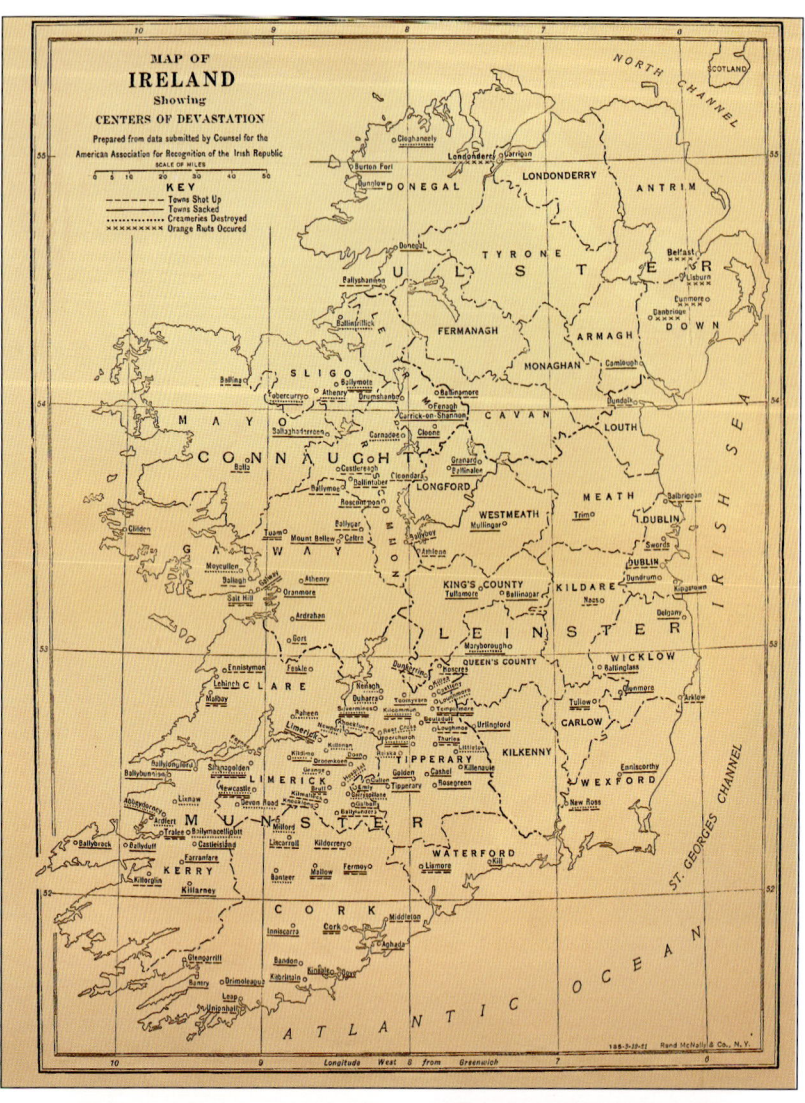

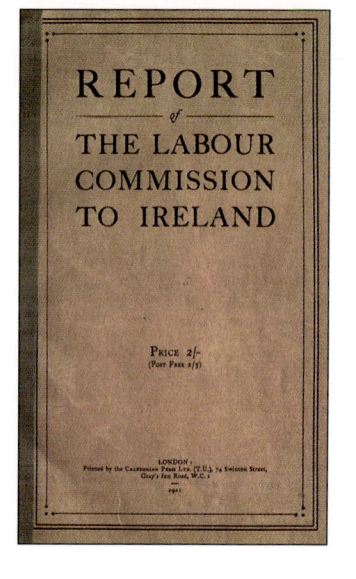

There was a spate of reports about the situation in Ireland and the actions of the Crown forces.

In November 1920 an American Commission of Inquiry on Conditions in Ireland began hearings, and took testimony from witnesses. The Interim Report, published in early 1921 (map from report, left) detailed atrocities, and proved hugely embarrassing to the British government.

The British Labour Party was against the partition of Ireland, but also opposed a republic – it wanted to maintain the connection between the two islands. Amidst the uproar in Ireland, however, the leadership was assailed for its timidity. As a sop, a commission of enquiry on Ireland was proposed in November 1920.

After duly making investigations, it published a report (near left) which detailed reprisals and atrocities. It concluded: 'Things are being done in the name of Britain which must make her name stink in the nostrils of the whole world...'.

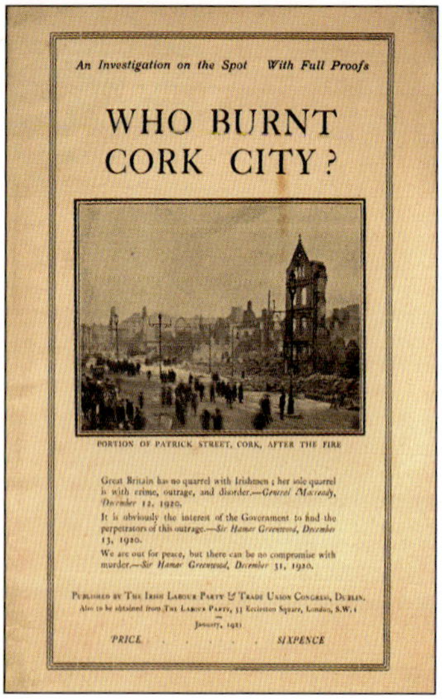

Far left: the Irish Labour Party published 'Who Burnt Cork City?' in January 1921. It apportioned full blame to the Crown forces.

Right: part of the document proclaiming martial law.

On 29 December 1920 a flying column ambushed an RIC patrol on the main street in Midleton. Three constables died as a result. A reprisal followed – seven houses were destroyed. There had been many reprisals but this was the first 'official' reprisal, allowed for under martial law. In the following months, official reprisals across Munster became commonplace.

Right: the 'Graphic' reports on the first official reprisals in Ireland at Midleton. In the photograph of the burnt-out Midleton Engineering Works and Garage, the caption primly notes: 'The destruction of these premises is not included in the official list of reprisals'.

193

A reprisal at Meelin, Co. Cork, followed soon after Midleton. Six houses were burnt and a teenager killed in retaliation for an ambush there (led by Seán Moylan) on 4 January 1921.

Left: this photograph from Meelin is captioned: 'Widow Brown's daughter in charge of the furniture after the destruction of their home'.

On 5 January 1921 martial law was extended to cover the counties of Clare, Waterford, Kilkenny and Wexford.

Left: Shemus' view of reprisals. Entitled 'Perhaps?', it depicts a woman at a shooting gallery offering Hamar Greenwood and General Nevil Macready a go at 'Reprisals'.

194

The British Army official history of the war relates: 'In February 1921 some extensive operations were carried out by troops and police in Dublin. Areas of the city were surrounded by cordons and troops and systematically searched'.

Right: Auxiliaries load up drums and other material confiscated in a Dublin raid.

Right: the back page of 'La Domenica de Corriere' (Milan) depicts what they term an official reprisal in Dublin – 'soldiers demolish a house in the area that was the recent scene of an ambush by Sinn Féiners'. As the troops energetically flail with their picks, the armoured car looks like a Peerless which has metamorphosed into having only one turret.

195

Above: in Dublin Castle, 'F' Company, of the Auxiliaries, with their two Rolls-Royce armoured cars, as depicted in an IRA intelligence book.

On 21 January 1921, eight ASU members of the 1st Battalion, Dublin Brigade, headed to Tolka Bridge and opened fire on two approaching RIC tenders. However, the IRA position had been given away (the alleged informer was executed five months later). The Auxiliaries of 'F' Company were alerted and attacked the ASU as they were dispersing. Two Volunteers escaped. One died of his wounds and the remaining five were captured – four of whom were later executed in Mountjoy.

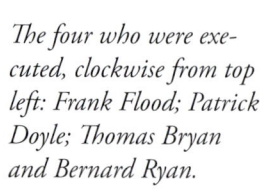

The four who were executed, clockwise from top left: Frank Flood; Patrick Doyle; Thomas Bryan and Bernard Ryan.

196

On the night of 27 January 1921, Captain Frank Busteed and 68 Volunteers set up at Dripsey (memorial, right), planning to ambush a patrol from Macroom to Cork. The next morning, Mrs Mary Lindsay, a loyalist, hearing of the ambush, ordered her driver to bring her to Ballincollig where she informed the military. A strong force of soldiers arrived and encircled the ambushers. Eight IRA men were captured, five of whom were sentenced to death. On 17 February Mrs Lindsay and driver were seized. She was forced to write a letter saying she would be shot if the prisoners were executed. Nevertheless the prisoners were executed at the end of February. On 11 March, Mrs Lindsay and her driver were shot.

In his military service pension application (above right), Busteed (right, with Lewis gun) details how: '...we arrested Mrs Lindsay and driver as spies. Both were executed later'.

Below: Mrs Lindsay.

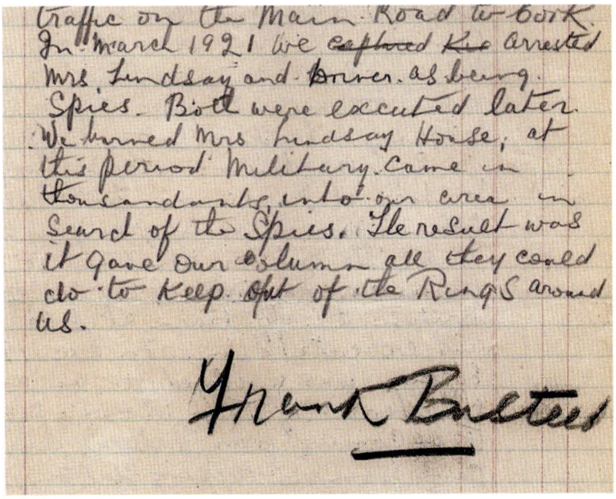

Left: the south signal box at Mallow - behind is the railway bridge from where the Volunteers had fired.

On the night of 31 January 1921, Volunteers lay in wait near Mallow station. In the darkness they fired from a bridge at RIC County Inspector King and his wife who were walking by. King was wounded but his wife later died. Infuriated RIC and Auxiliaries charged into Mallow station. They shot up a train, then ordered staff to run for their lives. Two men died and another was mortally wounded.

On 2 February 1921, 17 members of 'M' Company, ADRIC, were returning from Granard to Longford. At Clonfin, as the road dipped down approaching a small bridge, a mine exploded under the leading tender. In a well-planned ambush, the North Longford flying column, led by Seán Mac Eoin, opened fire on the second tender. After 20 minutes four Auxiliaries lay dead and eight were wounded. Mac Eoin prevented the survivors from being executed and chivalrously ensured that the wounded were cared for.

Left: the ambush site at Clonfin, Co. Longford.

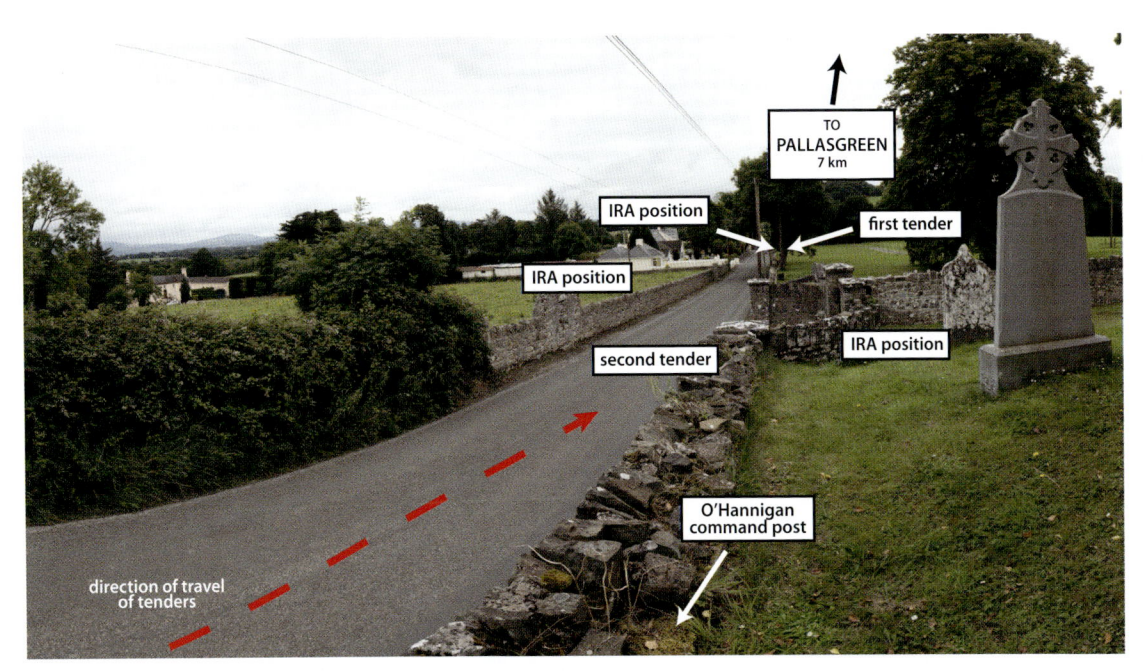

Above: ambush site at Dromkeen. Plaque (right).

The flying columns of the East and Mid-Limerick Brigades, IRA (under Donncha O'Hannigan) ambushed an RIC patrol here as it returned to Pallasgreen on 3 February 1921. It was a bloody encounter for the Crown forces, resulting in 11 dead. The first tender came under heavy fire and crashed into a wall. The second was fired on from the cemetery and the opposite side of the road. Eight RIC died immediately. An impromptu court martial was held in situ and the resulting vote was to execute the remaining Black and Tans.

Right: an RIC patrol in Co. Limerick.

Left: troops search a train on the Tralee branch.

On 11 February, Volunteers entered the cab of the Mallow to Tralee train (carrying a party of soldiers) at Rathcoole station. Approaching Drishanbeg, the driver was ordered to give a whistle blast. As the train stopped the IRA commander demanded that the soldiers surrender. There was a volley of shots in reply. In the darkness, the North Cork Brigade poured fire at the military in the train. With two dead, the British surrendered. The IRA collected their rifles and ammunition, and withdrew.

A disastrous train ambush occurred at Upton, Co. Cork, on 15 February 1921. Volunteers lay in wait at the station, expecting just 20 soldiers of the Essex Regiment, but another 30 had joined at Kinsale. After Drishanbeg, troops had been ordered to be spread out in trains. As the train arrived the IRA opened fire at the centre carriage where they thought the British were located. The soldiers replied with heavy fire from all along the train. The death toll was eight civilians, and three IRA men.

Left: a dramatic Italian depiction of the ambush.

Right: a depiction of an attack by Crown forces on a farmhouse.

The 4th Battalion of the 1st Cork Brigade was billeted at a small farmhouse at Clonmult, Co. Cork, where, unwisely, they had spent five weeks. On 20 February 1921, acting on intelligence, soldiers set out there from Midleton. They shot two Volunteers who were outside the farmhouse, then surrounded it and opened fire. After an hour, five men made an attempt to escape. Three were shot dead, one retreated back inside and, one, Captain O'Connell managed to escape. Two truckloads of ADRIC now arrived. The thatched roof was set on fire. The remaining occupants decided to surrender and exited the house. One was clubbed to the ground. The Auxiliaries shot the rest. By the end of the action, twelve IRA men lay dead.

Right: the burnt-out farmhouse at Clonmult.

Below: sign near the site.

On 5 March 1921, Brigadier-General HR Cumming (left, centre) was returning to Brigade HQ from an inspection tour in Kerry. His touring car was escorted by three Crossley Tenders and a Rolls-Royce armoured car.

Below left: a Rolls Royce armoured car.

Around 100 Volunteers from the Cork and Kerry brigades lay in wait at Clonbanin (near Banteer, North Cork). An earlier attempt to detonate a mine, as a west-bound convoy passed, had failed. Cumming's convoy, spaced out along 800m, approached from the west. The IRA opened fire. A bullet (from a captured Hotchkiss machine gun) entered the driver's slit of the armoured car and wounded the driver. The armoured car crashed, but continued firing with its Vickers. Cumming was shot as he ran for cover. After three hours of battle, the IRA withdrew. Cumming and three soldiers were killed.

Left: ambush site at Clonbanin.

Right: Mountjoy death book. Six Volunteers were hanged at Mountjoy Jail on 14 March 1921. Three others were also hanged that year (Thomas Traynor for killing an Auxiliary in Dublin, as well as Edmond Foley and Patrick Maher for the 1919 Knocklong rescue). In 2001 their remains (as well as that of Kevin Barry) were transferred to Glasnevin Cemetery in a State ceremony.

The English hangman, John Ellis (who had hanged Roger Casement and Kevin Barry), officiated on 14 March. Executed were: Patrick Moran and Thomas Whelan (for Bloody Sunday events); Patrick Doyle, Bernard Ryan, Thomas Bryan and Frank Flood (captured at Drumcondra on 21 January).

Middle right: looking unaccountably jolly on the day before he was hanged, Thomas Whelan strides between his captors. Whelan had been sentenced to death for the Bloody Sunday killing of Captain Baggallay at Baggot Street.

Right: thousands knelt in the rain outside Mountjoy on the morning of the executions.

203

At 6 am on 14 March, Patrick Moran and Thomas Whelan were led from their cells, bound and hooded, placed on the double trap doors, and simultaneously hanged. The other four were hanged in pairs in the following two hours.

Left: a poignant sketch 'Scene at 11:45 pm in the condemned cell on the Eve of the Execution of Thomas Bryan and Frank Flood', the last pair to be hung. Bryan is seen by the door singing 'The 'Soldiers Song'; Flood is writing a letter; an Auxiliary is lying down, while another sketches and a warder reads.

Left: the safety key at the hanghouse. When the prisoners were positioned on the trapdoors, the hangman withdrew the key, then pulled the lever operating the trapdoors.

Below: a postcard from Germany reflecting the general outrage at the six executions on 14 March.

Above: a group of Auxiliaries at Union Quay Barracks, Cork in 1921.

Early in the morning of 7 March 1921, men in civilian dress burst into the homes of the Limerick Mayor, Seoirse Clancy, and his predecessor, Michael O'Callaghan, and shot them dead. The assassins had collars turned up, caps over faces and wore goggles. Suspicion immediately fell on the Auxiliaries.

Right: the funerals of Clancy and O'Callaghan. Inset: memorial to Seoirse Clancy at St Munchin's Catholic Church, Limerick.

Left: memorial at Crossbarry, around 18 kilometres south-west of Cork city.

Tom Barry, with 104 men of his 3rd West Cork flying column, had spent a miserable St Patrick's Day in 1921 lying in wait along the Bandon-Kinsale road, awaiting a British patrol which never showed up. By the night of 18 March they had reached their HQ north of Crossbarry village and billeted there in several houses. However, the Crown forces had just extracted information on their location from a Volunteer captured at the Upton ambush some weeks before, and planned a vast sweep to capture Barry's column. At around 1 am on 19 March, the Crown forces massed, amounting to around 1,000 men.

At Crossbarry, Barry was wakened at 2:30 am – the lookouts had noticed the lights and sounds of lorries. At 3 am he paraded his men and decided to attack one side of the encirclement, at the Crossbarry road. This turned out to be a weak part of the cordon. His Volunteers were in place by 5:30 am.

Left: Tom Barry

Above: the barracks at Bandon, HQ of the Essex Regiment. Soldiers had been drafted from the regiment here and Kinsale. More came from Ballincollig and Cork. Auxiliaries also travelled from Macroom.

At around 8 am, lorryloads of troops drove along the road at Crossbarry. A mine was detonated and IRA rifles opened up. The British took heavy casualties and many soldiers fled. After several fierce exchanges the IRA withdrew to the north-west (map, right). Three Volunteers (as well as Charlie Hurley, OC 3rd Cork Brigade, killed at a nearby farmhouse) were dead – the British admitted ten killed. This large-scale battle was the most successful carried out by the IRA.

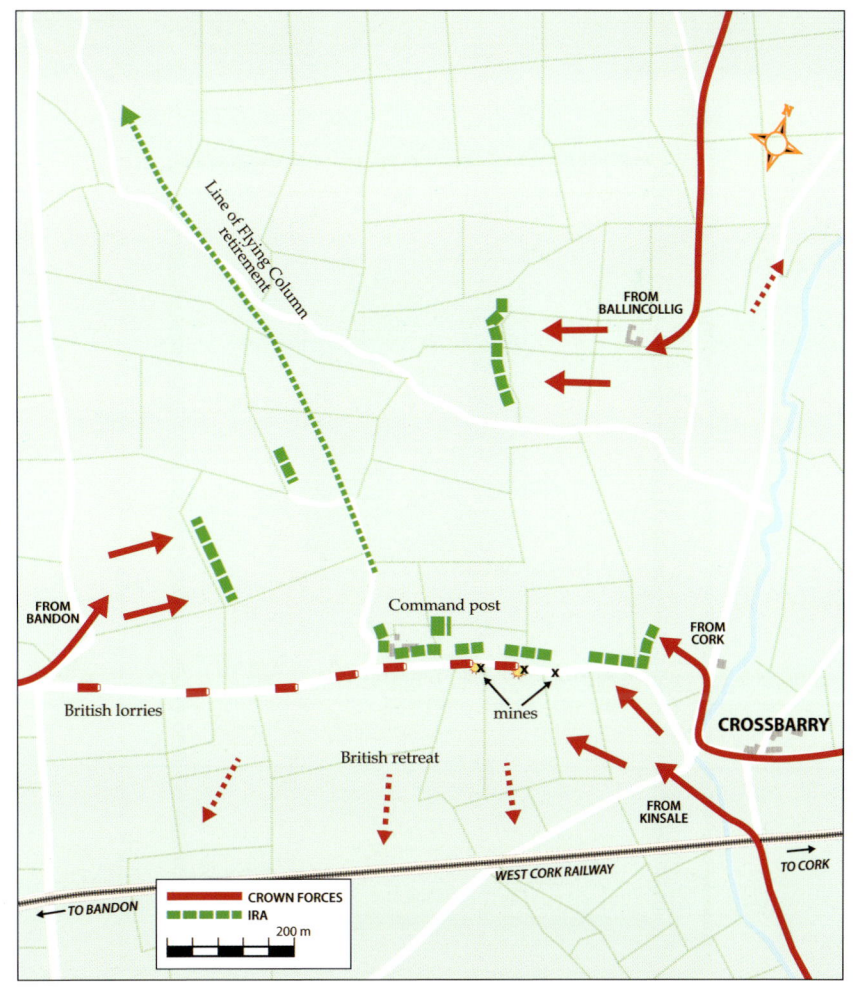

Above: Royal Fusiliers in Kerry, with a Vickers machine-gun truck in front of a locomotive.

On 21 March, at Headford Junction, the 2nd Kerry Brigade awaited a train from Kenmare, carrying a party of Royal Fusiliers. As the train arrived, the Volunteers opened fire. A Vickers in the front carriage was put out of action. When the connecting train from Mallow pulled in (also with troops aboard, and a machine-gun truck in front), the IRA withdrew. Lying dead were: eight British soldiers; two civilians and two IRA men.

Left: memorial for Commandant Dan Allman, killed at Headford.

"If death come to me, it will be because of my great love for Ireland."—St. Columcille

In Loving Memory of
Commandant Daniel J. Allman,
East Kerry Brigade Column, I.R.A.
Killed in Action at Headford, Co. Kerry,
On the 21st MARCH, 1921.
Aged 30 Years.
R.I.P.

"Greater love than this no man hath that a man lay down his life for his friends."

'Q' Company, of the Auxiliaries was based at the London & North Western Railway (L&NWR) Hotel at North Wall. Mostly made up of former naval and merchant navy men, their mission was to control port security.

Right: Auxiliaries pose at the side of the hotel after the attack.

On the morning of 11 April, Tom Ennis led an IRA attack, opening fire at the front and sides of the hotel. A mine placed at the front door failed to explode. Grenades were thrown through the windows. These included small bottles of phosphorus in carbon bisulphide. The Auxiliaries, suffering from the noxious fumes, burst out of the building, firing at the attackers. A whistle blew and the IRA withdrew, having suffered one dead.

Right: cadets in celebratory mood in the aftermath.

Near right: the L&NWR Hotel. Far right: the Scherzer bridge at Spencer Dock. Volunteer Garry Holohan was detailed to lift the electrically-operated bridge to block off the road. He failed to lift it but closed the road gates, which delayed the Crown forces.

209

On 15 April 1921, Major MacKinnon (left) commander of the Auxiliaries, was playing golf at Tralee. As he reached the third green, he was shot twice in the head. During his time in Tralee, this tall hero of the Great War had earned notoriety, burning houses with great zeal and personally killing two Volunteers.

Middle left: the premises of the 'Kerryman' newspaper. After MacKinnon's death, reprisals occurred in the Tralee district. The newpaper's works were destroyed after a refusal to print with a black border.

Early in the morning of 23 April, the RIC encircled a barn near Clogheen, Co. Cork, where six Volunteers (all from Blarney Street) of 1st Battalion, Cork No. 1 Brigade, were asleep. All were shot dead – the bodies were badly mutilated. They had been betrayed by an informer, who fled to New York. In April 1922, he was shot four times near Central Park by Cork IRA men, and later died of his wounds.

Left: memorial at Clogheen (around 5km north-west of Cork City).

In Spring 1921, the IRA GHQ decided to introduce a decentralised divisional structure. The idea was that this would result in better cooperation across boundaries and simpler management. First to be established was the 1st Southern.

Right: the eventual IRA divisional structure.

Below: the most effective division of all – the 1st Southern. Here officers of the division meet at the Mansion House in April 1922. At the centre front, fourth from the left, is Divisional Commander Liam Lynch.

Above: at Clonakilty in West Cork, a joint patrol of the RIC and the 1st Battalion, Essex Regiment, about to set off on their bicycles. The naval rating in the background is most likely a wireless operator assigned to the army.

One effective tactic employed by the IRA was to dig up roads and destroy bridges, to disrupt the movement of military patrols. Here, members of the Crown forces observe while men begin the repair of a damaged bridge at Ballinspittle, Co. Cork.

Above: bare terrain – Lough Mask and the Partry Mountains.

On 3 May 1921, the South Mayo Brigade flying column, under Tom Maguire, ambushed the RIC at Tourmakeady, killing four. The Volunteers then withdrew into the Partry Mountains. The Border Regiment, arrived at Tourmakeady (map, right) hours later and gave chase. Lieutenant Ibberson, in command, assigned other parties under Lieutenants Smith and Craig to encircle the mountain. Ibberson himself raced directly up the mountain, so fast that he moved well ahead of his men. Spotting the IRA, Ibberson fired and Tom Maguire (near right) fell wounded. Adjutant Michael O'Brien (far right) who had been helping Maguire, shot at Ibberson, who returned fire, killing O'Brien. Volunteers blazed at Ibberson, who sustained several wounds. With difficulty he made his way down the mountain to safety.

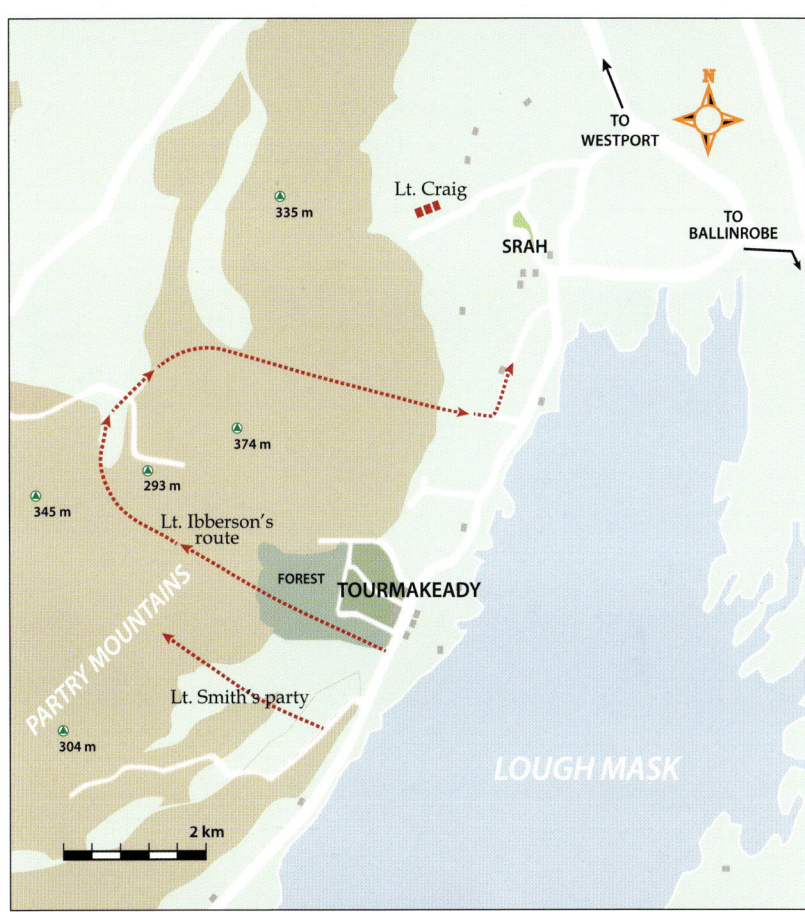

213

LA DOMENICA DEL CORRIERE

Anno XXIII. — Num. 12. — 20-27 Marzo 1921.

Uno spettacolo di guerra, nell'Isola senza pace. In Irlanda, gli aviatori sventano un'imboscata di ribelli contro autocarri carichi di truppe, e uccidono cinque degli assalitori.

(Disegno di A. Beltrame).

Right: RAF aerial weapons – a Cooper 20 lb aerial bomb and below, a Lewis machine gun.

Left: as Bristol fighters soar, 'La Domenica del Corriere' of March 1921 stirringly relates: 'the airmen foil an ambush by rebels...killing five assailants'. However, the reality was more prosaic. RAF activity was a lesser strand of the war effort in Ireland. RAF planes, were not allowed to fire at rebels, due to government nervousness about hitting civilians. Thus their role was to transport mail and senior officers between barracks. Escorts and reconnaissance were also carried out.

Finally on 24 March 1921 approval for armed attack was given. However, in the closing months of the War of Independence, there were very few attacks. RAF records for June list a few instances where the Lewis was fired from planes at ground targets: at Gort (on 11 June – bombs also dropped); Woodford (on 15 June) and during a major drive in Kerry. No casualties were recorded.

Right: in November 1920, a plane delivering mail for the nearby barracks crashed onto a roof at Waterford.

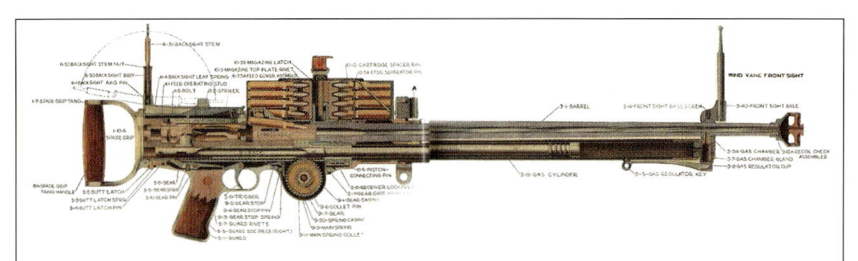

215

Seán Mac Eoin (left) was imprisoned in Mountjoy Gaol. Michael Collins planned an escape. It was to take place when Mac Eoin was scheduled to be in the Governor's office at a given date and time. On 14 May, Volunteers seized a Peerless armoured car, part of an escort for rations lorries. They then drove to Mountjoy with Emmet Dalton and Joe Leonard, dressed as British officers.

Left: a Peerless armoured car.

On arrival at the gates, Dalton waved an official paper and they were allowed to drive in. They deliberately parked so as to keep the gate jammed open. They were brought to the Governor's office, but Mac Eoin was not there. Dalton presented a prisoner removal order – but the governor proceeded to ring Dublin Castle for confirmation. Smashing the phone, the 'officers' drew their revolvers. They heard firing outside. A soldier on the roof had opened fire, but had been shot by one of the men in the Peerless. The 'officers' withdrew as Auxiliaries and soldiers closed in. The Peerless and occupants made off safely at speed.

Left: Mountjoy Gaol

On Sunday 15 May, District Inspector Major Biggs was driving with some companions in the direction of Newport, Co. Tipperary. Biggs had won a reputation for brutal behaviour and the IRA were determined to get him. As the party drove down a dip at a small bridge at Coolboreen, the local IRA opened up. Biggs was killed, as was Winifrid Barrington (right) from a prominent Limerick family.

Another District Inspector was shot on the same day, near Gort, Co. Galway. On 15 May, District Inspector Captain Blake and a party, including his wife, were leaving Ballyturin House. As they approached the gate, there was a shout: 'Hands up!' The IRA opened fire. Blake and his wife were killed, as were two other officers (depiction, right).

On 19 June, 2nd Lieutenant Donald Breeze was stopped by the IRA, while motoring near Carrickmines Co. Dublin. There was an altercation, where Breeze was wounded and was then taken off by car as a prisoner. It appears that en route Breeze tried to grab a revolver; the IRA stopped and shot him (depiction, right).

217

Above: watchful menace. As painted by Mick O'Dea – an Auxiliary, armed with revolver and Lewis machine gun, outside Hynes' public house in Dublin. For this elite force, life as a temporary cadet offered danger, but for these (mainly) young ex-officers, there was an occasional touch of the high life, and, sometimes, opportunities for unsupervised violence and excess.

Left: WF Martinson. This experienced veteran was promoted to be Adjutant of the Auxiliary Division RIC in April 1921.

Right: 'The Illustrated Police News' of May 1921 dramatically depicts the attempted rescue of an IRA prisoner from police custody. An Inspector Johnston was killed.

The IRA in Britain effortlessly swam within the large Irish community. They supplied many weapons and explosives, transshipped from ports like Liverpool to Ireland – sourced from Britain, and elsewhere. The IRA in Britain made sporadic attacks on infrastructure, which resulted in economic damage but little of military value. Nevertheless, the existential danger of IRA attack was a source of anxiety for the authorities.

Below right: members of the Liverpool IRA who were released from Dartmoor in 1922.

Below: at the end of November 1920, the IRA set fire to cotton warehouses and timber yards in Liverpool and Bootle, causing huge damage.

DARING SINN FEIN OUTRAGE IN GLASGOW.

Members of the Liverpool Coy. I.R.A.
Released from Dartmoor Prison, 14th February, 1922.

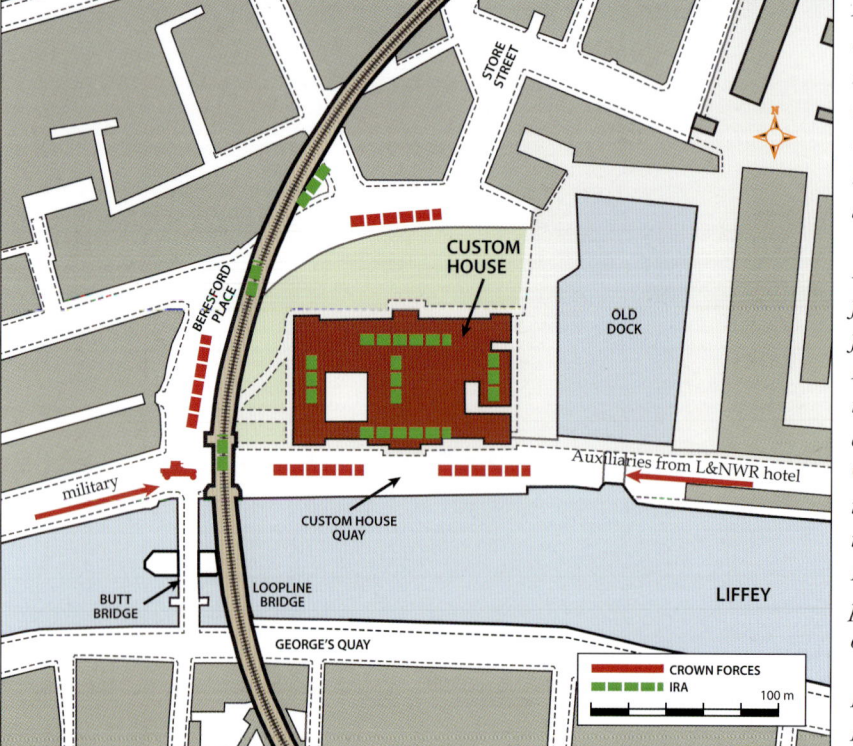

Above: the fire blazes in the Custom House, at the heart of civil administration of Ireland. The building contained all local government records and tax files.

De Valera, now returned from the USA, was in favour of large battles. Early in 1921 possible targets were considered by the IRA Army Council. Destruction of the Custom House was the choice. The Dublin Brigade began detailed preparations for the operation.

Left: map of the Custom House area.

On Wednesday 25 May, 270 Volunteers of the Dublin Brigade mustered. At 12:55 pm, 120 men of the 2nd Battalion (including some Squad members) under the command of O/C Tom Ennis, entered the Custom House. Others spread out in the surrounding area to protect the operation. Inside the Custom House, staff were rounded up and Volunteers poured paraffin on piles of files, setting them on fire.

The Auxiliaries arrived and surrounded the Custom House, exchanging fire with IRA units outside. Later in the battle, truckloads of military also arrived.

Above right: the round-up at Beresford Place, with, on the ground, 17-year-old Dan Head, shot dead after throwing a bomb into an Auxiliary tender.

Right: troops arrest civilians.

The Auxiliaries entered the building. All inside were ordered to leave with their hands up. They were lined up outside to be identified. A few Volunteers managed to bluff their way out, but the majority were detained and herded onto tenders.

Right: Crown forces display a flag taken from the Custom House.

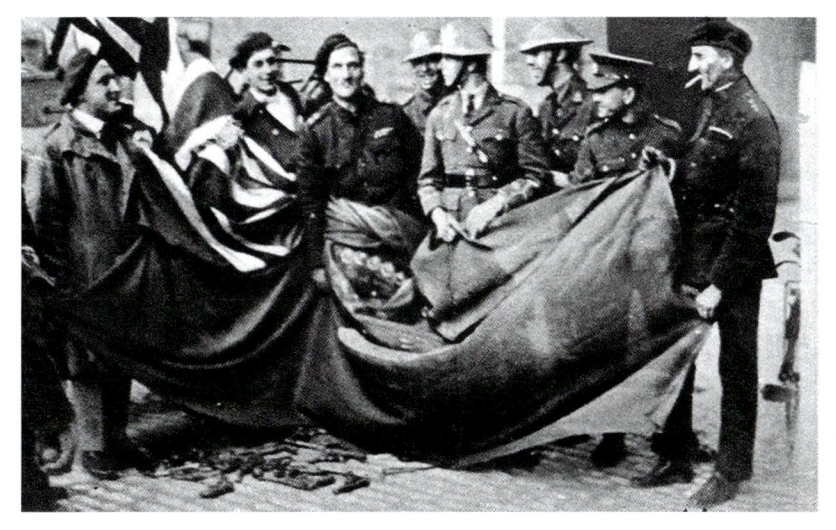

Above: a British officer, Mauser pistol in hand, stands next to a Peerless armoured car, in front of the Custom House.

Early in the action, the IRA had taken control of the Dublin fire stations. Many of the firemen were Volunteers or sympathisers. Callers on the phone were assured that help was on the way – but no firemen showed up. Eventually the Fire Brigade arrived (left) and when it was safe, they entered the burning building. However, as one fireman recalled: 'many parts of (the building) that were not on fire when we entered were blazing nicely in a short while'.

Right: the dome with melted copper sheeting. The building burned for ten days. Destruction was extensive.

This, the biggest IRA operation in the war, resulted in the death of four Volunteers (another died later of wounds). Four civilians were also dead. The capture of over a hundred experienced Volunteers was also a blow. However this must be seen against Dublin Brigade's nominal strength of 4,500. More were immediately recruited in the ASU – and the IRA deliberately intensified their Dublin activities in the aftermath.

Despite the loss of Gandon's masterpiece, subsequently rebuilt, the objective of destroying this vital administrative centre was achieved, another big step in making Ireland ungovernable. This 'spectacular' added to the pressure on the British to begin negotiations for a truce.

Right: a ruined corridor.

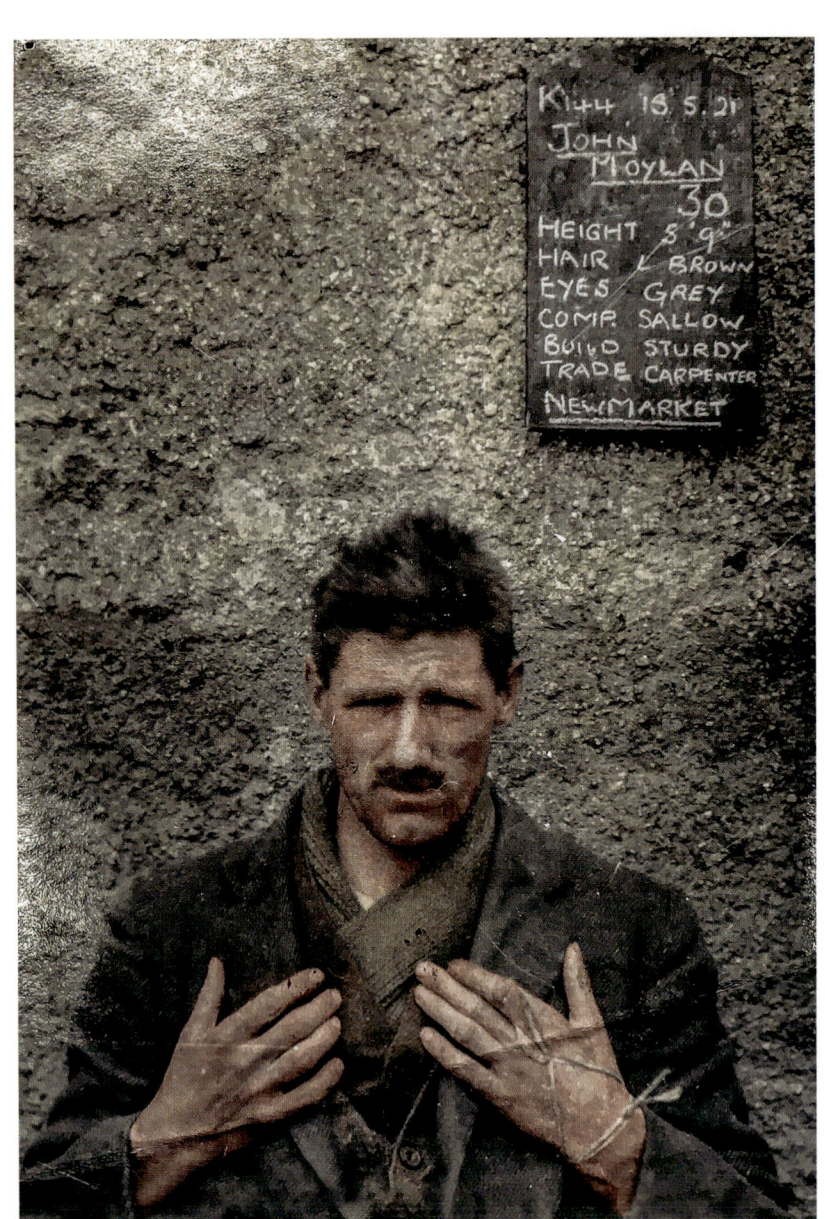

The Gloucestershire Regiment, deployed in north Cork, began to build up intelligence on the local IRA, led by Seán Moylan.

On 15 May 1921, in a well-planned raid, a party of troops captured Moylan and others at a farm near Kiskeam, north-west Cork. In a court martial, Moylan luckily escaped the death penalty, but got 15 years' penal servitude.

Left: Seán Moylan after capture. The strains of living on the run, as well as bouts of ill-health, can be seen.

On the morning of 31 May a company of the 2nd Battalion of the Royal Hampshires was being played by their band (below) down to the range for firing practice. On the way a mine was detonated as the band passed. Seven bandsmen were killed and around 20 wounded.

Right: a painting by Mick O'Dea of Michael Kilroy, West Mayo flying column, and his men.

On 2 June 1921 Kilroy led an ambush on an RIC patrol, in two Crossley Tenders, on the Leenane-Westport road at Carrowkennedy. The battle raged for several hours. Eight RIC men (including D/I Stevenson, killed as he drove the first tender) died as a result. Sixteen surrendered and these were later released.

Right: RIC men pose, with tenders, in front of a burnt-out barracks.

On 16 June, at Rathcoole, Co. Cork (map, below), a large IRA force attacked Auxiliaries returning from Banteer. Mines were detonated under a Lancia and two tenders. After two hours, the IRA withdrew, leaving two Auxiliaries dead and several wounded.

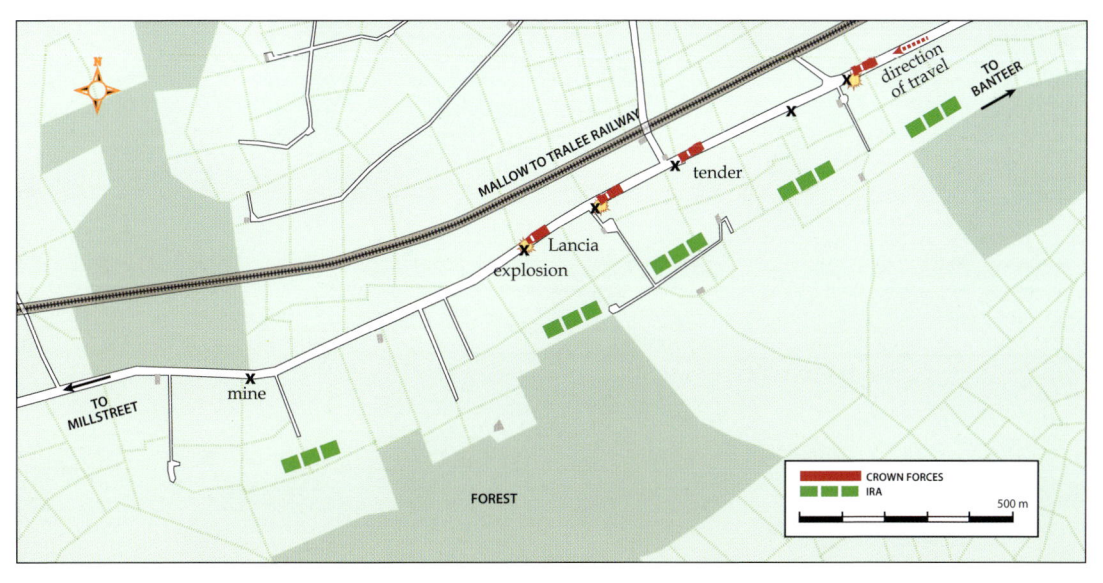

225

Since 1919, the 1st Battalion Essex Regiment had been stationed in West Cork. This, the most pro-active of the British regiments, was in an area where the IRA was intensively active. Major Arthur Percival (left, detail from a painting by Mick O'Dea), who, later, as general, surrendered Singapore in WWII. Percival garnered notoriety during his service in West Cork. Percival adopted IRA flying columns' tactics. His soldiers spread out on foot in units over the countryside, sleeping in barns or tents. They surrounded houses at nightfall, closing in at daybreak.

Below: a party of the Essex Regiment resting by a road in Co. Cork.

Near right: Brigadier-General Ormonde Winter, at the centre of the British spy web in Ireland since May 1920.

Winter reorganised intelligence, improved coordination and obtained an influx of secret service men. New groups were set in place to track down the 'Sinn Féiners'. One was the 'Igoe Gang' in Dublin (led by Eugene Igoe, far right) who shadowed suspects and arrested or, on occasion, shot them.

As IRA Director of Intelligence, Michael Collins (right) established a GHQ Intelligence staff at Crow Street. At an early stage, he cultivated a string of valuable informers. Collins established a system of safe houses, pubs and hotels across the city, where he and his shadowy operatives functioned.

Below: Dame Court, across from Crow Street. Informants met Collins in the nearby Stag's Head.

227

T/C JACK DUNNE

SECTION LEADER SCHOFIELD "F" COY. AUX. CASTLE

CAPT. JAMES J. WALSH. SECRET SERVICE

Collins' intelligence service maintained records on important aspects of the British military and civil grasp on Ireland. On the left are two extracts from an IRA intelligence photo book (1919-1921) maintained by Frank Thornton, Deputy Assistant Director of Intelligence. The contents of the book were extensive. These ranged from newspaper clippings to stolen or captured photographs. The indexed pages included 'spies', British military, Auxiliaries, RIC, DMP as well as judges and even a typist.

By mid-1921, Dublin was flooded with the forces of the Crown. Searchlights pierced the sky as night raids and round-ups continued.

Right: a ring of steel. At Kildare Street, in front of the National Museum: soldiers with bayonets; a truck with mounted searchlight and two Peerless armoured cars.

On 30 May 1921 Lloyd George announced the strengthening of Crown forces in Ireland. By mid-1921 the British cabinet was vacillating between a drive to intensify the war ('stick, not carrot') and the urge to negotiate a truce. In the peace camp were the Liberals, unhappy about the British atrocities in Ireland.

Right: wise masters of all they surveyed? British troops look out over the Liffey from the roof of the Four Courts. The statues on the pediment are of Justice (centre) and Wisdom (in background).

Left: a Shemus cartoon entitled 'The Six Counties' – the new Northern Prime Minister James Craig, reclines on six bubbles blown by Edward Carson, as Lloyd George and Hamar Greenwood peer in.

Under the Government of Ireland Act, an election for the 'Northern Ireland House of Commons' was held on 24 May 1921. Of the 52 seats, Unionists won 40; nationalist parties won 12. For the 'Southern Ireland House of Commons', no polling took place – all candidates were returned unopposed. Of the 128 seats, Sinn Féin won 124.

On 22 June the Northern parliament (left) was opened by King George V (inset). The coming into existence of the parliament meant that the partition of Ireland was now copper-fastened. The event was attended by Unionist members – but not by the nationalists. Reflecting a mood for conciliation, the King made a nuanced speech which asked for all Irishmen 'to pause...to forgive and forget'.

Two days later, a train carrying the 10th Hussars, who had been part of the royal escort in Belfast, was blown up near Dundalk (left). Many horses and three soldiers were killed.

There was a new mood for peace. Against the background of the international opprobrium that Britain was earning as news of atrocities by Crown forces circulated, the British decided to negotiate.

On 24 June Lloyd George invited Éamon de Valera and James Craig, the northern premier, to go to London to explore the possibility of a settlement.

In response, de Valera called a conference for 4 July in Dublin to discuss Lloyd George's proposal for London talks. Prime Minister Craig refused to come. De Valera, 'spokesman of the nation', as he described himself, met the southern Unionists at the Mansion House. Another meeting was held on 8 July. General Macready (Commander-in-Chief, Ireland) met de Valera there and terms for a truce were agreed.

Above right: General Macready (with a pistol bulging in his pocket) is cheered as he arrives at the Mansion House. Later, in his autobiography, Macready made reference to de Valera as a 'half-breed Spaniard.'

Right: de Valera (hatless, in central foreground, back to camera) returning to his car after the meeting, amidst a vast crowd.

Left: the bodies of four off-duty British soldiers lie in a quarry near Cork city. On 10 July 1921, on the eve of the Truce, they were captured and executed by Volunteers of Cork No. 1 Brigade, possibly in retaliation for the killing of a Volunteer a day earlier.

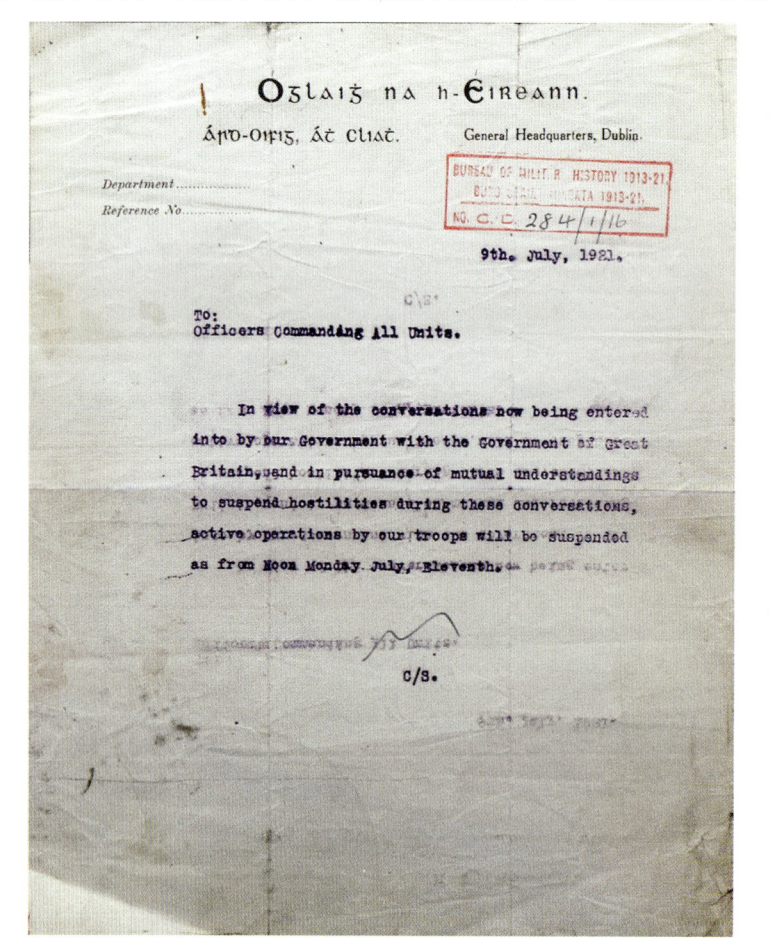

The Truce came into force on 11 July 1921. Under its terms, the British ended military manoeuvres, raids and searches. The IRA were to cease attacks on Crown forces.

Left: the order to all units of the IRA to suspend hostilities, issued by Richard Mulcahy, Chief of Staff.

Chapter 4
From Truce to Treaty

There was general relief amongst the public after the Truce was agreed on 11 July 1921. In the uneasy peace the British ended their activities and the IRA stopped their attacks on Crown forces. The IRA set up a Chief Liaison Office, assigning officers throughout the country to liaise with their British military counterparts. From now on, Volunteers could emerge from their clandestine existence. Wary of a return to conflict, the IRA's GHQ instituted a major programme of training during the Truce, establishing training camps nationwide. As the IRA had always been woefully short of arms, the GHQ redoubled its efforts to procure weapons – imports of which accelerated in the months after the Truce.

The Crown forces mainly stayed in their barracks, keeping a low profile, during the Truce period. However, they still maintained low-level intelligence operations, keeping an eye on IRA activities. The Truce did not prevail in Belfast. On the eve of its signing, loyalists attacked Catholic enclaves after the IRA ambushed police. Gun battles between the IRA, loyalists and police followed. Sixteen civilians were killed, mostly Catholic – more were killed in the following week. Hundreds of houses were destroyed.

A Belfast Boycott was in place, following a vote in Dáil Éireann. One motive was to respond to the pogroms against Catholics in Belfast (including the expulsion of Catholics from their workplaces because of their religion). Another was to alert Unionist businesses to the economic damage that partition would cause them.

Immediately after the Truce came into effect, Éamon de Valera went to meet the British Prime Minister in London. He was accompanied by, amongst others, Arthur Griffith, Robert Barton and Count Plunkett. Michael Collins had been offended at not being asked to travel. Huge enthusiastic crowds greeted the Irish delegation as they arrived. Having requested a personal meeting with Lloyd George, de Valera was received on 14 July in the cabinet room at No. 10 Downing Street. The wily Lloyd George had arranged for a large map, marked with the British Empire in red, to be hung on the wall. The eloquent Welshman tried to dazzle his visitor with a theatrical tour-de-force. However, de Valera remained unimpressed. At the same time as he grappled with de Valera, this adroit politician had to manage his recalcitrant colleagues in an unstable coalition. He was politically weak in the face of Tory opposition, firm believers in the inviolability of the British Empire. When de Valera said he would reject British proposals, Lloyd George threatened war. He noted that Britain's reduced global commitments meant it could now move more troops to Ireland and that 'the struggle would bear an entirely different character'. The series of meetings continued and at the end Lloyd George presented a formal offer. This gave the 26 counties dominion status (partition and hence 'Northern Ireland' remaining in place), with control over home defence, taxation, finance and policing – but with the Royal Navy still in control of Irish waters. De Valera was displeased but brought the offer back to Dublin where there was much discussion in cabinet. The Minister for Defence, Cathal Brugha, in particular, was concerned about the fundamental aspect which would mean the abandonment of the Republic declared at Easter 1916.

On 6 August 1921, the British agreed to release all members of the Dáil who were prisoners, but not Seán Mac Eoin, who was under sentence of death in Mountjoy. Sinn Féin made his freedom a precondition. The British relented and released him. Dáil Éireann met on 16 August in the Mansion House, where de Valera began his report on the negotiations.

Lloyd George invited de Valera to 'enter a conference to ascertain how the association of Ireland with the community of nations known as the British Empire can best be reconciled with Irish national aspirations'. On 9 September the Dáil cabinet approved the sending of a delegation. De Valera decided not to attend and later explained that this was in order to better prepare people for compromise. Plenipotentiaries were sent to London in October. The odds were stacked against the Irish delegation: they had unclear terms of reference, they were not united and some members, including Erskine Childers, reported directly back to de Valera. Lloyd George identified the main movers and had one-to-one meetings with Collins and Griffith. The latter was not in the same league as Lloyd George, a master of manipulation. The negotiations crashed against the rock of British intransigence on the issues of allegiance to the King and membership of the British Empire, fundamental to the imperial mind-set. Tensions had been building up between the delegation and their colleagues in Dublin. De Valera maintained his distance. He toured the west at the end of 1921 while negotiations were ongoing in London.

In the face of Lloyd George's histrionics which offered only signing the Treaty or facing 'immediate and terrible war', within three days, should they refuse to accept the Treaty, the delegation did not consult with Dublin but signed the Treaty document in London on 6 December 1921. In a famous exchange Earl Birkenhead said to Collins, 'I may have signed my political death warrant tonight'. Collins replied: 'I may have signed my actual death warrant'.

The treaty they signed set out, in 18 succinct paragraphs, how an Irish Free State would be formed, as a self-governing Dominion within 'the Community of Nations known as the British Empire'. It included: defence by sea was to be undertaken by the British, who would also retain naval ports; members of the Free State Parliament were to take an oath of allegiance to the constitution of the Irish Free State and to be "faithful to HM King George V"; the right of the Northern Ireland Parliament to opt out of the Irish Free State (which, to no one's surprise, it promptly did) and the sop of a Boundary Commission to be set up, if Northern Ireland did withdraw. In essence the Treaty comprised the same terms that Lloyd George had offered to de Valera in July 1921. An agreement for an imperfect and partial exit of the British from (most of) Ireland had thus been painfully achieved.

As agreed, after the Treaty was signed, IRA prisoners were released. On 8 December, the releases began and around 5,000 were freed. However, when the cabinet met at the Mansion House in Dublin on the same day, there was instant disagreement about the terms of the Treaty. The President of the Republic, Éamon de Valera, immediately came out against it. On 14 December, the cabinet held a vote, which resolved by four to three to recommend the Treaty to Dáil Éireann. In London on 16 December the British House of Commons overwhelmingly approved the Treaty. In Dublin, the Treaty debates that ensued ran on into January 1922. De Valera, led the supporters of the anti-Treaty position. Secret sessions were held on several occasions in an attempt to mask the discord. Much personal bitterness manifested itself in the debates and the die was cast for a Civil War in Ireland, which broke out six months later.

*Left: let joy be unconfined. Auxiliaries and military celebrate. The location is most likely at their HQ, Beggar's Bush Barracks.
During the Truce the Crown forces mainly stayed in their barracks keeping a low profile. However, they still maintained low-level intelligence operations, keeping an eye on IRA activities.*

Left: off for a swim. Auxiliaries relax after the declaration of the Truce.

A Chief Liaison Office was set up by the IRA, headed by Commandant Éamon Duggan. Liaison officers were appointed throughout the country.

Right: Duggan, Chief Liaison Officer, clarifies details of the Truce for the Athlone liaison officer, Fintan Murphy.

The Truce did not go smoothly in Cork. Tom Barry (bust, below right) had been appointed as Chief Liaison Officer in the martial law area. He was arranging a meeting with Brigadier-General Higginson (far right), Commanding 17th Infantry Brigade in Victoria Barracks, when the starchy general insisted that Barry should not show up in uniform. Barry duly showed up in mufti, whereupon he was informed that neither the IRA nor its officers were recognised; Barry replied that he would not deal with the British except in the status of an IRA officer. The impasse continued, Barry instructing his Liaison Officers to deal with the British only as IRA officers and not to co-operate with them until he heard from GHQ.

Óglaiġ na h-Éireann.

General Headquarters, Dublin.

Department CHIEF LIAISON OFFICE:
Reference No.

66, Dame Street,
Dublin.

Telephone 4888:   26th July, 1921.

TO:
Commandant Fintan Murphy.
Prince of Wales' Hotel,
ATHLONE.

A Chara,

    Yours of the 23rd instant received this morning.

RE CARRYING OF ARMS:

    I note what you say and shall take the matter up with British General Head-Quarters. I may mention for your information that there are no such armed guards operating in Dublin and I cannot therefore see why they should be necessary in other places.

RE BELFAST BOYCOTT:

    The destruction of property is a distinct breach of the Truce and you should issue instructions to that effect. Of course that does not mean that the Boycott is not to continue.

RE REPUBLICAN POLICE:

    The activities of the Republican Police in the discharge of the ~~other~~ ordinary civil police duties is no more a breach of the Truce than the activities of enemy police in the discharge of similar duties.

1.

Left: Linda Kearns, Eithne Coyle and Mae Burke at a training camp at Duckett's Grove, Co. Carlow. All three had escaped from Mountjoy Jail in October 1921. Demonstrating their republican zeal, they trample on a Union Jack.

Conscious of the need to improve discipline and standards, GHQ instituted a major programme of training during the Truce. Training camps were established all over the country.

Left: a group of Volunteers being trained at Killakee House, Co. Dublin. A variety of weapons are laid out on the steps. The IRA were always woefully short of arms and GHQ redoubled its efforts to procure weapons during the Truce period.

Right: the Mid-Clare Brigade, on a training exercise, parade at Kilfenora during the Truce period. From now on, Volunteers could emerge from their clandestine existence.

Right: No. 2 Battalion, Cork No. 1 Brigade.

Right: a rifle section of 3rd Battalion, Waterford Brigade, after the Truce.

There was no truce in Belfast. On 10 July loyalists attacked Catholic enclaves after the IRA ambushed police. There were gun battles between the IRA, loyalists and police. Sixteen civilians were killed, mostly Catholic – more were killed in the following week. Hundreds of houses were destroyed.

Left: in Belfast two wounded RIC constables are being carried to a lorry commandeered by an officer.

Left: a March 1921 black list detailing those who were distributing Belfast goods. In August 1920 Dáil Éireann had voted for a boycott of Belfast goods. One motive was to respond to the recent pogroms against Catholics in Belfast (including the expulsion of Catholics from their workplaces because of their religion). Another was to alert Unionist businesses on the economic damage that partition would cause them.

Right: grenade production at Rogers Brothers foundry at Bailieboro, Co. Cavan. The men sit behind their output of cast grenade cases and some wooden moulds. Grenade cases were filled with gelignite and fused with detonators.

The IRA had a variety of rifles, some purchased from British soldiers – or captured in raids or ambushes. GHQ had been able to import a minimal amount during the War of Independence – in reality most IRA units had to depend on weapons that they captured themselves. The pace of imports radically accelerated over the six months following the Truce.

Right: in Dublin, a Volunteer, dubbed 'TNT Mick', with a holstered revolver at hand, poses as he produces components for grenades.

Right: an experimental mortar made by IRA Captain Matt Furlong. In October 1920, Furlong first experimented using dummy shells. Then he fired a live round which exploded in the tube, mortally wounding him.

Above: the .303 calibre Lee Enfield SMLE Mk III. A very effective rifle, it was standard issue in the British Army. It was also used by Volunteers (when they could get their hands on them) during 1916 and the War of Independence. It was issued to the National Army during the Civil War.

Top left: some weapons of 1916 – the heavy (Howth) Mauser 71, bolt-action single shot rifle, first issued to the Prussian Army in 1872, and one of the few pike heads that were prepared, evoking memories of the 1798 rebellion.

Middle left: the Mauser C96 (Peter the Painter) semi-automatic pistol with detachable wooden stock, used to good effect by Volunteers.

Above left: popular with the IRA, a 9mm Luger Parabellum semi-automatic pistol.

Left: Thompson submachine guns were purchased in the US – some reached Ireland in mid-1921 and saw limited service up to 1923.

Near right: British officer's service weapon – the Webley .455 calibre six-shot revolver.

Far right: easier to conceal – the Webley MP Model .32 automatic, issued to DMP detectives.

Right: Vickers machine gun. This was the regular heavy machine gun of the British during WWI and for many decades afterwards. Solid and reliable, it was water-cooled and fed by a 250-round (.303 calibre) canvas belt. Both the Vickers and Lewis guns were used by the National Army in the Civil War.

Right: Lewis machine gun, with ammunition pan. This relatively light machine gun (air-cooled using an aluminium barrel radiator) fired .303 bullets at 550 rounds per minute.

Right: the 18-pounder field gun, standard British field artillery gun on the western front. This type was used to bombard Sackville Street in April 1916. First use of these in the Civil War was when the army of the Provisional Government shelled the Four Courts at the end of June 1922.

243

Some of the heroines of the Irish Revolution, from 1916 onwards.

Far left: Kathleen Lynn. A captain and medical officer of the Irish Citizen Army (ICA), she was at City Hall on Easter Monday, 1916. She assumed command there after Seán Connolly was killed. In 1919 this courageous woman founded a hospital for infants, St Ultan's.

Above near left: Rosie Hackett. She lost her job in the 1913 Lockout. A member of the ICA, she saw action at the College of Surgeons.

On Easter Saturday, Elizabeth O'Farrell (left) of Cumann na mBan, went to British lines at Moore Street to request negotiations. She later brought the surrender agreement to the other garrisons around the city.

Near left: Min Ryan, Cumann na mBan, carried messages at the GPO in 1916. Seán MacDermott's girlfriend, she was the last to visit him on the eve of his execution. In June 1919 she married Richard Mulcahy, then IRA Chief of Staff.

Far left: Margaret Skinnider. From Glasgow, she fought with the ICA at the College of Surgeons. Skinnider was seriously wounded when she led a party against British positions.

244

Above: Cumann na mBan pin.

Right: Countess Markievicz in uniform, revolver in hand. Moving beyond her Anglo-Irish roots, she helped found, variously, Fianna Éireann, Cumann na mBan and the Irish Citizen Army. Second in command at the College of Surgeons 1916, she was sentenced to death, but this was commuted. In 1918, she was the first woman elected to the House of Commons.

Cumann na mBan provided essential support for the Irish Volunteers. They were behind the barricades at Easter 1916 and ferried ammunition and dispatches to the various garrisons. During the War of Independence, these women, the eyes and ears of the IRA, carried messages and weapons. They nursed wounded Volunteers as well as cooking for and maintaining the flying columns.

Right: a Cumann na mBan member, perhaps idealised by absence, in a sketch made in Frongoch camp in 1916.

245

Left: a Cumann na mBan unit. One estimate is that, by mid-1921, there was a membership of 20,000.

Left: Annie Derham. Joining in 1914, she was one of the first members of Cumann na mBan. She was in action during Easter 1916, but died in 1918.

Below: a Cumann na mBan cycle company at a Wolfe Tone Commemoration at Bodenstown.

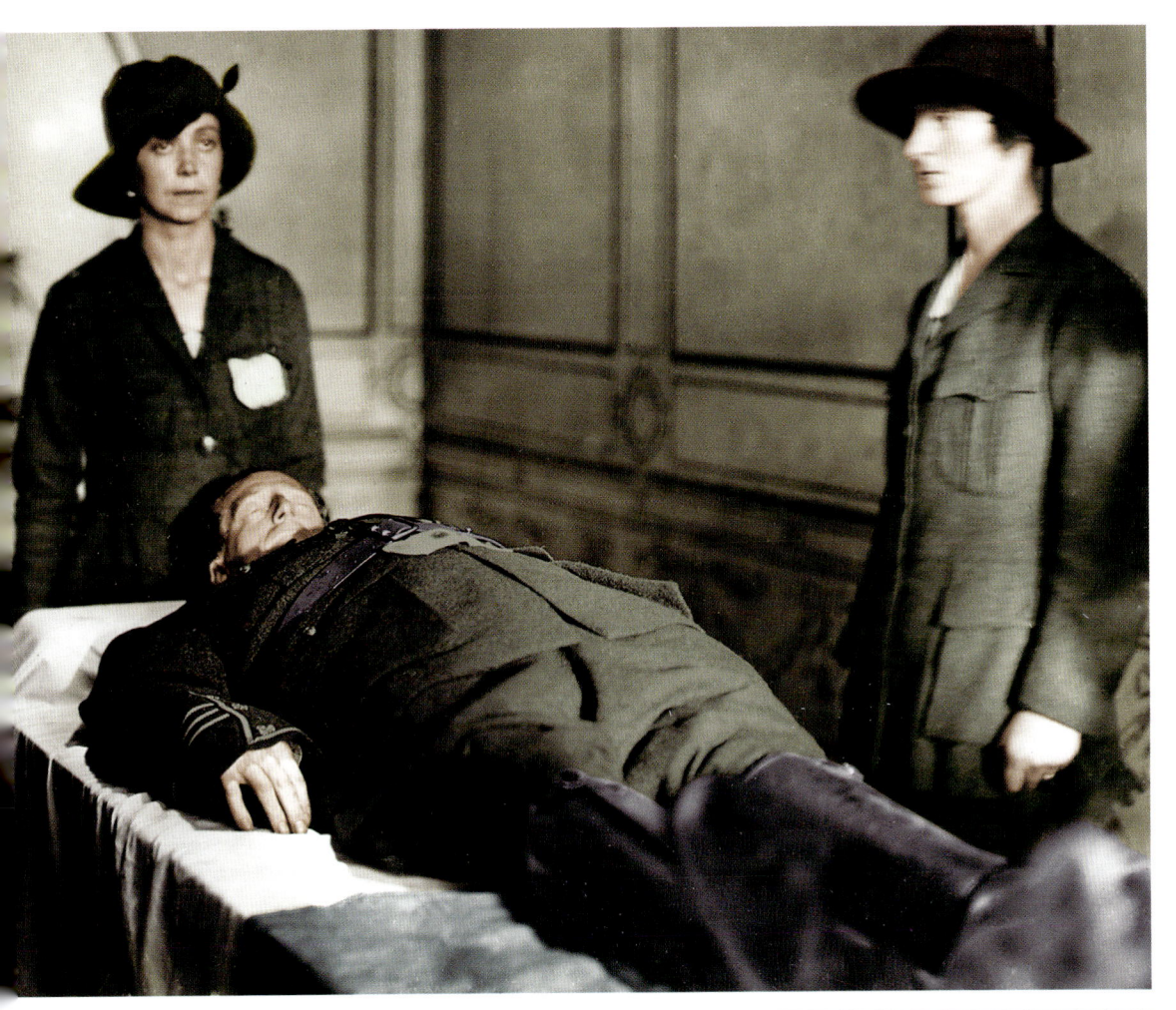

Above: Cathal Brugha was mortally wounded during the initial Civil War battle in central Dublin in July 1922. Here he is laid out in the mortuary of the Mater Hospital, flanked by a Cumann na mBan guard of honour. Most Cumann na mBan members backed the anti-Treaty forces.

Right: a Cumann na mBan certificate.

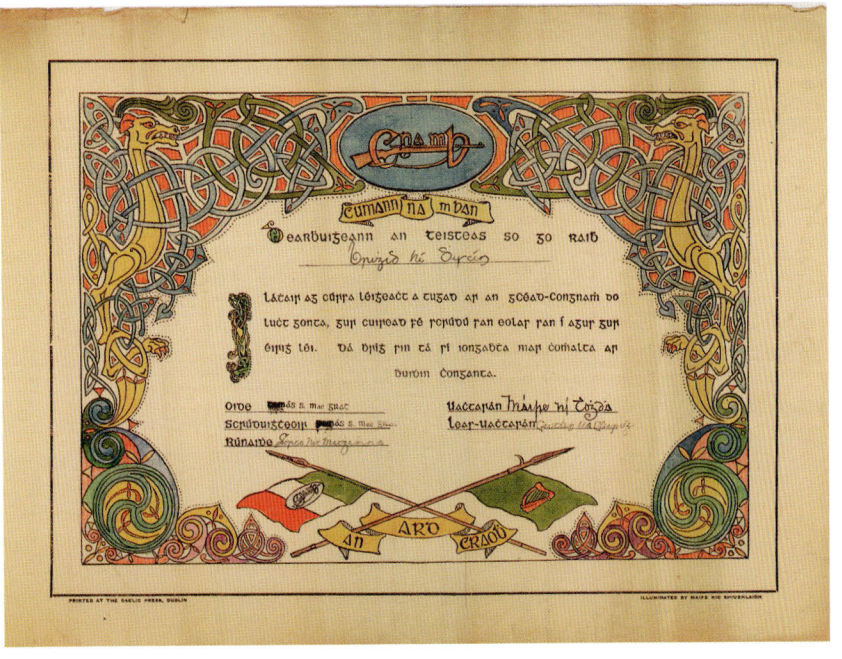

Above: a Republican 'Who's Who' at Tom Barry's wedding to Leslie Price in August 1921 at Vaughan's Hotel in Dublin.

The Truce period gave time to catch up with personal matters.

Left: in October 1921, Kevin O'Higgins got married. De Valera (on left) was in attendance; best man (on right) was Rory O'Connor. During the Civil War, O'Higgins was a member of the Free State Executive Council which, in December 1922, ordered O'Connor's execution.

Dan Breen didn't wait for the Truce. With a long-barreled Luger at hand, he married Brigid Malone, a Dublin Cumann na mBan member on 12 June 1921 (left). Seán Hogan (at rear) was best man.

Right: the Peace delegation at Kingstown (now Dún Laoghaire), en route to London in July 1921. De Valera was accompanied by, amongst others, Arthur Griffith, Robert Barton and Count Plunkett. (Michael Collins was offended at not being asked to travel.) Huge and enthusiastic crowds greeted the Irish delegation as they arrived.

De Valera arrives at London Euston (below right). Having requested a tête-à-tête with Lloyd George, de Valera was received on 14 July in the cabinet room at No. 10 Downing Street. The wily Lloyd George had arranged for a large map, marked with the British Empire in red, to be hung on the wall. The eloquent Welshman tried to dazzle his visitor with a theatrical tour de force. However, de Valera remained unimpressed. At the same time as he grappled with de Valera, this adroit politician had to manage his recalcitrant colleagues. He was politically weak in the face of Tory opposition, firm believers in the inviolability of the British Empire.

Right: crowds kneel and pray for peace as de Valera meets Lloyd George.

THE ILLUSTRATED LONDON NEWS

SATURDAY, JULY 23, 1921.

MAKING IRISH HISTORY AT 10, DOWNING STREET: MR. LLOYD GEORGE AND MR. DE VALERA MEET ALONE, TO DISCUSS PEACE.

The first meeting between Mr. Lloyd George and Mr. de Valera took place in the drawing-room at the Premier's official residence, No. 10, Downing Street, on July 14. The official statement issued afterwards said: "Mr. Lloyd George and Mr. de Valera met as arranged at 4.30 p.m. at 10, Downing Street. They were alone, and the conversation lasted until 7 p.m. A full exchange of views took place, and relative positions were defined." Other important conferences have followed. Sir James Craig has returned to Belfast, leaving Mr. Lloyd George and Mr. de Valera to work out their own solution for the South.

DRAWN BY OUR SPECIAL ARTIST, STEVEN SPURRIER. COPYRIGHTED IN THE UNITED STATES AND CANADA.

Left: the 'Illustrated London News' depicts a wary Lloyd George observing a gaunt de Valera. There was little meeting of minds between the two leaders at the peace negotiations. When de Valera said he would reject British proposals, Lloyd George threatened war. He noted that Britain's reduced global commitments meant that it could now move more troops to Ireland and that 'the struggle would bear an entirely different character'. The series of meetings continued and at the end Lloyd George presented a formal offer. This gave the 26 counties dominion status (partition and hence 'Northern Ireland' remaining in place), with control over home defence, taxation, finance and policing – but with the Royal Navy still in control of Irish waters.

De Valera was displeased but brought the offer back to Dublin where there was much discussion in cabinet. The Minister for Defence, Cathal Brugha, in particular, was concerned about the fundamental aspect which would mean the abandonment of the Republic declared at Easter 1916.

On 6 August, the British agreed to release all members of the Dáil who were prisoners, but not Sean Mac Eoin, who was under sentence of death. Sinn Féin made his freedom a precondition The British relented and released Right: 'The Daily Sketch' reports the release.

Below: Dáil Éireann met on 16 August 1921 in the Mansion House, where de Valera began his report on the negotiations.

McKEOWN RELEASED: TRUCE SAFE.

Mr. J. McKeown, the Sinn Fein M.P., whose release averts a threatened rupture of the Irish truce. This photograph, taken in Mountjoy Prison, with two of his guard, appeared in yesterday's late edition.
—(Exclusive.)

Lloyd George invited de Valera to 'enter a conference to ascertain how the association of Ireland with the community of nations known as the British Empire can best be reconciled with Irish national aspirations'. On 9 September the Dáil cabinet approved the sending of a delegation. De Valera decided not to attend and later explained that this was in order to better prepare people for compromise.

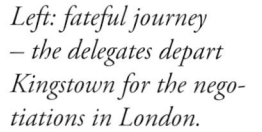

Left: fateful journey – the delegates depart Kingstown for the negotiations in London.

Left: some members of the Irish delegation on the mailboat en route to London for the October conference.

Right: member of the delegation, Michael Collins, in London.

On 11 October 1921 large crowds and newsreel cameras assembled as the Irish delegation entered No. 10 Downing Street to begin negotiations. Right: Michael Collins and Arthur Griffith.

PUNCH, OR THE LONDON CHARIVARI.—September 14, 1921.

THE PROBLEM PLAY.

Our ever-jeune Premier (conning his part): "NOW HERE AM I, A WELSHMAN, LOOK YOU: AND I HAF TO COME ON IN A HIGHLAND 'SET,' AND PLAY A SCENE IN ENGLISH—ALL ABOUT IRELAND—WITH A SPANISH AMERICAN—AND LEAD UP TO A HAPPY ENDING. WELL, WELL, I HOPE IT WILL BE ALL RIGHT ON THE NIGHT!"

Left: Punch's view of Lloyd George's dilemma, preparing for the complex Anglo-Irish negotiations.

Below: the might of the Empire – with Lloyd George in the middle of the British negotiating team (left). Facing them (right), the Irish delegation – (front to back) George Gavan Duffy, Robert Barton, Michael Collins, Arthur Griffith and Éamon Duggan. Standing, Erskine Childers (principal secretary to the delegation).

De Valera toured the west at the end of 1921 while negotiations were ongoing in London. Above: he reviews the IRA at Sixmilebridge, Co. Clare.

Right: the body language between the two gaunt men in the middle says it all. Here at a review in Co. Galway are Éamon de Valera, and on his left, Richard Mulcahy, Chief of Staff of the IRA. In 1922 de Valera emerged as the political leader of the anti-Treaty group; Mulcahy was to build up the new army of the Provisional Government and then lead it to victory in the Civil War.

Left: the Irish delegation in London. The odds were stacked against them: with unclear terms of reference, they were not united and some members like Childers reported directly back to de Valera. Lloyd George identified the main movers and had one-to-one meetings with Collins and Griffith. The latter was not in the same league as Lloyd George, a master of manipulation. The negotiations crashed against the rock of British intransigence on the issues of allegiance to the King and membership of the British Empire, fundamental to the imperial mindset.

In the face of Lloyd George's histrionics which offered only signing the Treaty or facing renewed war, the delegation did not consult with Dublin but signed the Treaty document in London on 6 December 1921.

Left: the strain is showing – an exhausted Irish delegation heads for home.

Right: the Anglo-Irish Treaty sets out, in 18 succinct paragraphs, how an Irish Free State would be formed, as a self-governing Dominion within 'the Community of Nations known as the British Empire'. It included: defence by sea was to be undertaken by the British, who would also retain naval ports; members of the Free State Parliament were to take an oath of allegiance to the constitution of the Irish Free State and to be 'faithful to HM King George V'; the right of the Northern Ireland Parliament to opt out of the Irish Free State (which, to no one's surprise, it promptly did) and the sop of a Boundary Commission to be set up, if Northern Ireland did withdraw.
In essence the Treaty comprised the same terms that Lloyd George had offered to de Valera in July 1921. An agreement for an imperfect and partial exit of the British from (most of) Ireland had thus been painfully achieved.

in Southern Ireland since the passing of the Government of Ireland Act, 1920, and for constituting a provisional Government, and the British Government shall take the steps necessary to transfer to such provisional Government the powers and machinery requisite for the discharge of its duties, provided that every member of such provisional Government shall have signified in writing his or her acceptance of this instrument. But this arrangement shall not continue in force beyond the expiration of twelve months from the date hereof.

18. This instrument shall be submitted forthwith by His Majesty's Government for the approval of Parliament and by the Irish signatories to a meeting summoned for the purpose of the members elected to sit in the House of Commons of Southern Ireland, and if approved shall be ratified by the necessary legislation.

December 6, 1921.

The cabinet met at the Mansion House in Dublin on 8 December. There was immediate disagreement about the terms of the Treaty.

However, in one area there was cause to rejoice. As agreed in the Treaty, prisoners were to be released. On the same day, 8 December, the releases began and around 5,000 were freed.

Left: after the order had been made for release of the interned prisoners, a crowd waits outside Kilmainham Gaol.

Left: celebrating their freedom and flying a tricolour, prisoners freed from the internment camp at Maryborough (Portlaoise), ride on a locomotive.

Chapter 5
Civil War

The Anglo-Irish Treaty was signed on 6 December. The Dáil debates on the Treaty that followed were punctuated by bitter uproar. These debates were protracted and soon descended to scenes of great rancour. The vote on the Treaty took place on 7 January 1922. It was narrowly ratified, by 64 votes to 57. The IRA was mainly anti-Treaty. Under the Treaty provisions a Provisional Government was established and a new army was formed. As the British troops left, during the takeover of barracks, there was friction between both sides. Recruitment to the new army was stepped up. The IRA met to form an Executive which rejected the authority of the new Government. In April 1922, it took over the Four Courts and other prominent buildings in Dublin.

There was little Government authority in place across the country and disorder prevailed in some areas. By May 1922, the British had withdrawn their troops from most of the 26 counties, leaving around 5,000 stationed in the Dublin area.

Elections in the 26 Counties were planned for 16 June 1922. Both sides made a pact in May and arrived at an agreed list of candidates. In the event, the anti-Treaty side fared badly: only 36 of their candidates were elected, while 58 of the pro-Treaty side were successful. Labour together with others who generally supported the Treaty, gained 34 seats.

The flare-ups between the opposing sides continued, increasing the likelihood of conflict. The assassination of Sir Henry Wilson in London resulted in near panic amidst the British Cabinet. Lloyd George wrote to Michael Collins stating that the IRA were to blame. He insisted that the continuing Four Courts occupation, as well as the ambiguous situation of the IRA, could no longer be tolerated.

In retaliation for the capture of an IRA commander during a raid at Baggot Street, Lieutenant-General JJ O'Connell, Deputy Chief of Staff of the pro-Treaty army, was kidnapped and brought to the Four Courts. This abduction proved to be the final event which propelled the Provisional Government to decide to mount an assault. Bombardment of the Four Courts commenced on 28 June 1922. Days of shelling ended with the storming of the buildings. A massive explosion followed by a fire sent the contents of the Public Record Office into smoke and aerial oblivion. The anti-Treaty IRA took over buildings in central Dublin including the so-called 'Block' on Upper Sackville Street. By 5 July, the Block, now in ruins, was cleared of resistance by the pro-Treaty army, using armoured cars and artillery. Republicans fled the city and the war moved to the rest of the country.

As the main conflict moved out of Dublin, there were clashes between pro- and anti-Treaty forces across the country. Limerick, on the Shannon, was a strategic point between Munster and Connacht. In a rerun of the Dublin conflict, the Provisional Government army took the city from the anti-Treaty IRA and the fighting moved to the nearby Bruree and Kilmallock region. After large-scale encounters the pro-Treaty side prevailed. With the help of an artillery piece, Waterford was easily captured from the Republicans. As towns were taken along the River Suir, the anti-Treaty 'Munster Republic' was beginning to be reduced. There was shock on both sides after the prominent Republican, Harry Boland, was mortally wounded in Skerries.

With much of Munster and the west under Republican control, the generals of the Provisional Government army decided in July 1922 to mount a series of amphibious landings on the southern and western coasts. Cross-channel steamers were commandeered and loaded with troops, armoured cars and artillery. Such landings could be perilous, but, by dint of some planning, a poor strategic response from the Republican side and a lot of luck, they were all successful. With the taking of Cork in August, the core of the anti-Treaty 'Munster Republic' faded away. However, danger still lurked in the countryside, as happened when Michael Collins, travelling in a convoy through West Cork, was shot dead in an ambush on 22 August 1922. His death was marked by universal sorrow. On 28 August his funeral cortège passed by enormous crowds along the Dublin streets to Glasnevin Cemetery where he was buried.

Under the terms of the Anglo-Irish Treaty, the Royal Navy patrolled at will through Irish waters. On many occasions, the Royal Navy gave discreet support to National Army troops in 1922. On occasion, along the Atlantic coast, they transported troops or fired starlight shells or shone searchlights when National Army outposts came under attack.

Few people realise the full extent of the damage inflicted on the railway system during the Civil War. At that time the railways were perceived by Republicans as a very visible symbol of government. As the war unfolded there were waves of destruction on the network – derailments and the wrecking of stations and bridges. One of the most spectacular examples was the blowing up of the Mallow Viaduct in August 1922. Railway engineers resolutely struggled to repair damage, aided from October 1922 by a special army corps set up to protect and repair the network. Due to increasing competition from road, railways had been in decline from their golden age – a decline which was hastened by the damage inflicted during the Civil War.

Autumn 1922 was the beginning of the end. The Government (which became the Free State Government on 6 December) had captured the cities and was gaining control of the towns. Anti-Treaty fighters still roamed the mountains, particularly those of Kerry, Cork and Mayo. A cycle of ruthless executions of Republicans started in November 1922, which generated reprisals in return – many Anglo-Irish 'big houses' were burnt by the anti-Treaty IRA, who perceived their owners as pillars of the Free State.

The veteran Republican and author, Erskine Childers, was captured in early November 1922 and was sentenced to death. He was executed at Beggar's Bush Barracks, meeting his death bravely and with dignity. The shooting of Seán Hales TD on 7 December incensed the Provisional Government, who ordered the execution of four prominent Republicans, the next morning, as a reprisal. With Government forces facing a wave of Republican 'hit-and-run' attacks, the CID, based at Oriel House in Dublin, resorted to a series of extra-judicial killings, in the period 1922-23.

The nadir of the Civil War came in early 1923 when the slaughter of pro-Treaty troops by a trap mine in Kerry led to the brutal murder of prisoners at Ballyseedy, also using a mine. As 1923 dawned, the anti-Treaty struggle was ebbing away. Liam Lynch, Chief of Staff of the IRA, was mortally wounded on a lonely mountainside in Co. Tipperary. The conflict juddered to an inconclusive end when Frank Aiken issued a ceasefire order to the IRA on 24 May 1923. A national election was called for August 1923. The election result proved surprisingly good for Sinn Féin, which won 44 seats. The pro-Treaty party, Cumann na nGaedheal, gained 63 seats. Labour and others won 46.

Left and below: anti- and pro-Treaty posters. Controversy immediately arose over the terms of the Treaty. Those in favour of it took the pragmatic approach that, while it was not perfect, it gave a form of independence. For those on the other side, giving up the Republic declared in 1916 and asserted by the 1919 Dáil, for a lesser form of independence, was a principal objection to the Treaty. An Irish Republic had been the shining goal in the struggle for independence since the time of Wolfe Tone.

BEFORE THE TREATY — 1921
READ "THE REPUBLIC OF IRELAND"

AFTER THE TREATY — 1922
READ "THE REPUBLIC OF IRELAND"

THE TREATY GIVES IRELAND

1. A PARLIAMENT RESPONSIBLE TO THE IRISH PEOPLE ALONE.
2. A GOVERNMENT RESPONSIBLE TO THAT PARLIAMENT.
3. DEMOCRATIC CONTROL OF ALL LEGISLATIVE AFFAIRS.
4. POWER TO MAKE LAWS FOR EVERY DEPARTMENT OF IRISH LIFE.
5. AN IRISH LEGAL SYSTEM CONTROLLED BY IRISHMEN.
6. AN IRISH ARMY.
7. AN IRISH POLICE FORCE.
8. COMPLETE FINANCIAL FREEDOM.
9. A NATIONAL FLAG.
10. FREEDOM OF OPINION.
11. COMPLETE CONTROL OF IRISH EDUCATION.
12. COMPLETE CONTROL OF HER LAND SYSTEMS.
13. POWER AND FREEDOM TO DEVELOP HER RESOURCES AND INDUSTRIES.
14. A DEMOCRATIC CONSTITUTION.
15. A STATE ORGANISATION TO EXPRESS THE MIND AND WILL OF THE NATION.
16. HER RIGHTFUL PLACE AS A NATION AMONG NATIONS.

**DUBLIN CASTLE HAS FALLEN !
BRITISH BUREAUCRACY IS IN THE DUST !
IS THIS VICTORY OR DEFEAT ?**

SUPPORT THE TREATY

Right: how the IRA split. The response to the Treaty varied widely in this army consisting of a federation of independent units. Often it depended on the attitude of the local leader. In general, the areas that had been most active during the War of Independence were more strongly anti-Treaty.

From mid-December the Dáil met to debate the Treaty, in both public and private sessions. These were held at Earlsfort Terrace in the Council Chamber of University College Dublin, now known as the Kevin Barry Recital Room of the National Concert Hall.

The debates on the Treaty were protracted and soon descended to scenes of great rancour and personal recrimination.

Right: four of the six women TDs outside the Dáil: (from left) Kathleen Clarke (widow of Thomas), Countess Markievicz, Kathleen O'Callaghan and Margaret Pearse (mother of Patrick). All of the women TDs voted against the Treaty.

Above: a Republican policeman guards the entrance at Earlsfort Terrace.

Left: the Dáil sits in the Council Chamber at Earlsfort Terrace.

Left: The pro-Treaty cartoonist Shemus disdainfully depicts de Valera as a scarecrow, with Document No. 2 in his pocket. De Valera had presented the document as an alternative to the Treaty. It proposed external association as a substitute to membership of the British Empire — in the event, the concept was too nuanced to garner real support.

The vote on the Treaty took place on 7 January 1922. It was narrowly ratified, by 64 votes to 57.

Right: protagonists for the Treaty stride out purposefully — (from left) Kevin O'Higgins, Arthur Griffith and WT Cosgrave.

On 9 January, de Valera stepped down as President, saying that he did not have the House's confidence. The following day, a motion to re-elect him was narrowly defeated. He and his supporters then left the chamber. Arthur Griffith was elected President of the Dáil by the remaining TDs. Below: de Valera (on right) and supporters outside the Dáil.

265

On 14 January, the 'Southern Ireland Parliament' met in Dublin's Mansion House, in the absence of anti-Treaty members of the Dáil. In accordance with the terms of the Treaty, they elected a Provisional Government, with Michael Collins as Chairman.

Left: the new Provisional Government, along with supporters, assemble for a photograph in front of the Mansion House.

Left: in those febrile times, the 'Washington Times' writer had been enthused by this dynamic new leader. He eulogises Collins' qualities, including 'virility', the 'contagious enthusiasm of youth' and 'damn-the-consequences directness'! He even adds the dubious accolade that 'Mick' Collins rivals Boss Croker (of Tammany Hall fame), as a politician.

Right: as large crowds gather outside the gates, Michael Collins arrives by taxi at Dublin Castle on 16 January 1922. He and the other members of the new Government were received by the last Viceroy of Ireland, Lord FitzAlan. The Dublin Castle press office recorded that 'The Lord Lieutenant congratulated Mr Collins and his colleagues and informed them they were now duly installed as the Provisional Government.' Another official statement, signed by Collins struck a different tone: 'The members of the Provisional Government received the surrender of Dublin Castle...today. It is now in the hands of the Irish nation'.

Right: obviously not impressed by the events at Dublin Castle — an anti-Treaty cartoon by Grace Plunkett (widow of the executed Joseph).

At the end of January, the British Army evacuated City Hall (adjacent to Dublin Castle), in the process taking away the flagpole. Alderman WT Cosgrave, TD (right), hoists the municipal flag at City Hall on a replacement flagpole, after receiving the building from the military.

THE GUARDS-BEGGARS BUSH--IRISH REPUBLIC
THE MEN WHO FOUGHT FOR THE FREEDO
(THE FIRST UNIT OF I.R.A. IN

Above: on 4 February the Dublin Guards line up at Beggar's Bush with Commandant Paddy O'Daly, (by the drum). Lieutenant Pádraig O'Connor stands to his right. The new army of the Provisional (later Free State) Government had taken over Beggar's Bush Barracks, in Dublin, from departing British troops on 31 January 1922 and set up headquarters there. In the following months, local forces (either pro- or anti-Treaty, depending on the locality), occupied barracks as they were evacuated.

Left: eyes right — British military during the evacuation, as they march past the soldiers of the new Provisional Government.

The anti-Treaty IRA flexed their muscles in their local areas during the first half of 1922. In the meantime, the Provisional Government endeavoured to rapidly build up its army. Outnumbered by the anti-Treaty IRA at the beginning of the Civil War (one estimate for these was around 13,000 men), the new army rapidly grew in size. By July 1922 an establishment of 35,000 was authorised. At its peak in mid-1923, the army of the Free State amounted to around 55,000.

Right: new recruits for the Provisional Government army receive their kit at Beggar's Bush Barracks.

269

Above: Commandant-General Seán Mac Eoin raises the tricolour after the handover at Athlone Barracks on 28 February 1922. Alluding to Custume's heroic defence of the bridge there in 1691, he said that it was over 300 years since an Irish flag had been hauled down —'the flag of Ireland was being unfurled that day, also under fire, and they meant to keep it there'.

Left: Cork Lord Mayor Dónal O'Callaghan taking over Union Quay RIC Barracks.

Right: dominating Thomond Bridge across the river Shannon, King John's Castle in Limerick. This proved one of the first flashpoints on the road to conflict. In early March, on hearing that Clare pro-Treaty units under Commandant-General Michael Brennan were moving to take over barracks in Limerick, the local IRA (with assistance from the Tipperary and Cork IRA), moved to pre-empt this. While King John's Castle remained in GHQ hands, the anti-Treaty IRA were in occupation of all the other Limerick strongpoints.

The vast Templemore Barracks, Co. Tipperary, was another highly strategic location. It was taken over by the local IRA; of uncertain allegiance, they refused to allow a Provisional Government detachment to enter the barracks. When GHQ sent an armoured car there in April, it was captured by the now openly anti-Treaty occupants.
Right: the Rolls Royce armoured car, now renamed 'The Mutineer', after being transferred to the Four Courts by order of Ernie O'Malley.

Left: Richard Mulcahy, at Portobello (now Cathal Brugha) Barracks, GHQ of the Provisional Government Army. As the new Minister of Defence, he endeavoured to prevent a split during the months of turmoil after the signing of the Treaty. On 20 March 1922 he went to Mallow to meet the leaders of the 1st Southern, the strongest of the IRA divisions, who had declared against the Treaty. The only agreement that was reached was to delay a planned convention.

In a daring act of piracy, the British vessel 'Upnor', (below), returning surplus armaments, was captured by the IRA on 29 March 1922, about 50km off the Irish coast, en route from Haulbowline to Devonport. Hundreds of cases of rifles and machine guns, along with ammunition, were off-loaded at Ballycotton, Co. Cork, which boosted the anti-Treaty armoury in the region. Collins was outraged, as indicated in his telegram to Winston Churchill, which blamed the British (left).

```
    WITH REFERENCE TO THE UPNOR CAPTURE IT IS
GENERALLY BELIEVED HERE THAT THERE WAS COLLUSION
BETWEEN THOSE RESPONSIBLE ON YOUR SIDE AND THE
RAIDERS.  ALSO GENERALLY BELIEVED THAT THE CAPTURE
WAS ENORMOUSLY LARGER THAN IS STATED IN YOUR WIRE.
HAVE YOU MADE INQUIRY AS TO THE EXACT PROPORTIONS
OF THE CAPTURE?  THE INCIDENT WAS UNDOUBTEDLY A
BREACH OF THE TRUCE BUT PROVISIONAL GOVERNMENT
STRONGLY FEEL THAT THE SAFETY OF THESE ARMS ENTIRELY
A QUESTION FOR YOUR ADMIRALTY.



                    MICHAEL COLLINS
```

The IRA held a convention on 26 March 1922 where it re-affirmed its allegiance to the Republic and elected an Executive.

Right: Oscar Traynor, O/C Dublin Brigade, (with Rory O'Connor, left) speaks at a parade at Smithfield, on 2 April 1922, to express support for the anti-Treaty IRA Executive.

At the end of March, following what they regarded as misleading reports on the army convention, the anti-Treaty IRA destroyed the presses of the 'Freeman's Journal'. In the edition of 22 April this Shemus cartoon (right) was included, depicting a Phoenix rising from the ashes of the wrecked plant.

The IRA Executive ordered that certain strategic buildings in Dublin be occupied. Among these was the great Four Courts complex on the north Liffey quays (right), which was taken over as their headquarters on the night of 13 April. After the occupation, the complex was progressively fortified; law books and ledgers were stuffed into windows. It was a formidable fortress but, like the GPO in 1916, it was not ideal for having a leadership bottled up within.

273

Left: Arthur Griffith at Longford, en route to Sligo for a public meeting on Easter Sunday, 16 April 1922. Liam Pilkington, in charge of the 3rd Western Division, had proclaimed the meeting and the anti-Treaty IRA took over public buildings in the town. In response Commandant-General Seán Mac Eoin led his Provisional Government troops from Athlone, even wielding an axe himself to cut through trees felled to block the road to the town.

Left: a watchful Seán Mac Eoin, Webley at the ready, overlooks the meeting in Sligo on Easter Sunday, from the first-floor window of a hotel. In the event, with Sligo flooded by pro-Treaty troops, the IRA did not interfere with Griffith's meeting.

Dublin's Wellington Barracks (now Griffith College) was occupied by Provisional Government troops on 12 April 1922. Eight days later there was an hour-long attack by the anti-Treaty IRA (depicted by 'La Tribuna Illustrata', right). Later in November there was a sustained attack. A soldier and a civilian were killed, 17 soldiers wounded — a fleeing Republican was captured nearby and shot dead.

LA TRIBUNA ILLUSTRATA

Anno XXX — Num. 19 — 7 Maggio 1922 — Centesimi 20 il numero

Nell'Irlanda senza pace, gli estremisti repubblicani hanno tentato d'impadronirsi della caserma Wellington, a Dublino, occupata dalle truppe dello Stato libero irlandese.

(*Disegno di A. Minardi*)

At around 2:30 in the morning on 26 April 1922, members of the local IRA, led by Michael O'Neill, knocked at the door of the Hornibrook residence (near Farran on the Cork-Macroom road). One account says that they wanted to commandeer the family car. After the party climbed in a window, O'Neill was shot dead. Later the occupants, Thomas Hornibrook, his son Samuel and Herbert Woods (a champion boxer and former British officer, centre left) were seized, brought to an isolated spot and shot. Over the following days, ten more Protestants were shot dead in and around the Bandon valley. It is likely that revenge featured highly amongst the motives of local Volunteers. For them, unrestrained by any authority in those lawless times, there may have been an underlying latent sectarianism. However this was not the policy of the anti-Treaty IRA, whose local leader, Tom Hales, was away in Dublin attending conciliation meetings.

Over the first months of 1922, sectarian violence in Belfast had spiralled out of control.

Left: in a Belfast street, a statue of the Virgin, used for target practice by the B-Specials (USC).

Thousands of Catholic refugees from northern pogroms flooded south. In Dublin, the anti-Treaty IRA had already seized Fowler Hall (Parnell Square, Orange Order HQ), and the Kildare Street Club, which they regarded as synonymous with Loyalism. To house refugees, they also took over Freemasons' Hall and the YMCA.

Right: Bridie Gallagher, a refugee, stands outside the Kildare Street Club.

The partition of Ireland had not been central in the Treaty negotiations. A Boundary Commission was promised, giving Nationalists the hope that the northern state would wither away. Nevertheless, the Northern Ireland Government had become an established fact – and it was underpinned by the Ulster Special Constabulary (USC), who, unlike the now superseded (and disbanded) RIC, were blatantly anti-Catholic. Craig and Collins reached an agreement at the end of March which was intended to dampen down tensions (cartoon, right) — but all the initiatives soon ran into the sand. Collins next planned a covert campaign against the six-county state, in the hope that it would prove to be a unifying factor with the anti-Treaty forces.

Left: all smiles in Kilkenny after agreement was reached.

Throughout early 1922 there were skirmishes all over the State, as both sides jostled for control. One of the most serious incidents occurred in early May when anti-Treaty IRA units assembled in Kilkenny and set up in Ormond Castle and the City Hall. In response, 200 troops of the Dublin Guard were dispatched by train. There was a day-long confrontation, with some casualties. As the fighting was about to escalate, there was a meeting of a truce committee (made up of senior leaders of both sides) in Dublin, which arrived at a compromise: both sides were to garrison different positions in the city.

Left: Two prominent members of the truce committee pictured outside the Mansion House, Dublin, in early May. Senior anti-Treaty leader, Seán Moylan is with Commandant-General Seán Mac Eoin (on right).

Part of the May agreement between the sides was that the anti-Treaty IRA evacuate Freemasons' Hall and the Kidare Street Club.

Right: photograph taken just after the IRA evacuation of the Grand Chapter room of Freemasons' Hall. No damage had been inflicted on the building.

Right: the Grand Chapter Room, decorated in Egyptian Pharaonic style, as it is today. The Grand Lodge of Ireland is one of the oldest in the world. Its headquarters, Freemasons' Hall in Molesworth Street, is replete with elaborately themed rooms.

On 2 May 1922, the anti-Treaty IRA took over the Ballast Office, strategically located facing O'Connell Bridge; it housed the Dublin Port offices, which collected port import duties.

Right: the building was evacuated later in May and handed over to the Lord Mayor, Lawrence O'Neill, photographed (right) demanding admittance, accompanied by associates.

279

Above: Free State men march to the Curragh Camp for the handover on 16 May 1922. Lieutenant-General JJ O'Connell climbed the water tower to erect a giant tricolour, using an improvised flagpole, replacing one cut down by the departing British. Left: an intense-looking General Eoin O'Duffy (Assistant Chief of Staff), with Emmet Dalton on his left, takes the salute during the handover of Portobello (now Cathal Brugha) Barracks in Dublin on 17 May. By now, British troops had withdrawn from most of Ireland, leaving around 5,000 stationed in the Dublin area.

Right: Hazel Laverton, at the helm of the 'Lady of the Lake', which ferried the B-Specials (USC) along Lower Lough Erne during the May events.

At the end of May 1922 there was a major confrontation in the Belleek-Pettigo salient, along the new border, between the IRA (both pro- and anti-Treaty) and the USC, who had mounted an attack on Belleek (within the new 'Northern Ireland'), after a reported (but not proven) kidnap of four of their members. Following an exchange of fire with Volunteers, the USC had to be evacuated by boat, with Mrs Laverton's steamer involved in operations. A convoy of USC was ambushed by IRA units just inside the Co. Donegal border line — the USC retreated, abandoning vehicles. Despite Collins' and Lloyd George's wish to damp down the conflict, Winston Churchill ordered a large force of British military and USC to the area, with tanks, artillery and RAF support. These proceeded to encircle Pettigo. After fierce exchanges, the IRA, vastly outnumbered, withdrew in early June.

Right: a captured Lancia armoured vehicle.

BELFAST TELEGRAPH, WEDNESDAY, MAY 31, 1922

THE LANCIA CAR CAPTURED FROM THE SPECIALS NEAR BELLEEK, NOW IN THE HANDS OF THE I.R.A.

281

Left: the workers' Soviet at Cleeve's mill and bakery at Bruree, Co. Limerick, August 1921.

Influenced by revolutions in Europe (principally that in Russia), workers occupied their places of work to protest against poor conditions. In 1922 this included the Cleeve's dairy works across the south. With a few exceptions, there was little sympathy for the plight of workers' from the anti-Treaty IRA and none from the pro-Treaty side. These actions, against the background of events in Bolshevik Russia, made bourgeois Ireland nervous about the current disorder.

Left: a Shemus cartoon in the 'Freeman's Journal' of August 1922, shows Trotsky saying to the ailing Lenin: 'Cheer up Comrade Lenin: I've just learned, Ireland is ours for the taking!' Lenin – very sick: 'I seem to have heard that before!'

Elections were planned for 16 June 1922. Both sides made a pact in May on an agreed list of candidates. In the event, the anti-Treaty side fared badly: only 36 of their candidates were elected, while 58 of the pro-Treaty side were successful. Labour and others (who generally supported the Treaty) gained 34 seats.

Right: 'Le Petit Journal' dramatically portrays Wilson's assassination.

Longford-born Field Marshal Sir Henry Wilson had been Chief of the Imperial General Staff and was vociferous in his opposition to the Treaty. As security advisor to the newly created entity of Northern Ireland, which was riven by sectarian pogroms, he became a hate figure to all shades of nationalist opinion. On 22 June 1922, after a WWI memorial ceremony, Wilson had been trailed back to his home at Eaton Terrace by two London-based IRA Volunteers, who shot him there. (They were soon captured and later hanged). The British Cabinet met immediately, in a state of agitation. Lloyd George wrote to Michael Collins stating that the IRA were to blame; the continuing Four Courts occupation, as well as the ambiguous situation of the IRA, could no longer be tolerated.

Right: the 'Illustrated London News' depicts the pursuit of the assassins by 'shirt-sleeved policemen with truncheons, and enraged civilians'.

After Wilson's assassination, the British Cabinet — urged on by Winston Churchill (left), Secretary of State for the Colonies — issued an order for attack by British forces on the Four Courts on 25 June 1922. However, the Cabinet were dissuaded by the commander of British forces in Ireland, General Macready, and the order was rescinded.

The next significant event occurred on 26 June. The anti-Treaty IRA raided Ferguson's motor garage, a branch of a Belfast firm, on Lower Baggot Street, and commandeered cars, (considered as imported in defiance of the Belfast Boycott, then being organised by anti-Treaty forces). Pro-Treaty troops arrived and surrounded the premises, (below left). The leader of the raiding party, Commandant Leo Henderson, director of the Belfast Boycott, was captured and transferred to Mountjoy Gaol.

Later that night, in retaliation, Lieut.-General JJ O'Connell, Deputy Chief of Staff, was kidnapped and brought to the Four Courts. This abduction proved to be the final event which propelled the Provisional Government to decide to assault the Four Courts.

On the evening of 27 June 1922, the Dublin Guards, under Paddy O'Daly, sealed off the area surrounding the Four Courts. An ultimatum to evacuate the building was given to the occupants at 3:40 am on 28 June. The first shells were fired from Winetavern Street shortly after 4 am The Civil War had begun.

Right: shelling from Winetavern Street. Two 18-pounder guns (provided by the British the day before) are in operation, shielded by Lancias. The bombardment is well under way, as seen by the pockmarks on the Four Courts buildings opposite.

At an early stage, high-explosive shells ran short and shrapnel shells had to be used. A resupply of high-explosive shells allowed the eventual creation of large breaches in the Four Courts. Right: shells, ready and laid out in woodshavings.

Right: shell recovered from the grounds of the Capuchin Friars in Church Street, a short distance away from the Four Courts complex.

285

STOP PRESS
POBLACHT NA h-EIREANN

Wednesday, June 28th, Seventh Year of the Republic.

No 1

COMMUNIQUE FROM THE FOUR COURTS

We have received the following message from Major General Rory O'Connor, I.R.A.:

9 a.m., Wednesday, June 28th

At 3.40 a.m. this morning we received a note signed by Tom Ennis demanding on behalf of "The Government" our surrender at 4 a.m. when he would attack.

He opened attack at 4.07 in the name of his Government, with Rifle, Machine and field pieces.

THE BOYS ARE GLORIOUS, AND WILL FIGHT FOR THE REPUBLIC TO THE END. HOW LONG WILL OUR MISGUIDED FORMER COMRADES OUTSIDE ATTACK THOSE WHO STAND FOR IRELAND ALONE?

Three casualties so far, all slight. Father Albert and Father Dominic with us here.

Our love to all comrades outside, and the brave boys especially of the Dublin Brigade.

(Signed) RORY O'CONNOR,
Four Courts. Major General, I.R.A.

The Republic is fighting for its life.
The Republic proclaimed in arms at Easter, 1916, established by law in January, 1919, defended by an army and people with heroic bravery and sacrifice through Terror, torture, and devastation in 1920 and 1921: the Republic consecrated by the blood of Pearse, Connolly, and the dearest and noblest of our patriots: the Republic once more is fighting for its life.
Citizens, defend your Republic!
The enemy is the old enemy, England; using new weapons lent her, to their shame, by traitors to the Republic in our midst. Mr. Churchill cracked the whip in his speech on Monday night when he ordered the Provisional Government to attack the Four Courts. His Free State agents have obeyed. Shame on them — Shame!
Mercenaries wearing Irish uniform, paid, equipped, and armed by England, and acting under England's orders, are attacking our brothers of the Irish Republican Army, who defend the living Republic, and will defend it to the death.
In the Four Courts, bombarded by guns borrowed from Churchill, and attacked by troops armed by Churchill, stand the men who have refused to foreswear their allegiance to the Republic, who have refused to sacrifice honour for expediency, and sell their country to a foreign King. In Rory O'Connor and his comrades lives the unbought, indomitable soul of Ireland.
Irish citizens, give them support! Irish soldiers, bring them aid!

Left: the initial communiqué from the Four Courts defenders, which exhibits a degree of self-confidence and optimism for the future. It was published in 'Poblacht na hÉireann', a broadsheet which presented the war from the Republican viewpoint for the rest of 1922 and into 1923.

It was incongruous for what was essentially a guerrilla army (and their leadership elite) to set up in a static, easily besieged position. Most of this leadership was captured when the Four Courts fell. However, the defenders of the Four Courts, for most of the siege, had some communications with the outside. They could send and receive a limited number of messages, usually conveyed by members of Cumann na mBan.

Left: map of the Four Courts area.

286

The Provisional Government Army took over the next-door Four Courts Hotel as HQ (right). They also placed a Lancia against the front gates of the courts to prevent the exit of the 'Mutineer', the Rolls Royce armoured car that had been captured.

Below right: rifles and sandbags — a photo taken on the Four Courts roof, during the early days of the occupation. During the assault at the end of June, the IRA sniped at the opposing artillery positions from on high.

Pro-Treaty gunners deliberately created two major breaches in the walls. After 3 pm on 29 June, troops stormed the Four Courts through these newly created gaps. One was at Morgan's Place, where the assault proved difficult. Another was at Church Street (the breach created by an 18-pounder at Hammond Lane). Commandant Pádraig O'Connor led his troops through this breach and captured some surprised defenders. O'Connor explored the Record Office and saw that it had been prepared for fire. Holes had been cut in floors, with blankets draped through.

Right: the breach at the Record Office at Church Street.

Above: flames and smoke billow upwards in the conflagration.

On the morning of 30 June, with the Headquarters Block on fire, O'Connor's troops readied to advance. At around 12:30 pm there was an enormous explosion at the western end of the Headquarters Block, where munitions had been stored. Many pro-Treaty troops were injured. Two more explosions went off at around 2 pm. The defenders surrendered at 3:45 pm.

Left: devastation — ground zero, with the Bridewell and Land Registry Office just discernable in the background.

After the battle for the Four Courts, fire had become widespread and the buildings lay in total ruin. In the Central Hall, the dome had collapsed. Right: the statue of Henry Joy, Chief Baron of the Irish Exchequer, casts a ghostly pall over the rubble.

During the occupation the Republicans had commandeered a large collection of vehicles, intended for an expeditionary attack on the North. These had been stored in the grounds of the Four Courts.

Right: in the aftermath a car lies submerged under rubble amidst the devastation.
In the background is the ruined Record Treasury section of the Public Record Office where Irish medieval documents, maps, census, administrative and court records had been stored. The building erupted into flames after the huge explosion that occurred nearby on 30 June.

Documents from the Public Record Office wafted over the city.

Near right: a document recovered after the conflagration, being restored in the National Archives.

Far right: passers-by on Sackville Street pick up documents.

Above: a view of the Four Courts, looking west along Inns Quay. As rubble lies strewn about, the Lancia is still at its forlorn station, blocking a main gate of the, by now, devastated complex.

Capuchin priests attended at the Four Courts during the siege. As well as giving spiritual comfort and helping with evacuating the wounded, they acted as intermediaries in negotiating surrender by the Republican occupiers.

Left: Fr Dominic O'Connor after the siege.

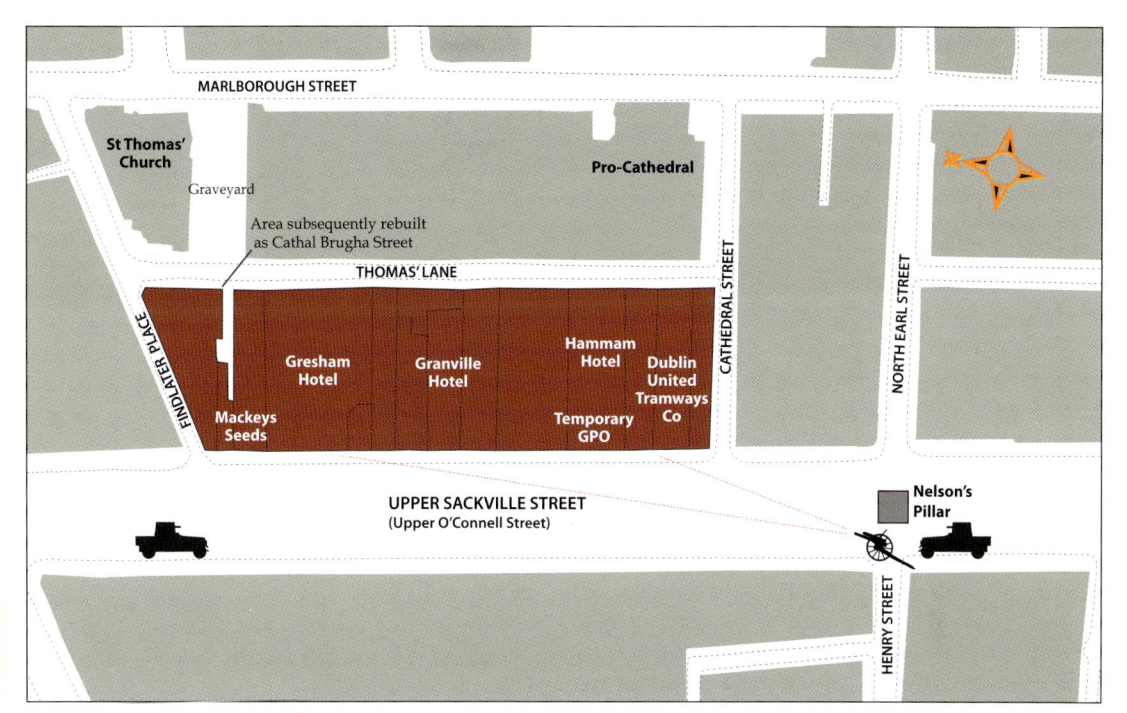

Above: map of the 'Block' area. As the siege of the Four Courts entered its endgame on 29 June, the IRA took over buildings in central Dublin to relieve the pressure. The 'Block' on Sackville Street was the principal objective. It ranged from Findlater Place to Cathedral Street and included the Gresham and Granville Hotels as well as the Hammam Hotel where Oscar Traynor, OC, set up his headquarters.

Above right: Moran's Hotel on Talbot Street was taken over by the anti-Treaty IRA, as was an outpost south of the Liffey at the Swan, a licensed premises (right) on Aungier Street. These outlying positions were soon overcome.

By the evening of 2 July, with outlying areas cleared, pro-Treaty forces now had the Block surrounded. As the attacks intensified, the main IRA force withdrew on 3 July, leaving a small group under Cathal Brugha. Eventually, on the evening of 4 July, an 18-pounder (above), was set up at the corner of Henry Street to shell the Block.

Left: the position was shielded by Lancia armoured personnel carriers.

Right: seen here on Henry Street, this Rolls Royce armoured car has been named 'Custom House' in memory of the IRA action there in 1921 during the War of Independence. Bitterness at the beginning of the Civil War is evident from the figure of 'Rory Boy' with a noose around its neck. Rory O'Connor had just been captured at the Four Courts. Armoured cars played a significant part in the conflict around Sackville Street. Fourteen of these Rolls Royce armoured cars had been acquired from the British. These formidable armoured vehicles were over five metres long and weighed around four tonnes. The protective shutters over the radiator at the front can be clearly seen – closed here during the fighting.

Right: at Henry Street, the chalked slogan on the protective Lancia refers to the nickname 'Trucers'. This reflected the pro-Treaty perception that many flocked to join the anti-Treaty IRA after the truce in 1921, having played no part in the War of Independence. The other side harboured a similar opinion about their pro-Treaty opponents.

Above: ready for ignition. In front of the Mackey's Seeds premises and guarded by two watchful comrades standing by containers of petrol, a pro-Treaty officer fires through a window of the adjacent Gresham Hotel. The intention is to place incendiaries and flush out the opposing forces within.

Left: smoke billows from the buildings of the Block. As a Rolls Royce armoured car maintains station, a horse-drawn unit of the Dublin Fire Brigade races along the street.

Above: a staged photograph during the fighting around Sackville Street. The symmetry and composition of these two soldiers, posing, in what looks like a yard, on a timber frame with their Lee Enfield Mk III rifles, is excellent.

Right: Two Lancias are parked on the street outside the Hammam Hotel, which has a gaping hole in the entrance caused by shells. By nightfall on 5 July, the Hammam Hotel, pounded by shells and then set ablaze, was razed to the ground.

Left: memorial plaque to Cathal Brugha, at the southern end of the former Block at the corner of O'Connell Street and Cathedral Street.

Principled and determined, Cathal Brugha was one of the foremost protagonists on the anti-Treaty side. As the pro-Treaty forces gained the upper hand in the fighting at the Block, most of the Republican defenders had managed to escape. On 5 July, Brugha was in charge of a small rearguard group, having retreated to the Granville Hotel. At around 7 pm, with the hotel in flames, Brugha ordered his men to surrender. Then he emerged into Thomas' Lane, behind the hotel, pistol in hand, and ran towards a party of troops. Shots rang out and he was hit by a single bullet. Wounded in a femoral artery, he died two days later.

Left: in the aftermath of the fighting, firemen are at work on the ruins of the Dublin United Tramway Company's offices at the corner of Cathedral Street. A crowd of Dubliners, eternally curious, looks on.

Above: a temporary GPO (note the new 'An Post' branding) had been set up on Upper Sackville Street while the GPO was being rebuilt after the destruction of 1916. This post office (part of what became the Block) was also devastated in the fighting of July 1922.

Right: Provisional Government troops receive medical assistance during the fighting.

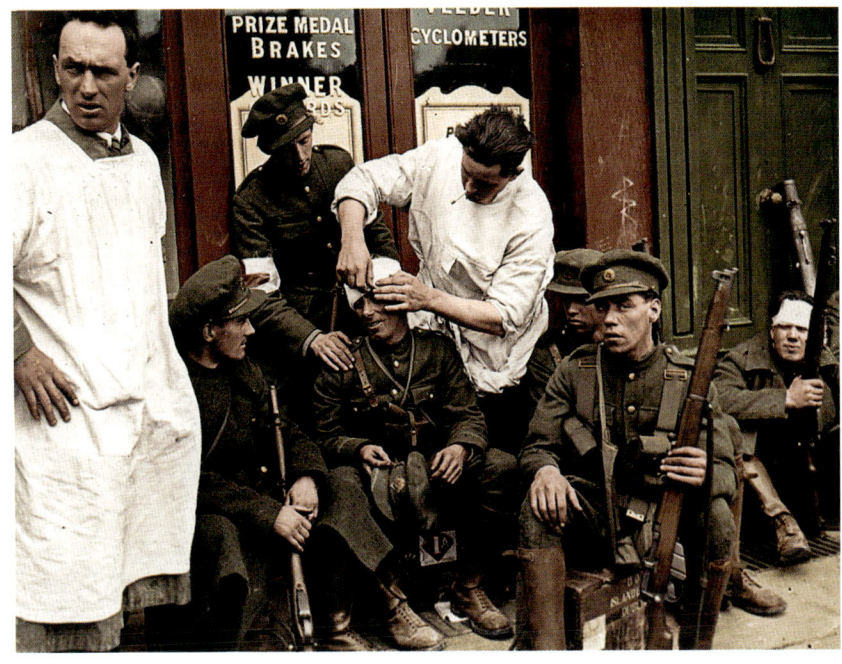

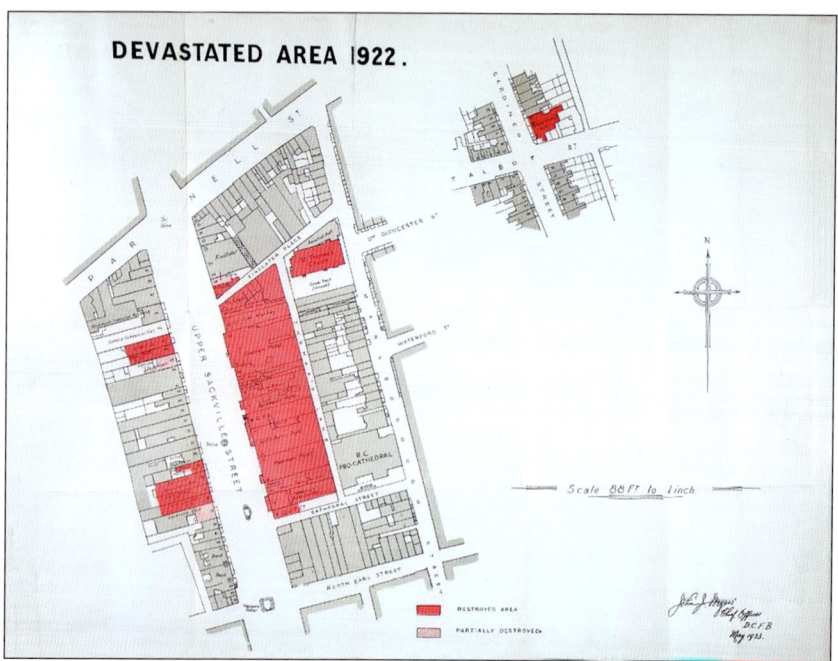

Above: the last to surrender after Brugha was shot, anti-Treaty men emerge under guard from the Edinburgh Life Assurance building on the west side of Upper Sackville Street. They had tunnelled from an outpost at the nearby Thwaites Mineral Water Plant to here.

Left: map of the devastation after the fighting at Upper Sackville Street, prepared by John Myers, Chief Officer, Dublin City Fire Brigade.

Above: repairs to the track of the Dublin & Blessington Steam Tramway, damaged by the IRA. The South Dublin Brigade, IRA, destroyed Rathfarnham police station on 30 June and travelled to meet up with other Republicans regrouping at Blessington, where the original plan was to march on Dublin.

Right: charabanc at Crooksling, on the Blessington road, on 5 July. When Provisional Government troops converged on Blessington, there was little resistance and they found the Republicans had dispersed.

Above: a view from Mount Misery. Republican forces had occupied strongholds in Waterford City and raised the bridge over the River Suir. On 19 July 1922, Comdt-General Prout's forces set up an 18-pounder here on the escarpment to bombard the anti-Treaty strongholds across the river (including the Post Office, left). Troops crossed in boats and seized the Quay. The bridge was lowered and the main force took the city. Right: when Government troops reached the Granville Hotel on the Quay they discovered a mine in the hall and cut its wires. Here, in the portico outside the hotel, they proudly display the mine.

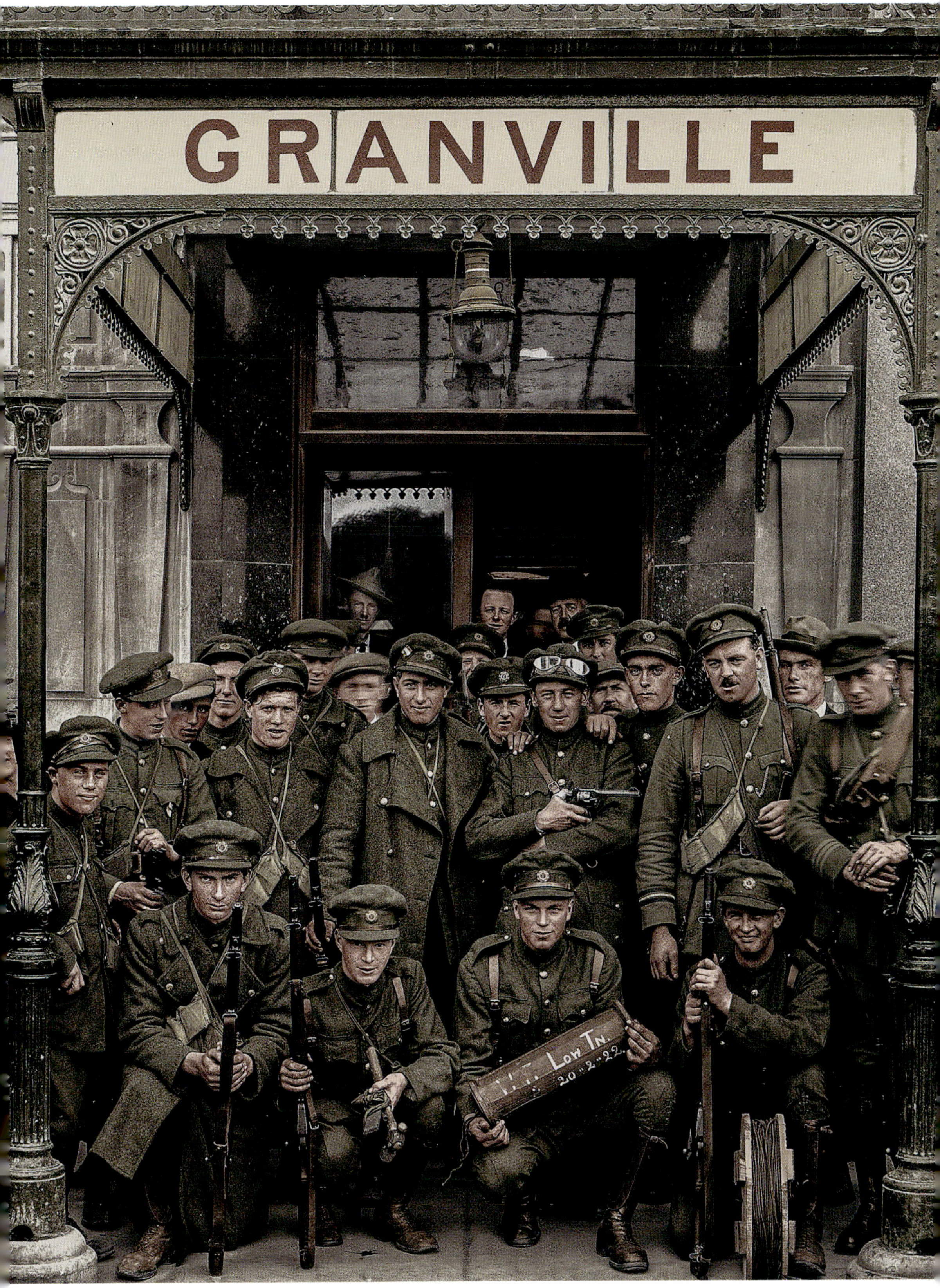
GRANVILLE
Low Tn.
20.2.22.

Above: barricades and barbed wire on O'Connell Street.

Limerick controlled approaches to the south-west and the north-west. Republican forces were entrenched in most strongholds in the city. Pro-Treaty Comdt-General Michael Brennan agreed a truce on 4 July with Liam Lynch (Chief of Staff of the anti-Treaty IRA). This bought time for the pro-Treaty side, allowing troops and arms to be sent to Limerick.

Left: anti-Treaty forces park their commandeered cars in front of the Imperial Hotel in Limerick.

The Limerick truce ended on 11 July, when the Provisional Government forces, on the pretext that a soldier had been shot, spread out along the barricaded streets of the city and opened fire on the Ordnance Barracks.

As fighting continued in Limerick, General Eoin O'Duffy left Dublin with troops, weapons, an armoured car and an 18-pounder. He reached Killaloe and fought his way into Limerick on 19 July.

Right: pro-Treaty troops pose after their capture of Limerick.

Above: after shelling in the city, Republicans withdrew from the New Barracks and set it on fire. Civilians can be seen looting.

An 18-pounder shelled Strand Barracks, and on 20 July it was stormed. Next came Castle Barracks. In face of the onslaught, Liam Lynch sent an order to the anti-Treaty forces to abandon their now-untenable positions and burn them.

Left: pro-Treaty troops sit on the rubble at a Limerick barracks around an improvised fire in a battered tin bath.

In the last week of July, after consolidating his hold on Limerick, General O'Duffy sent troops to the Kilmallock-Bruree area (close to the border with anti-Treaty Cork), where the Republicans had regrouped after withdrawing from the city. There was also an advance on Adare on 4 August. The town was taken that evening, by pro-Treaty troops.

Pro-Treaty troops headed out of Limerick to the 'South-Western Front', as the newspapers dubbed it. Right: soldiers pose in front of a charabanc, packed with their colleagues.

Above: as a pro-Treaty convoy passes through a village in the south-west, the men are offered cigarettes by a local supporter.

There was fierce fighting across a wide front in the Kilmallock-Bruree area. Eventually Kilmallock was taken on the morning of 5 August. Most of the defenders had withdrawn. The Kerry IRA Brigades had previously left to face the pro-Treaty forces that landed at Fenit on 2 August.

Left: a convoy of pro-Treaty troops in Bruff.

As the war proceeded, abuse and propaganda flowed as freely as bullets. While the mainstream press, national and foreign, was universally pro-Treaty, a type of 'mosquito press' emerged on the Republican side. The most authoritative was 'Poblacht na hÉireann, War News' (right). After the Dublin fighting of July 1922, it was produced in the Republican heartland near Ballingeary along the Cork-Kerry border. The editor was Erskine Childers, who had to lead a peripatetic existence, moving from hideout to hideout.

Constance Markievicz produced a series of propaganda drawings on cyclostyled paper, supporting the Republican side, and had them posted around Dublin.

Right: a Markievicz drawing. Here, Hibernia, represented by the bound maiden, is harassed in turn by: Desmond FitzGerald (Minister for Publicity, in Union Jack waistcoat); a threatening Michael Collins; a plump Bishop and WT Cosgrave (in clown attire).

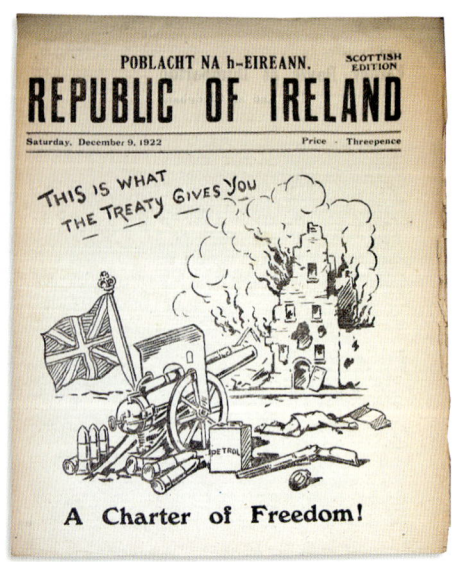

Near left: the most professional of the anti-Treaty publications was 'Poblacht na hÉireann, Scottish Edition', produced in Glasgow

Far left: there were many impromptu cyclostyled anti-Treaty newsletters, as evidenced by the 'Republican War Bulletin'. Interestingly, this and most of the others (as did 'Poblacht na hÉireann, War News', on the previous page) carry the strapline 'seventh year of the Republic', thus emphasising that, in the Republican viewpoint, the Republic proclaimed in 1916 had not been abolished and was still in existence.

Left: a rare pro-Treaty flier. Handbills promoting the pro-Treaty viewpoint are scarce. A constant theme on the pro-Treaty side was that those on the opposing side had not done much during the recent War of Independence, as was previously seen in the reference to 'Trucers' chalked on the Lancia on page 293. The handbill here makes this allegation – that many of the Republicans were inactive in 1921 and emerged to fight only in 1922.

Right: the Martinsyde Type A1 Mk II aeroplane, purchased during the Treaty negotiations, at Baldonnel (HQ of Irish military aviation) with the Irish tricolour being painted on its fuselage.

The Army Air Service (known as the 'Army Air Corps' from October 1924) was established in mid-1922. It acquired its first fighter in early July. By the end of October 1922 there were 15 aircraft in service. Fighters included the Bristol F.2B (below) and the DH.9 DII (bottom).

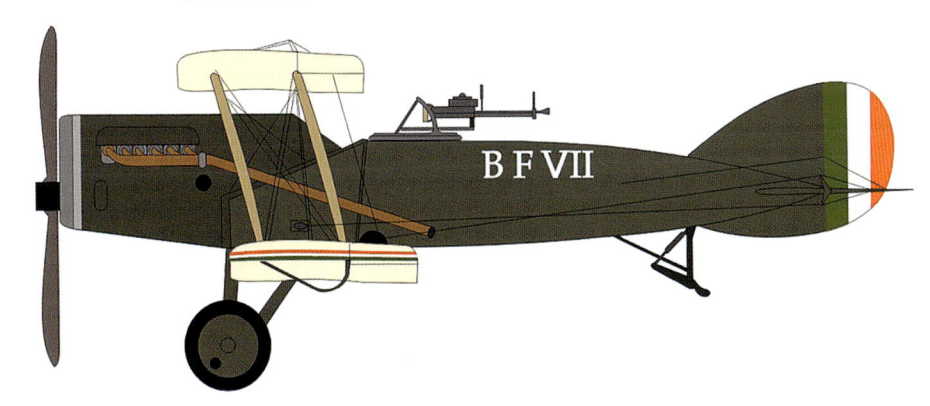

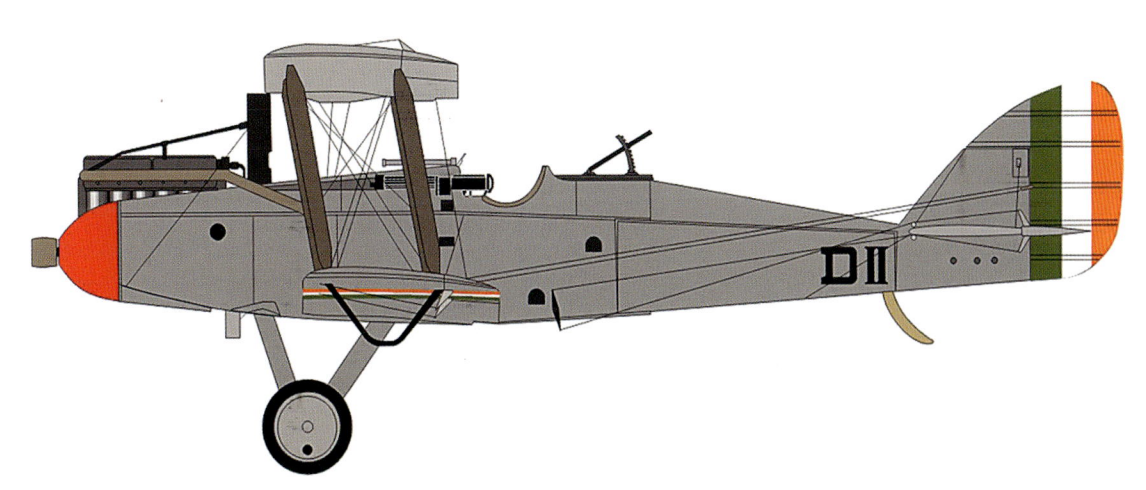

Above: a line-up of Army Air Service planes.

Left: a Bristol F.2B at Baldonnel Aerodrome. This type had been one of the most successful fighters during WWI. By the end of October 1922, six had been acquired.

Air Service fighters were extensively used during the south-west campaigns of the Civil War. Duties included reconnaissance, patrolling railway lines and dropping propaganda leaflets. Unlike the RAF's reluctance during most of the War of Independence, Air Service pilots had no hesitation in strafing gatherings of 'Irregulars' on the ground.

Left: an Avro 504K trainer, seen here at Baldonnel. One of the first pilots in the Air Service, Lieutenant WP Delamere, is in the rear cockpit.

In mid-1922, seaborne landings were seen as the way to establish Provisional Government control in the west and south-west. The first landing by the pro-Treaty army was from the steamer 'Menevia' (right) at Westport Quay (below right) on 24 July 1922. On arrival, 400 troops with an armoured car spread out to capture towns in Co. Mayo. This provided useful experience of an amphibious operation and was a template for subsequent landings.

The next landing was made during the early hours of 2 August 1922 at Fenit. The cross-channel ferry 'Lady Wicklow' (below right) landed 450 soldiers, the 'Ex-Mutineer' armoured car (back in service after seeing action on the anti-Treaty side during the Four Courts siege) and an 18-pounder at Fenit Pier, Co. Kerry (below). There was heavy fighting during the advance to Tralee, which was taken later that day.

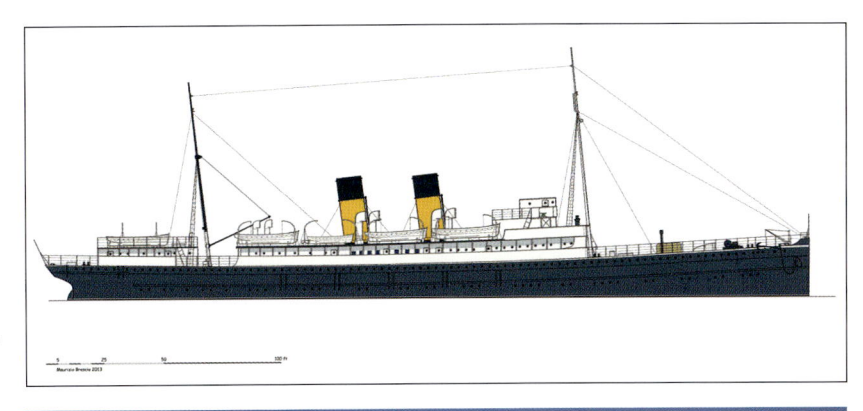

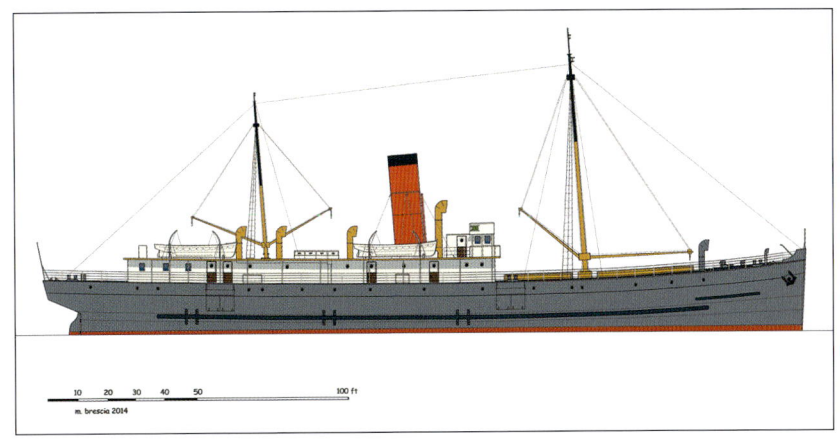

311

Kenmare was taken by pro-Treaty forces when 200 men under Brigadier Tom O'Connor 'Scarteen' (left) landed at the local pier on 11 August 1922, from the vessels 'Margaret' and 'Mermaid'. The troops spread out in the town and occupied strongholds like the bank and the Carnegie Library.

A month later on 9 September, the Republicans attacked and retook Kenmare. Tom O'Connor 'Scarteen' and his brother John were shot dead in their home on Main Street. (Left: their grave at Kenmare.) 130 prisoners were taken, but were soon released by their Republican captors. It took until 6 December 1922 for the town to come back under Free State control.

The pro-Treaty side was now effectively under military direction: a 'War Council' (composed of Generals Collins, Mulcahy and O'Duffy) had been announced by Collins at a Cabinet meeting on 12 July 1922. He requested an official instruction, which was issued by the Government in the following days.

Right: Portobello (now Cathal Brugha) Barracks, headquarters of the pro-Treaty army, 7 August 1922. Tension is evident on the faces of the officers (General Mulcahy, centre right) as one of the most decisive manoeuvres of the war is organised. With land communications blocked, it had been decided that the way to gain control of the important Cork region was by sea. The successful landings at Westport and Fenit gave them the experience and confidence to send a large expeditionary force to the region. The intention was to make a landing at Cork Harbour, with simultaneous landings at Youghal and Union Hall. A flotilla of steamers sailed from Dublin's North Wall that day.

Right: amphibious ambition, the principal landings by pro-Treaty forces during the period July-August 1922.

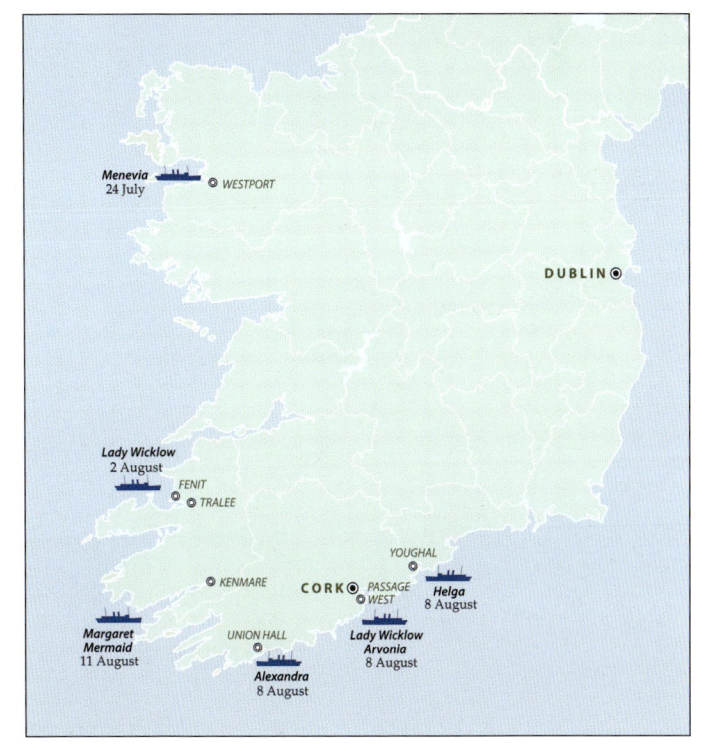

The cross-channel London & North Western Railway steamer 'Arvonia' (left), along with the 'Lady Wicklow', was commandeered by the Provisional Government for the landing in Cork Harbour. The crew of the 'Arvonia' were mostly Welshmen and, understandably, were reluctant to take part in the risky expedition to Cork.

Left: as they sail to Cork on board the 'Arvonia', soldiers clean an 18-pounder field gun. The scrawled letters on its shield show it is a veteran of the June shelling of the Four Courts and also of a brief and successful engagement on 4 July against anti-Treaty forces entrenched at Millmount, Drogheda.

Above: poignant, soldiers dance on the deck of the 'Arvonia', to the strains of a melodeon-player, perched on the 18-pounder. For men about to face the dangers of war, it was a way to pass the time on the long voyage south.

Unable to proceed upriver for fear of mines, the 'Arvonia' docked at the Queenstown Dry Docks pier at Passage West. Ironically, this spot had been the first landing point of Queen Victoria on her initial visit to Ireland in 1849 (engraving of the Royal Squadron anchored by Passage, right).

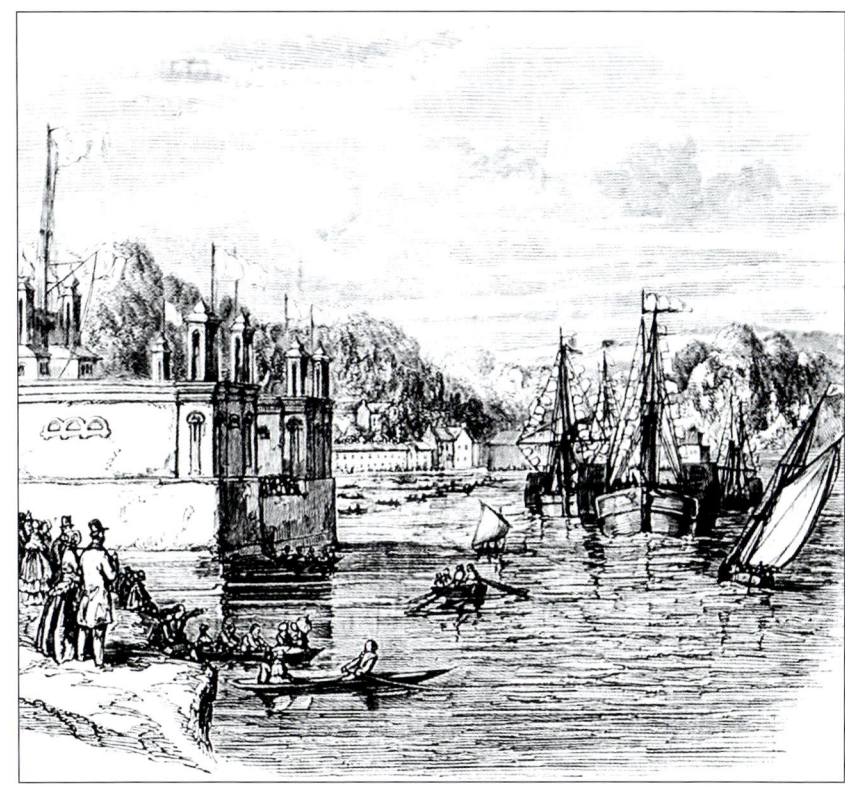

Left: safely ashore, soldiers assemble at the dockside, about to set off on the journey towards Cork City, around 10 kilometres upriver. They were to encounter fierce resistance on the way. The Lancia armoured personnel carrier tows the 18-pounder across the crane tracks towards the dockyard exit.

The expeditionary force at Passage West docks came under fire from positions across the water and from a machine gun ensconced on the hillside above the town.

Left: fighting in the streets of Passage West in August 1922. Here a pro-Treaty officer, revolver in hand, crouches as his troops shelter around the corner. The Peerless armoured car faces in the direction of opposing fire.

Republican forces rushed to the area to resist the incursion. There was heavy fighting amidst the rolling hills, fields and woods between Passage West and Rochestown over the following days.

Left: sketch map of battles on 8-9 August in the area around Rochestown College.

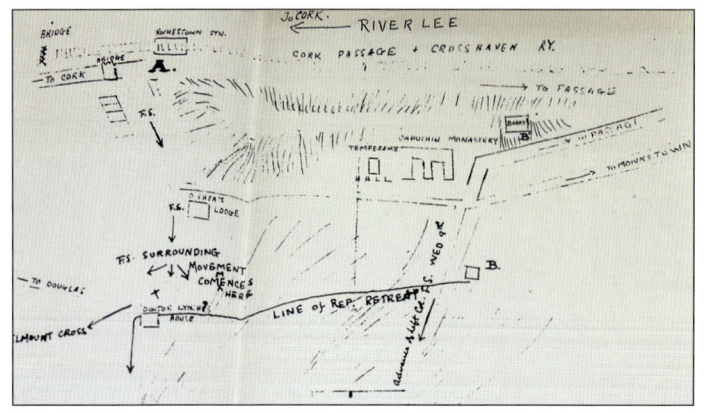

After fierce fighting on its approaches, Cork City was taken on the evening of 10 August. As the Republican forces withdrew, they made their way to Macroom and regrouped. From there the Republicans dispersed and the war in the south-west now entered a guerrilla phase.

Right: the 'Lady Wicklow', laden with troops, in the upper reaches of Cork Harbour. Smaller and slower than the 'Arvonia', it had been commandeered from the B&I Steam Packet Company. Before its voyage to Cork, it had carried troops for the Fenit landing on 2 August (page 311).

Right: after the taking of the city, ships could sail upriver to berth at the Cork quays. Here in Lough Mahon, Upper Cork Harbour, care is taken in navigating past the 'Gorilla' (a steamer) in the foreground and, just visible, the 'No. 1 Hopper' (a dredging barge). These had been sunk by Republicans to prevent passage upriver.

The Provisional Government army was now in command of Cork City. At the gangplank of the 'Lady Wicklow', Major-General Tom Ennis (with Thompson machine gun) looks relaxed. A more reserved-looking Colonel-Commandant Mac Craith, is on the right.

During the period of de facto Republican control in Cork, the 'Cork Examiner' was under censorship and had to publish anti-Treaty communiqués. Before the Republicans withdrew from the city, they smashed the newspaper's printing press with sledgehammers.

Left: soldiers mill around at Albert Street Station, with a Peerless armoured car in the background. A sandwich vendor finds a ready market for her wares.

Below: Cork 'Republican' silver. As Cork had been cut off from communicating with the Assay Office in Dublin, local silversmiths, William Egan & Sons devised their own unique assay marks, based on Cork's original marks of a ship between two castles.

Above: Chetwynd Viaduct on the West Cork railway was blown up by anti-Treaty forces, August 1922.

Douglas Viaduct of the Cork and Blackrock Railway was severely damaged by the Republicans, to deny transit by rail to the city by the pro-Treaty army. Right: men of the Railway Protection, Repair & Maintenance Corps at work repairing the viaduct in early 1923.

Below right: Belvelly Viaduct, south of Fota, on the Cork-Queenstown (Cobh) line, another of the railway bridges in the Cork Harbour area blown up in August. Below: Cork 'Republican' stamps. During the anti-Treaty control of Cork, a series was printed in the city. These proclaimed the postal service of 'Poblacht na hÉireann'.

319

As the reassuring news of the successful southern landings came, the Provisional Government was dealt a grievous blow. Arthur Griffith, President of Dáil Éireann, died of a cerebral haemorrhage at the age of 51 on 12 August 1922. This veteran of the nationalist struggle was one of the most eminent of the pro-Treaty leaders. Michael Collins, Commander-in-Chief of the Provisional Government army, had just begun a tour of the south when news came of Arthur Griffith's death. Collins returned for the funeral, held on 16 August (left). He himself had only six days to live.

Left: British officers (still stationed in Dublin barracks) enter the Pro-Cathedral to pay their respects to Arthur Griffith.

Right; an example of an open-topped Leyland Eight touring car, as used by Collins.

Collins resumed his southern journey and reached Cork City on the night of 20 August. He spent the next day trying to trace Republican funds lodged in the city's banks. At 6:15 am on 22 August he set out for a long day's tour of West Cork, with the intention of assessing the situation on the ground and meeting old comrades. The convoy travelled in the following order: a motorcycle outrider; a Crossley tender carrying soldiers armed with rifles and a Lewis machine gun; Collins with Maj.-General Emmet Dalton in a Leyland Eight touring car and, bringing up the rear, the 'Sliabh na mBan' Rolls Royce armoured car (right).

On the morning of 22 August, IRA officers were meeting upstairs in (the then) Long's public house (right), at the crossroads at Bealnablath. Collins' party stopped here to ask a man (who happened to be an IRA sentry) standing outside for directions, at around 9 am. Anticipating that the convoy would return the same way, the Republicans decided to set up an ambush about a kilometre up the road.

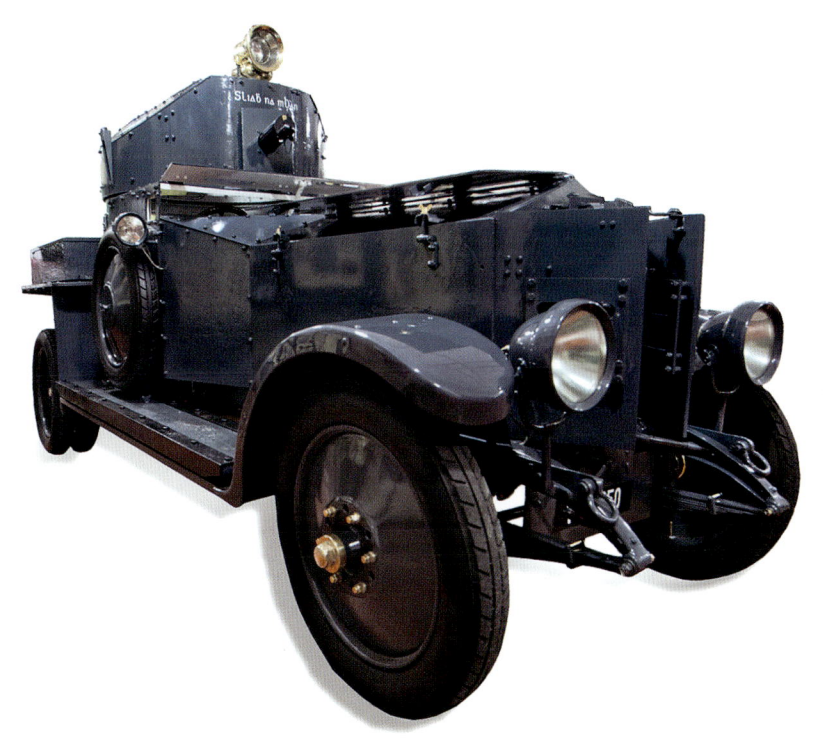

321

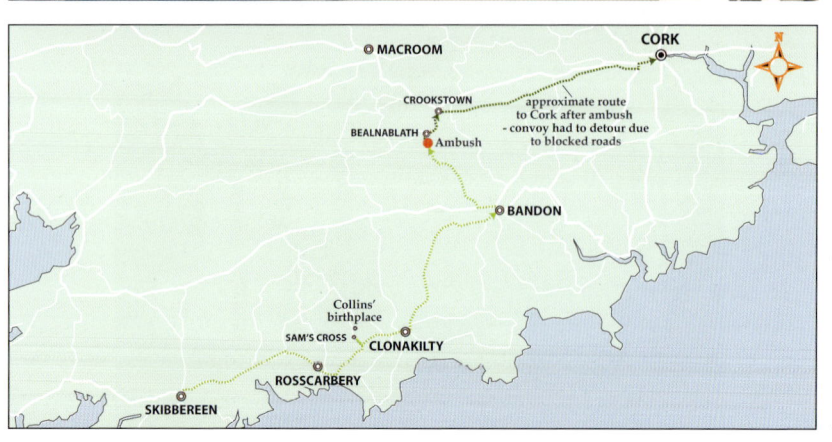

Left: at around 4:30 on the afternoon of 22 August, General Collins climbed into his Leyland touring car, after leaving the Eldon Hotel in Skibbereen, where he had a meal. This was the furthest point in his journey that day. The convoy embarked on the long and convoluted return journey to Cork City. At around 7:15 pm, in mist and fading light, the convoy approached the ambush site at Bealnablath. The ambushers, who had been lying in wait for hours, had just given up on the convoy returning. A few remained, about to clear away a dray-car barricade. Sighting the convoy, they ran to positions and opened fire.

Simple, spartan and effective. The view inside the turret of the 'Sliabh na mBan' (left). The armoured car proved to be an important component of the convoy on that fateful day, initially spraying the enemy positions with fire. It was to enjoy a chequered afterlife: it fell into Republican hands in December 1922, and was later found hidden at a farm in Gougane Barra.

Left: map of Collins' ill-fated return journey.

Above: the approximate positions at Bealnablath.

After the first shot was fired at the convoy, Collins countermanded Dalton's order to 'get out of there' (from the touring car), saying 'We'll fight them'. There was a heavy exchange of fire. Collins left the touring car and fired at the attackers with his Lee Enfield rifle, separated a little from his convoy. A shot rang out, and Collins fell, mortally wounded, with a gaping hole behind his right ear. His body was placed in the rear of the armoured car. Later it was transferred to the touring car. Following a nightmarish journey, the party reached Cork City after midnight.

Right: 'The bloody convulsions in Ireland': 'Le Petit Journal' of Paris imaginatively depicts the events.

323

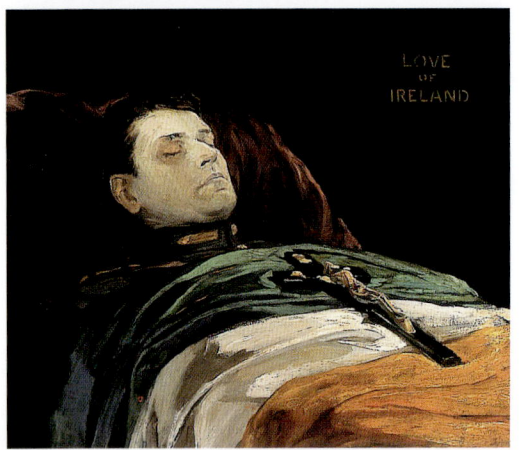

Left: Michael Collins' body was laid out in Shanakiel Hospital in Cork.

Emmet Dalton managed, with difficulty, to send the news of the death back to Army GHQ, Dublin, in the morning hours of 23 August. The message was sent by shortwave radio to Waterville, Co. Kerry, and cabled from there to New York. It was relayed to London and then to Dublin.

Left: in the Hugh Lane Gallery, Dublin, 'Love of Ireland', painted later in 1922 by Sir John Lavery.

Collins' remains were transported from Cork to Dublin on the cross-channel steamer 'Classic'. Later they were brought to lie in state at City Hall. There was universal sorrow at his death (even on the anti-Treaty side). On 28 August his funeral cortège passed through enormous crowds along the Dublin streets to Glasnevin Cemetery where he was buried.

Left: a commemoration ceremony by the National Army at Bealnablath, later in 1922. An army chaplain reads prayers near the simple wooden cross marking where Collins died.

Right: General Richard Mulcahy. Energetic, methodical, efficient and ruthless, the Minister of Defence and Chief of Staff was now the military supremo and was appointed Commander-in-Chief of the army. WT Cosgrave replaced Michael Collins as Chairman of the Provisional Government.

During the early hours on 23 August, after Richard Mulcahy heard of Collins' death, he at once wrote a message, as Chief of the General Staff, to the 'Men of the Army'. It starts: 'Stand calmly by your posts. Bend bravely and undaunted to your work. Let no cruel act of reprisal blemish your bright honour… Ireland! The Army serves – strengthened by its sorrow.'

Right: amidst the grief was this instance of reprisal, as depicted in this poster attributed to Countess Markievicz. A few days after Collins' death, two anti-Treaty Fianna youths were picked up at North Strand in Dublin, shot and their bodies dumped at Whitehall.

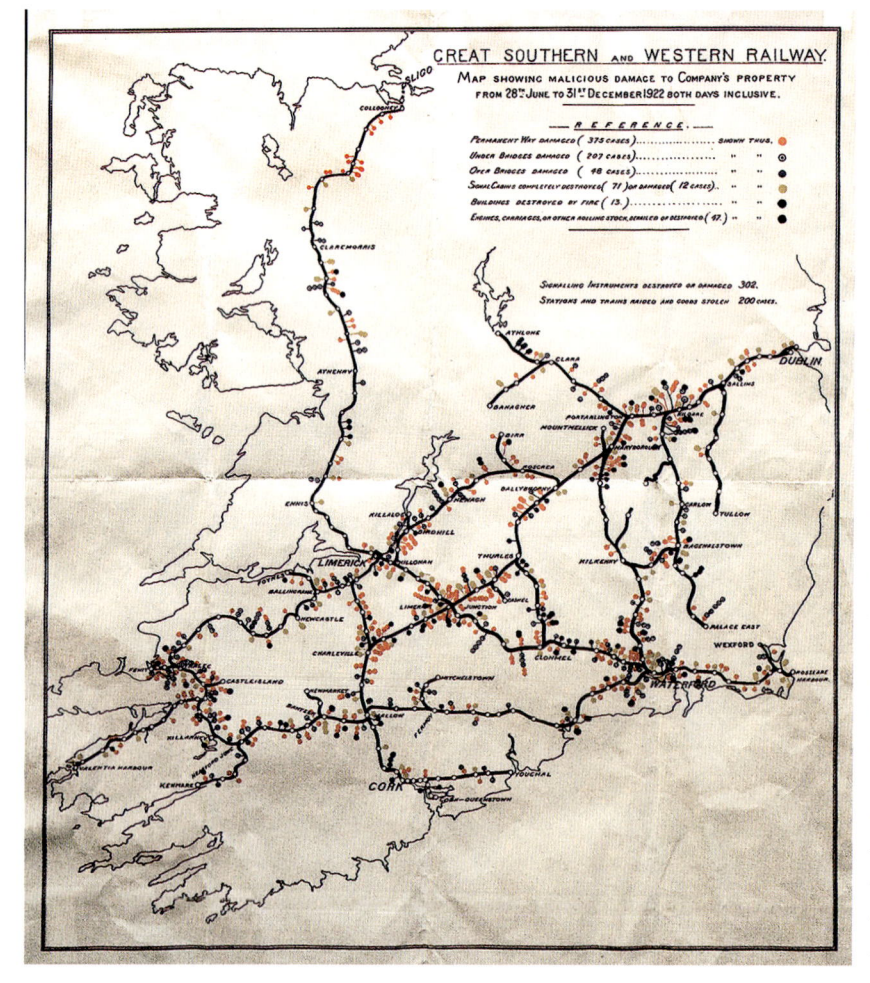

Left: soldiers on guard at a derailment at Ballyragget, Co. Kilkenny.

Initially, the IRA destroyed railways leading to the south to prevent pro-Treaty troop movements. Later, as the struggle moved to its guerrilla phase, the railways, a soft target, were sabotaged at will. In early twentieth-century Ireland the railway system still constituted an essential economic artery and localities suffered when the line was cut. In response, to guard the railways and repair damage, the Provisional Government set up the Railway Protection, Repair & Maintenance Corps (RPR&MC) in October 1922. It was staffed by a mixture of soldiers and railway workers

Left: as shown on this map, damage to the GS&WR system by the end of December 1922 was: 375 incidences of damaged track; 255 bridges damaged; 83 signal cabins destroyed or damaged; 13 buildings destroyed by fire; 47 locomotives and rolling stock derailed or destroyed. There was also damage to the other railways in Ireland. The mayhem on the entire network continued relentlessly into early 1923.

Above: a derailment on the GS&WR system, from the photo book kept by the Locomotive Foreman at Maryborough (Portlaoise). Here at Ballywilliam on 12 January 1923, derailed locomotive No. 45 lies upside down on the embankment, as the rescue crew pose.

Right a GS&WR breakdown steam crane lifts a damaged locomotive from the river at Foynes, Co. Limerick, April 1923.

Above: Edenderry Junction on the Midland Great Western Railway. The down Galway Express was derailed on 17 February 1923. The carriages remain on the track, but the tender has spilled onto the embankment with the locomotive lying in the adjacent field.

Left: rerailing a badly damaged locomotive.

Right: Ballyvoyle Viaduct was a multi-arch masonry bridge spanning the River Dalligan, on the Waterford to Mallow line, originally opened in 1878. The viaduct was initially damaged in August 1922. More destruction occurred the following January when the anti-Treaty IRA intercepted a ballast train and sent it backwards over the edge.

Right: at Ballyvoyle, the GS&WR rescue team have sprung into action. The locomotive and other equipment were recovered by the ingenious technique of laying a temporary track from the base and around the side of the abutment, then back along the steep ascent up to track level. While the permanent way men adjust the temporary track at the top of the slope, a supervisor inspects the arrangements, before the battered tender is winched up.

Right: the rebuilt viaduct at Ballyvoyle on the Waterford to Mallow line, now closed. Four steel lattice girders rest on high concrete piers. It was faster to reconstruct using concrete and prefabricated steel than to reconstruct the original eight-arch masonry structure.

The strategic ten-arch masonry viaduct (left) at Mallow, which carried the Dublin-Cork mainline over the River Blackwater, was destroyed in August 1922 (below left, after the attack). It caused great hardship across the region. A temporary station was put in place south of the river, with transfer by road to the station north of the river. Speed was of the essence in reconstructing the viaduct. As at Ballyvoyle, the quicker method of installing steel spans was employed – it took only 14 months to rebuild.

Below: reconstruction of the viaduct gets underway.

Right: a wildly dramatic scene in Co. Tipperary, as presented in the 'Illustrazione del Popolo' of February 1923. In this depiction, anti-Treaty forces are supposed to have demolished an arch of this multi-span railway viaduct. The express train, travelling at 70km per hour manages to cross the damaged span.

The 650m-span Barrow railway bridge (right). In February 1923 a young student, a Republican, rowed out, hand cranked the centre span into the open position, then dropped the crown-pinion wheel into the river. The Rosslare to Waterford line remained closed for the rest of the Civil War.

331

Above: at Mullingar, the armoured train of the RPR&MC dubbed 'King Tutankhamen', with soldiers and crew. Note the sheepdog next to the machine gun on top of the tender, to the left.

Left: RPR&MC equipment at sidings, Glanmire Road, Cork. The 'Grey Ghost' is behind in the middle siding, to the right.

Right: fitted out at Inchicore Railway Works of the Great Southern & Western Railway (GS&WR), an armoured Lancia, equipped with flanged steel wheels, which allowed it to travel on the rails (with top speed of around 70km per hour.) The RPR&MC used these to patrol the railway network. Two of the series had turrets, as in this example. The works was the centre of engineering excellence in Ireland. It has carried out armament work for all governments in Ireland from WWI onwards.

Right: armoured and ready to patrol, well-armed RPR&MC men pose by their Lancias at Glanmire (now Kent) Station, Cork.

Right: an illustration of the 'Grey Ghost', the only rail-mounted armoured Lancia that had camouflage. In mid-October 1922, while patrolling the railway line north of Fethard, it was ambushed and captured by the anti-Treaty IRA, who set it on fire. After relieving the crew of their arms, the IRA released them.

333

Above: most of the participants in the Civil War were surprisingly young. These two young National Army soldiers, billeted in the countryside, seem scarcely out of their teens.

Left: framed by the 'Big Fella' and the 'Fighting 2nd', officers pose at a Dublin barracks, July 1922. In the centre is Comdt-General Tom Ennis.

Above: the destroyer HMS 'Seawolf'.

Right: under the terms of the Anglo-Irish Treaty, the Royal Navy patrolled at will through Irish waters. On many occasions, the Royal Navy gave support to National Army troops in 1922 and maintained radio contact. Here, in an intelligence report, Captain Hugh Somerville, Senior Naval Officer, Haulbowline, recounts events along the south-west coast, including how HMS 'Ettrick' fired a blank round at Republican attackers at Fenit on the night of 23 September 1922. He also tells how, on the night of 22 September, HMS 'Seawolf' gave assistance to the pro-Treaty garrison at Caherciveen during an attack. Searchlights were shone and starshells fired, and 'Seawolf' provided weapons to the defenders.

Right: memorial to Hugh Somerville at St. Barrahane's Church, Castletownshend, Co. Cork. He was a brother of the writer, Edith Somerville.

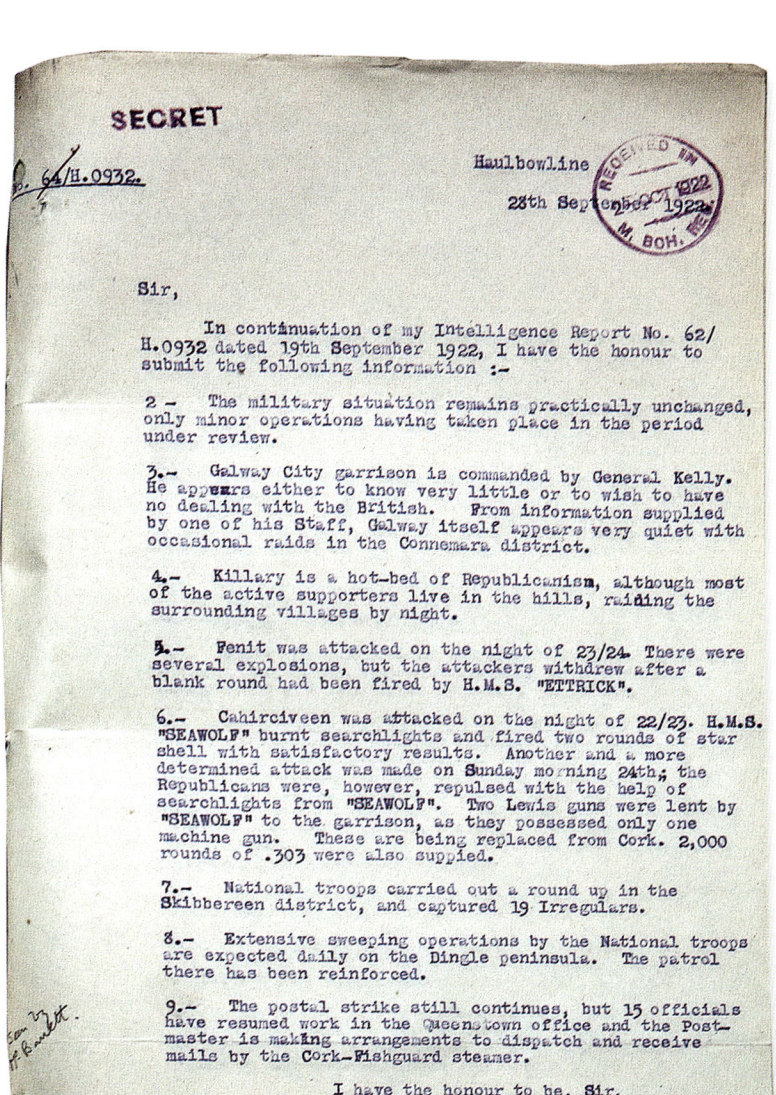

SECRET

No. 64/H.0932.

Haulbowline
28th September 1922

Sir,

In continuation of my Intelligence Report No. 62/H.0932 dated 19th September 1922, I have the honour to submit the following information:—

2.— The military situation remains practically unchanged, only minor operations having taken place in the period under review.

3.— Galway City garrison is commanded by General Kelly. He appears either to know very little or to wish to have no dealing with the British. From information supplied by one of his Staff, Galway itself appears very quiet with occasional raids in the Connemara district.

4.— Killary is a hot-bed of Republicanism, although most of the active supporters live in the hills, raiding the surrounding villages by night.

5.— Fenit was attacked on the night of 23/24. There were several explosions, but the attackers withdrew after a blank round had been fired by H.M.S. "ETTRICK".

6.— Cahirciveen was attacked on the night of 22/23. H.M.S. "SEAWOLF" burnt searchlights and fired two rounds of star shell with satisfactory results. Another and a more determined attack was made on Sunday morning 24th; the Republicans were, however, repulsed with the help of searchlights from "SEAWOLF". Two Lewis guns were lent by "SEAWOLF" to the garrison, as they possessed only one machine gun. These are being replaced from Cork. 2,000 rounds of .303 were also supplied.

7.— National troops carried out a round up in the Skibbereen district, and captured 19 Irregulars.

8.— Extensive sweeping operations by the National troops are expected daily on the Dingle peninsula. The patrol there has been reinforced.

9.— The postal strike still continues, but 15 officials have resumed work in the Queenstown office and the Postmaster is making arrangements to dispatch and receive mails by the Cork-Fishguard steamer.

I have the honour to be, Sir,

Your obedient Servant

H C Somerville
CAPTAIN.
Senior Naval Officer.

The Secretary of the Admiralty
(Copy to G.H.Q. Dublin)

IN LOVING MEMORY OF
VICE ADMIRAL H.G.C. SOMERVILLE C.B., D.S.O.
BORN 1873 . DIED 1950.
HIS LAST APPOINTMENT WAS SENIOR NAVAL OFFICER
HAULBOWLINE 1922 - 1923.
MARY.

Left and below left: Tom Keogh, commemorated in bronze and marble, on the impressive monument at his grave in Knockananna, Co. Wicklow.

Colonel-Commandant Tom Keogh and his six pro-Treaty army colleagues were blown up by a trap mine near Carrigaphooca Bridge near Macroom on 16 September 1922. Keogh, only 23 at the time of his death, had been a member of Collins' 'Squad'. He had led the pro-Treaty force which captured the Wexford area in early July 1922. Keogh was well commemorated: Richmond Barracks in Goldenbridge, Dublin was renamed after him, as were two Rolls Royce armoured cars.

Left: Carrigaphooca Bridge. As well as a memorial to Tom Keogh and his six colleagues who died, there is also a plaque on a nearby rock, commemorating a Republican prisoner, James Buckley, who was brought here afterwards and shot, and whose body was put in the hole caused by the explosion.

On 13 July 1922, there was an IRA ambush at Dooney Rock (memorial, above) near Lough Gill in Sligo. They seized the 'Ballinalee' Rolls Royce armoured car (right, seen here earlier in Provisional Government army service at Sligo during Arthur Griffith's visit in Easter 1922).

Right: Christy MacLynn, driver, with the captured armoured car, now renamed 'Lough Gill', which the IRA used on forays around the area. In September 1922 pro-Treaty forces mounted a large push on Sligo. The 'Lough Gill' was cornered in the lee of Benbulben on 19 September. The crew attempted to set it on fire, damaging the engine. Other Republicans hid by the southern base of the mountain that evening and fled up a gully the next morning.

Right: This grainy image shows Commandant Fallon in front of the now-recovered and burnt-out armoured car, with slogans scrawled by National Army soldiers.

337

National Army troops climbed up Benbulben in pursuit of the fleeing IRA men. They captured four of them on the foggy morning of 20 September and shot them on the mountain (at the point marked by a cross, above and left). They included Séamus Devins, TD, and Brian MacNeill, son of Eoin MacNeill. Two others were shot elsewhere on the mountain and it took two weeks to find their bodies (another cross marks this spot, below). The slain Republicans are popularly known as the 'Sligo Noble Six' (left).

In late October the editor of 'Poblacht na hÉireann', Englishman and Republican, Erskine Childers (near right), set out for Dublin. The pro-Treaty side had developed a phobia about him and regarded him as the eminence grise behind all major Republican 'outrages'. In reality Staff-Captain Childers had led a peripheral and peripatetic existence editing the paper, hiding in remote West Cork cottages.

Erskine Childers was captured at his cousin Robert Barton's house in Co. Wicklow on 10 November. Ten days later he was brought before a military court, found guilty of being in possession of a pistol and sentenced to death (under the recently enacted and draconian Public Safety Act).

Right: order to Commandant Pádraig O'Connor to receive Childers into his custody. O'Connor (top, far right) established a good rapport with his prisoner; he also was ordered to command the firing squad. Childers was executed at Beggar's Bush on the 24th. He shook hands with each member of the firing squad, and met his death bravely and with dignity.

Right: Beggar's Bush Barracks, Dublin.

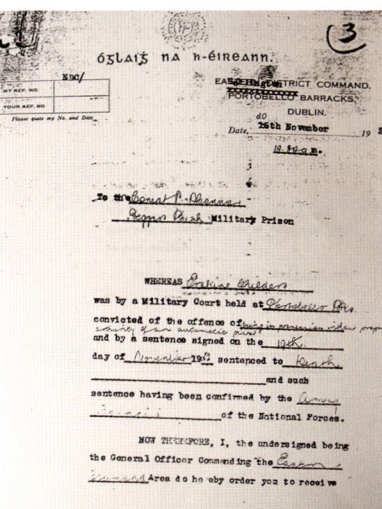

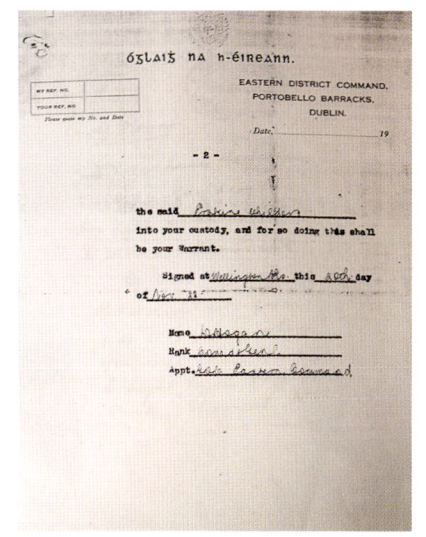

Executions of many captured Republicans continued apace, and this changed the IRA attitude to reprisals. On 27 November 1922, an alarmed Liam Lynch wrote to the Provisional Government protesting that his side had adhered to the rules of war and warning of consequences. Lynch issued an order on 30 November that 'all members of the Provisional 'Parliament' who had voted for the Murder Bill' be shot on sight. On 7 December a member of the IRA shot dead Seán Hales, TD, and wounded Pádraic Ó Máille, Leas-Cheann Comhairle of the Dáil, near the Ormond Hotel in Dublin (Depicted in this vivid illustration in 'Ilustrazione del Popolo', left).

Seán Hales had taken a prominent role in the IRA in West Cork during the War of Independence. He was a friend of Michael Collins – they had been interned together in Frongoch in Wales after the 1916 Rising. He took the pro-Treaty side and was TD for Cork South. His brother Tom was prominent on the anti-Treaty side and, ironically, commanded the IRA group that shot Collins.

Left. Seán Hales monument, Bandon, Co. Cork.

Right: Rory O'Connor, in happier times – at Bodenstown, June 1922, with Oscar Traynor, Countess Markievicz and Muriel MacSwiney.

The Government Executive Council met in an emergency session that evening after Hales' assassination on 7 December. After some debate, it concluded with an order to execute, as a reprisal, four prominent Republicans incarcerated in Mountjoy Prison. These had been captured after the taking of the Four Courts. The prisoners were roused from their cells the next morning and told that they were to be shot, as a reprisal, at 7:00 am. A firing squad shot the four together. The execution was conducted clumsily: nine revolver shots were required as coups de grâce. The prisoners had not been tried and these reprisal executions were not based on any law.

Above right: as well as Rory O'Connor, those executed were (from left), Dick Barrett, Joe McKelvey and Liam Mellows. Mellows, a socialist, was one of the few leaders, on either side of the Treaty divide, who had tried to articulate what an Irish Republic might actually comprise.

Right: remembrance in the Scottish edition of 'Poblacht na hÉireann'.

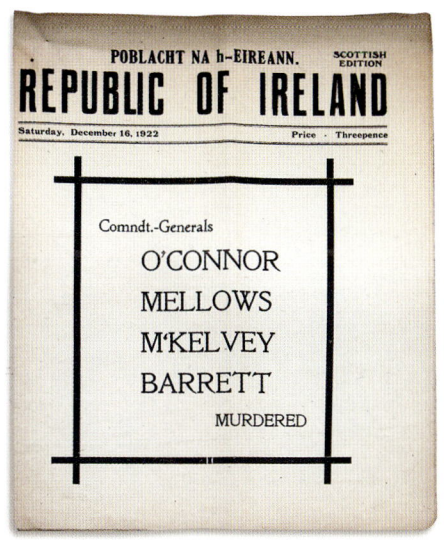

341

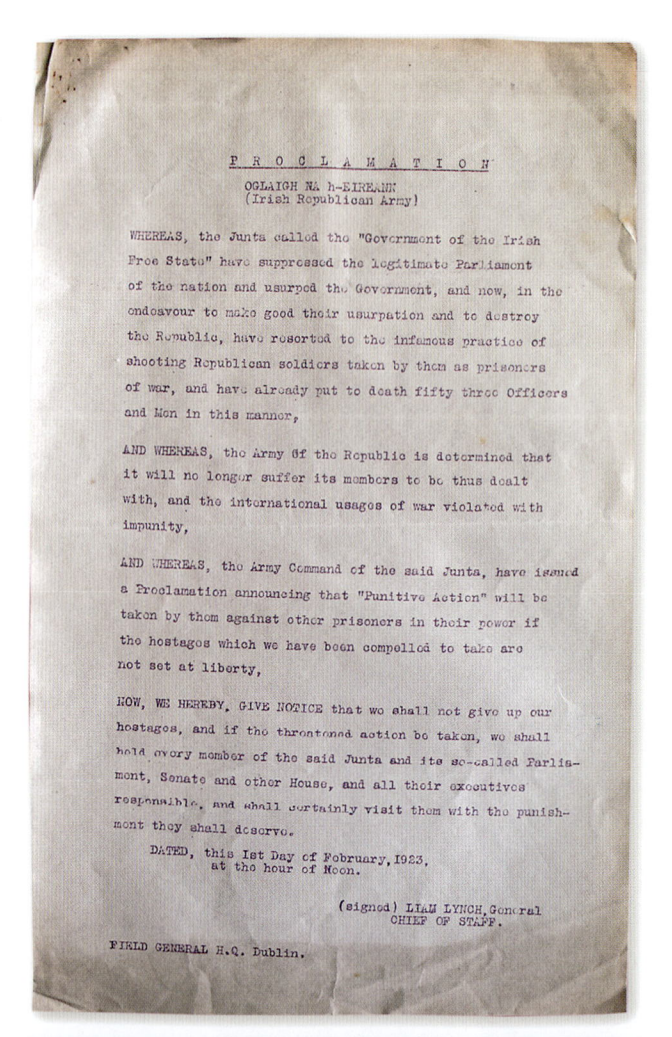

PROCLAMATION
OGLAIGH NA h-EIREANN
(Irish Republican Army)

WHEREAS, the Junta called the "Government of the Irish Free State" have suppressed the legitimate Parliament of the nation and usurped the Government, and now, in the endeavour to make good their usurpation and to destroy the Republic, have resorted to the infamous practice of shooting Republican soldiers taken by them as prisoners of war, and have already put to death fifty three Officers and Men in this manner,

AND WHEREAS, the Army of the Republic is determined that it will no longer suffer its members to be thus dealt with, and the international usages of war violated with impunity,

AND WHEREAS, the Army Command of the said Junta, have issued a Proclamation announcing that "Punitive Action" will be taken by them against other prisoners in their power if the hostages which we have been compelled to take are not set at liberty,

NOW, WE HEREBY, GIVE NOTICE that we shall not give up our hostages, and if the threatened action be taken, we shall hold every member of the said Junta and its so-called Parliament, Senate and other House, and all their executives responsible, and shall certainly visit them with the punishment they shall deserve.

DATED, this 1st Day of February, 1923, at the hour of Noon.

(signed) LIAM LYNCH, General
CHIEF OF STAFF.

FIELD GENERAL H.Q. Dublin.

Left: it was no longer an honourable war between former colleagues. On 1 February 1923, Liam Lynch, Chief of Staff, IRA, issued this proclamation. It notes 53 IRA men executed and the threat of punitive action by the Free State on prisoners if 'the hostages that we have been compelled to take are not set at liberty'. It warns the 'Junta' that they will not give up their hostages and if the threatened action be taken that all responsible will be visited 'with the punishment they shall deserve'.

Many Anglo-Irish 'big houses' were burnt by the anti-Treaty IRA, who perceived their owners as pillars of the Free State. Below left: the remains of Castlelboro House, Co. Wexford, burnt in February 1923, today.

Pro-Treaty TD Seán McGarry's house on Philipsburgh Avenue, Dublin, was burnt on 10 December 1922. His seven-year-old son, Emmet (below), died of burns sustained in the fire.

Above: the Chief State Solicitor, Michael Corrigan's house on Leinster Road in Rathmines, was blown up on 29 January 1923. The unfortunate gentleman surveys the ruins of his house.

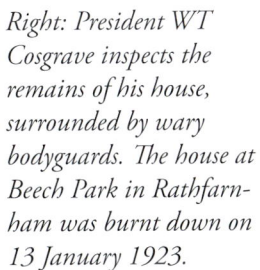

Right: President WT Cosgrave inspects the remains of his house, surrounded by wary bodyguards. The house at Beech Park in Rathfarnham was burnt down on 13 January 1923.

Left: great abundance – 18-pounder field guns, trucks and armoured cars in ready supply from the British. The weapons were battle proven and state of the art for their time. Their use gave the National Army a decisive advantage over the course of the Civil War. It had rapidly increased in size and, as 1923 began, had gained the upper hand across most of the country.

Left: a unit of the anti-Treaty IRA at Sligo. In contrast to National Army Troops, anti-Treaty men were short of supplies; many had to live in rough terrain, sometimes commandeering provisions. While they were still able to inflict damage on their enemy, they had lost much territory and local support. The executions towards the end of 1922 severely affected morale.

Right: British troops leave Dublin, December 1922.

By the end of 1922, confident that the Government of the Free State would prevail in the Civil War, the British made arrangements to evacuate the last of their troops. On 13 December a destroyer was sent to North Wall at Dublin Port to protect the ships carrying troops. National Army patrols were deployed north and south of the Liffey. Cross-channel steamers were engaged for the evacuation exercise (including the 'Arvonia' and the 'Menevia', veterans of the pro-Treaty amphibious landings months before). On 17 December, the last British installations were handed over, including the Magazine Fort, the Royal Hospital, Marlborough (now McKee) and Royal (now Collins) Barracks. The troops were played by their regimental bands to North Wall, where they boarded the waiting ships, cheered by a large crowd (right), some of whom waved Union Jacks.

During the early part of the Civil War, the Criminal Investigation Department (CID) was based at Oriel House on Fenian Street, Dublin (left). It was a shadowy quasi-military intelligence organisation. Founding members included those from Collins' 'Squad'. The CID, facing the wave of Republican 'hit-and-run' attacks, resorted to a series of extra-judicial killings in the period 1922-23, particularly in Dublin.

Left: memorial to Noel Lemass, in the Dublin Mountains. Lemass (older brother of Seán, a later Taoiseach) was abducted in broad daylight near Wicklow Street, Dublin, in July 1923. His badly decomposed body was found here three months later. A coroner's jury concluded that 'forces of the State' had been implicated in the murder of Noel Lemass (photo, below).

The cycle of atrocity and reprisal reached new levels of frightfulness in Kerry. It began at Barinarig wood near Knocknagoshel on 6 March 1923. Lured by a false tip-off, a party of eight pro-Treaty soldiers, led by Lieutenant O'Connor (a local man, who was the subject of Republican animosity), came to investigate a supposed Republican arms dump (right). It turned out to be a trap mine. O'Connor and four others were killed, including Captains Dunne and Stapleton, who were Dublin Guards, long-time comrades of Brigadier-General Paddy O'Daly, OC Kerry Command.

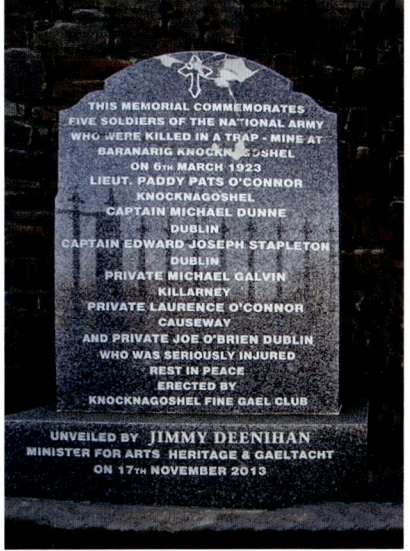

Right: memorial at Knocknagoshel. It has been vandalised several times.

What occurred next ranks among the lowest points of the Civil War. On 7 March 1923, the day after the Knocknagoshel trap-mine explosion, nine prisoners at Ballymullan Barracks (left, in earlier days) were brought by Free State soldiers to a barricade at Ballyseedy near Tralee, ostensibly to clear it. They were tied together and then blown up by a mine. Unbeknownst to the troops, one prisoner, Stephen Fuller, was blown into a field and survived. He was able to tell what happened and, despite efforts at a cover-up, the news of the massacre soon filtered out.

Right: the Ballyseedy Monument, by the Breton sculptor, Yann Renard-Goulet, unveiled in 1959. This tortured statue is one of the most dramatic sculptures in Ireland and aptly remembers the appalling atrocity that took place here.

Brigadier-General Paddy O'Daly, OC Kerry Command. Veteran of the Magazine Fort action during 1916 (see page 66) and a 'Squad' hitman during the War of Independence, he was in charge at Ballymullan Barracks when the murders occurred across his Kerry Command.

The frightfulness continued in Kerry. On the same day as the Ballyseedy explosion, soldiers of the Dublin Guards, stationed in the Great Southern Hotel in Killarney, brought five prisoners to the nearby Countess Bridge, over the railway line, again ostensibly to clear a barricade. Grenades were thrown and they were raked with machine-gun fire. Four prisoners died, one escaped.

On 12 March 1923, five prisoners were taken from the Baghaghs workhouse, near Caherciveen, by the Dublin Guards to a place nearby (memorial right). They were shot in the legs and placed on a booby-trapped barricade. The mine exploded and this time no one escaped – all five were killed.

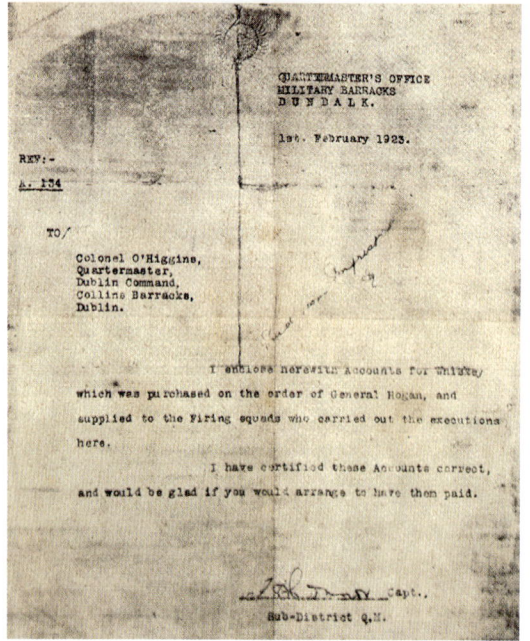

On 14 March 1923, Charlie Daly (above) and three other prisoners (like Daly, two were from the Kerry IRA) were marched from Drumboe Castle, Co. Donegal and executed in this nearby field (memorial, left). The prisoners had been tried the previous January, but no sentence had been imposed. Following the shooting of a Free State captain, an order to execute came by radio from GHQ in Dublin. Coincidentally, Stephen Fuller, the Ballyseedy 'escapee', had taken refuge in Daly's family home in Kerry, the day after the explosion.

Seventy-seven is generally known as the number of executions by the Free State in 1922-23, although in reality it was somewhat more. Being a member of a firing squad could be traumatic. Left: Quartermaster's note about whiskey purchased for members of the firing squad at Dundalk Barracks.

Above: the isolated Nire Valley in Co. Waterford. An IRA Executive meeting was held in the area in March 1923. The Chief of Staff, Liam Lynch (right), did not realise the game was up. Optimistically, he thought that acquisition of mountain artillery from abroad would make all the difference. The meeting culminated in a vote on 26 March 1923, on a motion by Tom Barry, that continued resistance would not further the cause of independence. It was defeated by six votes (including that of Lynch) to five. De Valera, also present, had no vote. Because of the diverging opinion, the IRA Executive agreed to meet three weeks later (extract from minutes, below right).

Around ten days later, Lynch passed through the Nire Valley again on his fatal journey, travelling for the planned meeting of the Executive at Araglin, Co. Cork.

```
Proposed by Comdt. Gen. Barry and seconded by O/C. 1st S/D:-
"That in the opinion of the Executive further armed resistance and
operations against F.S. Government will not further the cause of
Independence of the country."
FOR:- Comdt. Gen. Barry, O/C. 1st S/D, D/O, O/C. Kerry 1, Q/M.
Cork 1 - 5
AGAINST:- C/S., D.C/S., A.C/S., A/G., M/F, O/C. 2nd Southern - 6.
The proposal was defeated by one vote.

Proposed by C/S, seconded by A/G.
"That an Executive meeting be called in 3 weeks time". The proposal
was agreed to.
```

351

Left: the Liam Lynch Memorial in the Knockmealdown Mountains.

In early April 1923, Liam Lynch, Chief of Staff, was en route, accompanied by his aides, to the planned meeting of the IRA Executive at Araglin, intending to resume discussion on whether to continue the war. Pro-Treaty forces, alerted by intelligence gathered by the CID, prepared for a massive sweep of the Knockmealdown area.

On 10 April, as Free State troops began their early-morning sweep of the Knockmealdown mountains, Lynch and his companions were spotted running up a ridge of Crohan West. Following an exchange of fire, he was felled by a long-distance shot at around 9 am. Wounded in the abdomen, Lynch was captured and carried off the mountain with difficulty on an improvised stretcher comprising a greatcoat and rifles. He was eventually transported by ambulance to St Joseph's Hospital, Clonmel, where he died that evening.

Left: Liam Lynch laid out in a coffin at Clonmel.

Six Republicans had gone into hiding here in a cave at Clashmealcon (above), on the north Kerry coast. On 16 April 1923, two pro-Treaty soldiers climbing down to search the cave were shot. From the cliffs above, the troops tried to flush out the Republicans by burning hay and setting off landmines — all to no avail.

As night fell, two Republicans attempting to escape were drowned. At midday on the 18th, the leader, Timothy 'Aeroplane' Lyons, surrendered, but the rope parted as he climbed up and he fell to his death. Accounts say that he was shot as he fell. The other three surrendered and were brought back to the barracks in Tralee, tried by military court and executed on 25 April.

Near right: memorial near cave. Far right: 'Aeroplane' Lyons.

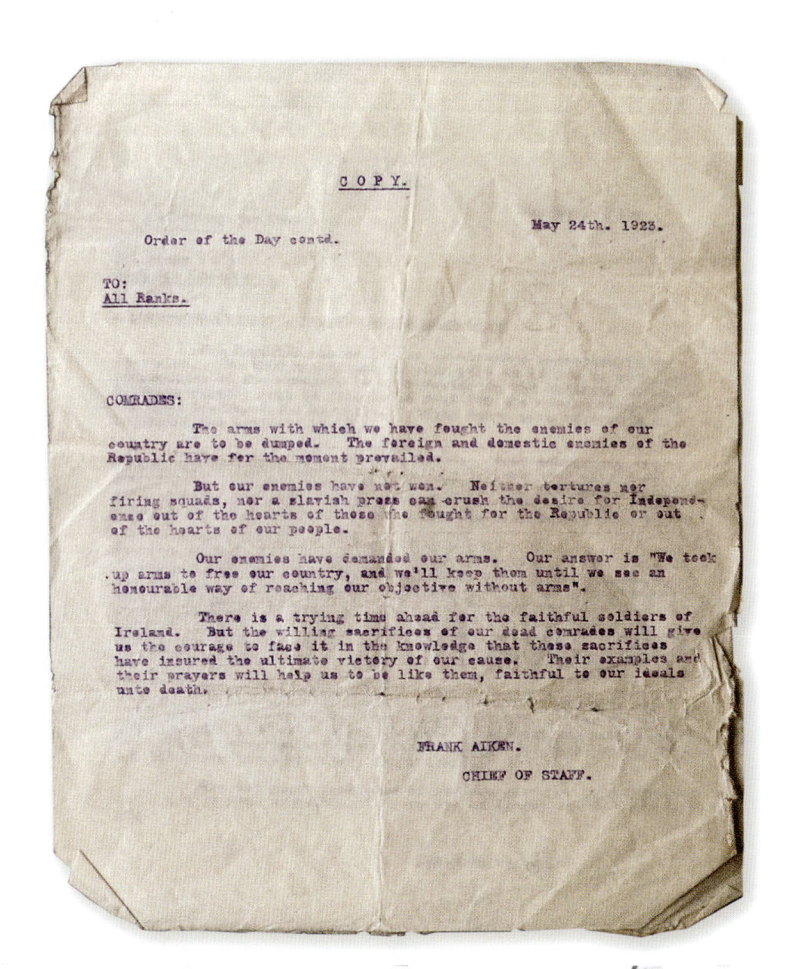

Left: the end came swiftly. In little over six weeks after Liam Lynch's death, the new IRA Chief of Staff, Frank Aiken, in an Order of the Day (left), wrote: 'The arms with which we have fought the enemies of our country are to be dumped. The foreign and domestic enemies of the Republic have for the moment prevailed.' It was accompanied by a message from de Valera to the 'Soldiers of Liberty – Legion of the Rearguard' stating that 'further sacrifices ...would now be vain and continuance of the struggle in arms unwise in the national interest'.

With the war won, the National Army began to reduce in size. In September 1923, the 5,000-strong Railway Protection, Repair and Maintenance Corps was disbanded. Many returned to employment in the railway companies; others joined the Engineering Corps of the army. Left: General Richard Mulcahy salutes at the stand-down ceremony.

Above: Éamon de Valera wearing a beard, useful when he was moving around trying to avoid capture. He shaved it off the evening before the Ennis meeting.

De Valera proposed that the Republicans participate in the General Election called for August 1923. On 15 August, he emerged from hiding to address a Sinn Féin election meeting at Ennis, Co. Clare. Shots were discharged and scuffles ensued as de Valera was seized by pro-Treaty troops (depiction, right) and dispatched to prison. He was to spend around a year in captivity.

Right: WT Cosgrave flies to the hustings at Carlow.

Despite many of their candidates being incarcerated, the election result was surprisingly good for Sinn Féin, at 44 seats. The pro-Treaty party in power, Cumann na nGaedheal, gained 63 seats. Labour and others won 46.

Above: de Valera playing chess in Kilmainham Gaol. He was the last prisoner, released on 16 July 1924.

Left: Dan Breen with his Free State captor.

In 1923 around 12,000 Republicans were in captivity. With no negotiated peace and no handover of arms, the Free State authorities were reluctant to release the prisoners.

Left: 'Le Petit Journal' depicts an October 1923 hunger strike by Republican prisoners sympathetically, comparing it with that of Terence MacSwiney. The hunger strike was called off in late November.

Emigration was the only option for many of the defeated. Below: at Cobh in 1923, Republicans en route to embarking on a Canada-bound ship.

Right: Kevin O'Higgins, Minister for Justice, addresses members of the Civic Guard at the Phoenix Park Depot. An armed police force had been established in February 1922, but was disbanded by the Provisional Government after a mutiny at the Kildare training barracks in May. A new Civic Guard was constituted in September 1922. As the Civil War ended this new unarmed force was essential in underpinning Government control across the country.

Kevin O'Higgins gave the victor's version: he recalled the early days as 'simply eight young men in the City Hall standing amidst the ruins of one administration, with the foundation of another not yet laid, and with wild men screaming through the keyhole'. However, there was also a powerful empire across the water, on watchful standby, providing assistance and ready to stamp out any hint of a Republic.

The ministers of the Free State (right – O'Higgins is on left) now had to face the task of reducing a swollen army and rebuilding a bankrupt, bitter and divided State.

357

The State had to reconstruct buildings and infrastructure damaged during the Civil War. Left: assessing the damage at the Four Courts. The dome was rebuilt in reinforced concrete and then clad with copper. The work was carried out in 1924–31, under the direction of TJ Byrne, principal architect in the Office of Public Works.

In this Punch cartoon (below left), Lloyd George points out to the dim (Irish) pig that there was no chance of a Republic. In 1923 after the Free State had won the Civil War, this was blindingly obvious. Only the Boundary Commission was left in play. In the Treaty negotiations, Lloyd George had dangled this to the Irish delegation, implying that it would result in border gains, leading to a reduced and unsustainable Northern Ireland. In the event, with ambiguous terms of reference and the commission set-up stacked against him, the unassertive Eoin MacNeill resigned in November 1925. A month later the Free State agreed to wrap it up, leaving the existing border intact, in effect bribed by the British promise to absolve them from servicing part of the Imperial Debt.

A TEST OF SAGACITY.

Mr. Lloyd George. "LADIES AND GENTLEMEN, WITH THE LETTERS I HAVE PLACED BEFORE HIM OUR LEARNED FRIEND WILL NOW SPELL OUT SOMETHING THAT SIGNIFIES THE GREATEST HAPPINESS FOR IRELAND."

The Pig. "I CAN'T MAKE THE BEASTLY THING SPELL 'REPUBLIC.'"

Right: soldiers of the Irish Defence Forces line up during the State Commemoration ceremony in 2016 at Arbour Hill, where the executed leaders of the Easter Rising are buried.

Commencing in 2012, the Irish Government organised a Decade of Centenaries programme, focussing on the many significant national centenaries of the events that occurred in the period 1912–1923. The stated objective of the programme was to ensure that this complex period of Ireland's history is remembered proportionately, respectfully and with sensitivity.

Right: the Republican Plot at St Finbarr's Cemetery, Cork, one of the largest in Ireland. It is a pantheon of prominent Cork Republicans from the 1920-23 period, including the two Lord Mayors, Tomás Mac Curtain and Terence MacSwiney. Tom Barry's grave is located nearby.

Three Volunteers crown the War of Independence memorial at Elphin, Co. Roscommon, one of the more spectacular of its type. Comdt-General Tom Maguire (1892-1993, veteran of the action at Tourmakeady, page 213) performed the unveiling ceremony here in September 1963.

Since its establishment in 1832, Glasnevin Cemetery has become a shrine for heroes of the national struggle.
The protagonists of the Civil War are now dead, remembered on plaques and headstones. Many of these former enemies now lie in close proximity for all eternity in Glasnevin. Those buried here include: Kevin O'Higgins, Rory O'Connor, Erskine Childers, Eamon de Valera, Arthur Griffith and Cathal Brugha. Also here is the most visited grave in Glasnevin (left), that of Michael Collins.

Bibliography

Principal Libraries, Museums & Archives consulted:
British National Archives, Kew; Cork Public Museum; Dublin City Library & Archive; Imperial War Museum, London; Irish Capuchin Provincial Archives, Dublin; Irish Railway Records Society, Dublin; Kilmainham Gaol Museum; Military Archives (Military Service Pensions Collection, Bureau of Military History Witness Statements), Dublin; Military Museum, Collins Barracks, Cork; Military Museum, The Curragh; National Archives of Ireland, Dublin; National Library of Ireland, Dublin; National Museum of Ireland, Dublin; RAF Museum, London; South Dublin Libraries, Tallaght; Trinity College Library, Dublin; UCD Archives, Belfield, Dublin; Ulster Folk and Transport Museum.

Periodicals:
An Cosantóir: The Defence Forces Magazine; *An tÓglach*; Capuchin Annual; History Ireland; Irish Historical Studies; Journal of the Irish Railway Record Society; The Irish Sword; Irish and British newspapers.

Books on the Irish Revolution recommended in the first instance:
Barry, MB, *Courage Boys We are Winning, an Illustrated History of the 1916 Rising*, Andalus Press, Dublin, 2015
Barry, MB, *The Green Divide, an Illustrated History of the Irish Civil War*, Andalus Press, Dublin, 2014
Barry, MB, *The Fight for Irish Freedom, an Illustrated History of the War of Independence*, Andalus Press, 2018
Barry, T, *Guerrilla Days in Ireland*, Mercier Press, Cork, 2012
Crowley, J, Ó Drisceoil, D, Murphy, M, *Atlas of the Irish Revolution*, Cork University Press, 2017
Dorney, J, *The Civil War in Dublin: The Fight for the Irish Capital, 1922–1924*, Merrion Press, Dublin, 2017
Fewer, M, *The Battle of the Four Courts*, Head of Zeus, London, 2018
Gillis, L, *May 25: Burning of the Custom House*, Kilmainham Tales Teo., Dublin, 2017
Hopkinson, M, *Green against Green, The Irish Civil War*, Gill & Macmillan, Dublin, 1988
Hopkinson, M, *The Irish War of Independence*, McGill-Queen's University, 2004
McCall, E, *Tudor's Toughs*, Red Coat Publishing, Newtownards, 2010
O'Brien, P, *Battleground, the Battle for the General Post Office, 1916*, New Island, Dublin, 2015
O'Malley, E, *On Another Man's Wound*, Mercier Press, Cork, 2013
O'Malley, E, *The Singing Flame*, Mercier Press, Cork, 2012
Townshend, C, *Easter 1916, The Irish Rebellion*, Penguin Books, London, 2006

Books:
(No author information: NA)
(NA) *A History of the Royal Air Force and the United States Naval Reserve in Ireland, 1913—1923*, Karl Hayes and Irish Air Letter, Dublin, 1988
(NA) *Cuimhneachán 1916*, National Gallery of Ireland, Dublin, 1966
(NA) *Sinn Féin Rebellion Handbook*, Irish Times, Dublin, 1916
(NA) *The forged 'Irish Bulletin'*, Aubane Historical Society, Millstreet, 2017
(NA) *The Rebellion in Dublin, April 1916*, Eason & Son, Dublin, 1916
Abbot, R, *Police casualties in Ireland, 1919—1922*, Mercier Press, Cork, 2000
Andrews, CS, *Dublin Made Me*, Lilliput Press, Dublin, 2001
Barton, B, *From Behind a Closed Door*, Blackstaff Press, Belfast, 2002
Bateson, R, *Dead and Buried in Dublin*, Irish Graves Publications, Dublin, 2002
Bateson, R, *Memorials of the Easter Rising*, Irish Graves Publications, Dublin, 2013
Bateson, R, *The Rising Dead: RIC & DMP*, Irish Graves Publications, Dublin 2012.
Bateson, R, *They died by Pearse's side*, Irish Graves Publications, Dublin, 2010
Béaslaí, P, *Michael Collins and the Making of a New Ireland*, Phoenix Publishing Company, Dublin, 1926
Beckett, JC, *The Making of Modern Ireland 1603–1923*, Faber & Faber, London, 1972
Begley, D, *The Road to Crossbarry*, Deso Publications, Bandon, 1999
Bennett, R, *The Black and Tans*, Edward Hulton, London, 1959
Borgonovo, J, *Spies, Informers and the 'Anti-Sinn Féin Society'*, Irish Academic Press, Dublin, 2007
Borgonovo, J, *The Battle for Cork*, Mercier Press, Cork, 2011
Bowyer Bell, J, *The Secret Army: the IRA 1916—1979*, Poolbeg, Dublin, 1990
Breen, D, *My Fight for Irish Freedom*, Anvil Books, Dublin, 1981
Brennan-Whitmore, W, *Dublin Burning*, Gill & Macmillan, Dublin, 1996
Brunicardi, D, *The Seahound*, Collins Press, Cork, 2001
Buckley, D, *The Battle of Tourmakeady: Fact or Fiction*, THP Ireland, 2008
Carey, T, *Hanged for Ireland, a Documentary History*, Blackwater Press, Dublin, 2001
Carroll, A, *Seán Moylan*, Mercier Press, Cork, 2010
Casey, C, *The Buildings of Ireland: Dublin*, Yale University Press, New Haven and London, 2005
Chambers, C, *Ireland in the Newsreels*, Irish Academic Press, Dublin, 2012
Clayton, X, *Aud*, GAC, Plymouth, 2007
Coakley, D, O'Doherty, M, ed., *Borderlands*, Royal College of Surgeons, Dublin, 2002
Collins, L, *James Connolly*, O'Brien Press, Dublin, 2012
Connell, JEA, *Dublin in Rebellion: A Directory 1913–1923*, Lilliput Press, Dublin, 2009
Connell, JEA, *Dublin Rising 1916*, Wordwell, Dublin, 2015
Connolly, C, *Michael Collins*, Weidenfeld & Nicholson, London, 1996
Coogan, TP, *1916: The Easter Rising*, Orion Books, London, 2005
Coogan, TP, *De Valera: Long Fellow, Long Shadow*, Hutchinson, London, 1993
Coogan, TP, *Michael Collins*, Arrow Books, London, 1990
Coogan, TP, *The Twelve Apostles*, Head of Zeus, London, 2016
Cooke, P, *A History of Kilmainham Gaol*, Brunswick Press, Dublin, 2005
Cottrell, P, ed., *The War for Ireland 1913–1923*, Osprey Publishing, Oxford, 2009
Cottrell, P, *The Irish Civil War 1922–23*, Osprey Publishing, Oxford, 2009
Crowe, C, ed., *Guide to the Military Service (1916–1923) Pensions Collection*, Óglaigh na hÉireann, Dublin, 2012

361

Crowley, B, *Patrick Pearse, a Life in Pictures*, Mercier Press, Cork, 2013
De Courcy Ireland, J, *The Sea and the Easter Rising 1916*, Maritime Institute of Ireland, Dún Laoghaire, 1966
Deasy, L, *Brother against Brother*, Mercier Press, Cork, 1998
Doherty, G, Keogh, D, ed., *Michael Collins and the Making of the Irish State*, Mercier Press, Cork, 1998
Dolan, A, *Commemorating the Irish Civil War*, Cambridge University Press, Cambridge, 2006
Dorney, J, *Peace after the Final Battle, the Story of the Irish Revolution*, 1912—1924, New Island, Dublin, 2014
Doyle, T, *The Civil War in Kerry*, Mercier Press, Cork, 2008
Doyle, T, *The Summer Campaign in Kerry*, Mercier Press, Cork, 2010
Dudley Edwards, R, *Patrick Pearse, the Triumph of Failure*, Gollancz, London, 1977
Duggan, JP, *A History of the Irish Army*, Gill & Macmillan, Dublin, 1991
Durney, J, *The Civil War in Kildare*, Mercier Press, Cork, 2011
English, R, *Ernie O'Malley: IRA Intellectual*, Oxford University Press, Oxford, 1999
Fallon, L, *Dublin Fire Brigade and the Irish Revolution*, South Dublin Libraries, Dublin, 2012
Fanning, R, *Fatal Path: British Government and Irish Revolution 1910—1922*, Faber and Faber, London, 2013
Farry, M, *Sligo 1914—1921, a Chronicle of Conflict*, Killoran Press, Trim, 1992
Farry, M, *The Aftermath of Revolution, Sligo 1921—23*, University College Dublin Press, Dublin, 2000
Farry, M, *The Irish Revolution, 1912—23, Sligo*, Four Courts Press, Dublin, 2012
Feeney, B, *Seán MacDiarmada*, O'Brien Press, Dublin, 2014
Ferguson, S, *GPO Staff in 1916*, Mercier Press, Cork, 2012
Ferriter, D, *A Nation and not a Rabble, the Irish Revolution 1913—23*, Profile Books, London, 2015
Ferriter, D, intro., *Dublin's Fighting Story 1916—1921*, Mercier Press, Cork, 2009
Fitzpatrick, D, ed., *Terror in Ireland*, Lilliput Press, Dublin, 2012
Fitzpatrick, D, *Politics and Irish Life, 1913—1921*, Gill & Macmillan, Dublin, 1998
Fox, R, *The History of the Irish Citizen Army*, James Connolly Debating Society, Belfast, 2013
Gallagher, M, *Éamonn Ceannt*, O'Brien Press, Dublin, 2014
Garvin, T, *1922: The Birth of Irish Democracy*, Gill & Macmillan, Dublin, 1996
Gibney, J, *Seán Heuston*, O'Brien Press, Dublin, 2013
Gillis, L, *Revolution in Dublin: A Photographic History 1913—23*, Mercier Press, Cork, 2013
Gillis, L, *The Hales Brothers and the Irish Revolution*, Mercier Press, Cork, 2016
Gillis, L, *Women of the Irish Revolution*, Mercier Press, Cork, 2014
Gillis, L, *The Fall of Dublin*, Mercier Press, Cork, 2011
Good, J, *Enchanted by Dreams*, Brandon, Dingle, 1996
Greaves, D, *Liam Mellows and the Irish Revolution*, Lawrence & Wishart, London, 1971
Greaves, D, *The Life and Times of James Connolly*, Lawrence & Wishart, London, 1986
Griffith, K, O'Grady, TE, *Curious Journey*, Hutchinson, London, 1982
Gwynn, D, *The History of Partition (1912—1925)*, Browne & Nolan, Dublin, 1950
Harrington, M, *The Munster Republic: The Civil War in North Cork*, Mercier Press, Cork, 2009
Harrington, NC, *Kerry Landing: August 1922*, Anvil Books, Dublin, 1992
Hart, P, ed., *British Intelligence in Ireland 1920—21: The Final Reports*, Cork University Press, Cork, 2002
Hart, P, *The IRA at War 1916—1923*, Oxford University Press USA, New York, 2005
Hart, P, *Mick: The Real Michael Collins*, Penguin, London, 2006
Hart, P, *The IRA and its Enemies: Violence and Community in Cork*, 1916—1923, Oxford University Press, Oxford, 1999
Herlihy, J, *The Dublin Metropolitan Police*, Four Courts Press, Dublin, 2001
Hittle, JB, *Michael Collins and the Anglo-Irish War*, Potomac Books, Washington DC, 2011
Holt, E, *Protest in Arms, the Irish Troubles 1916-1923*, Putnam, London, 1960
Hopkinson, M, ed., *The Last Days of Dublin Castle, the Mark Sturgis Diaries*, Irish Academic Press, 1999
Hopkinson, M, ed., *Frank Henderson's Easter Rising*, Cork University Press, 1998
Hughes, B, *Michael Mallin*, O'Brien Press, Dublin, 2012
Johnson, S, *Johnson's Atlas & Gazetteer of the Railways of Ireland*, Midland Publishing, Leicester, 1997
Joy, S, *The IRA in Kerry 1916—1921*, Collins Press, Cork, 2005
Kautt, WH, *Ground Truths*, Irish Academic Press, Dublin, 2014
Keane, B, *Massacre in West Cork*, Mercier Press, Cork, 2014
Kenna, S, *War in the Shadows*, Merrion Press, Kildare, 2014
Kenna, S, *Thomas MacDonagh*, O'Brien Press, Dublin, 2014
Kennealy, I, *The Paper Wall: Newspapers and Propaganda in Ireland 1919—1921*, The Collins Press, Cork, 2008
Keogh, D, *Twentieth-Century Ireland, Revolution and State Building*, Gill & Macmillan, Dublin, 2005
Kissane, B, *The Politics of the Civil War*, Oxford University Press, Oxford, 2005
Kostick, C, Collins, L, *The Easter Rising, a Guide to Dublin in 1916*, O'Brien Press, Dublin, 2012
Laffan, M, *Judging WT Cosgrave*, Royal Irish Academy, Dublin, 2014
Laffan, M, *The Resurrection of Ireland, the Sinn Féin Party*, 1916-1923
Langton, J, *The Forgotten Fallen, the Fallen of the Irish Civil War, Volume 1*, Kilmainham Tales, Dublin, 2019
Lawlor, P, *1920-1922, The Outrages*, Mercier Press, 2011
Lawlor, P, *The Burnings 1920*, Mercier Press, Cork, 2009
Lee, JJ, intro., *Kerry's Fighting Story 1916—1921*, Mercier Press, Cork, 2009
Lewis, M, *Frank Aiken's War*, UCD Press, Dublin, 2014
Litton, H, *Edward Daly*, O'Brien Press, Dublin, 2013
Litton, H, *The Irish Civil War: An Illustrated History*, Wolfhound Press, Dublin, 1995
Litton, H, *Thomas Clarke*, O'Brien Press, Dublin, 2014
Lynch, D, *The IRB and the 1916 Insurrection*, Mercier Press, Cork, 1957
Macardle, D, *The Irish Republic*, Merlin Publishing, 1999
Macardle, D, *Tragedies of Kerry 1922—1923*, Irish Freedom Press, 2004
MacCarron, D, *Wings over Ireland, The Story of the Irish Air Corps*, Midland Publishing, 1996
Martin, FX, ed, *The Irish Volunteers 1913—1915*, Merrion, Dublin, 2013
Martin, FX, ed., *The Howth Gun-Running and the Kilcoole Gun-Running*, Merrion, Dublin, 2014
Martin, K, *Irish Army Vehicles, Transport & Armour since 1922*, Karl Martin, 2002

Matthews, A, *Renegades, Irish Republican Women 1900—1922*, Mercier Press, Cork, 2010
Matthews, B, *The Sack of Balbriggan*, Balbriggan, 2006
Maxwell, J, Cummins, PJ, *The Irish Air Corps, An Illustrated Guide*, Max Decals Publications, Dublin, 2009
McCall, E, *The Auxies*, Red Coat Publishing, Newtownards, 2013
McCall, E, *The First Anti-Terrorist Unit, the Auxiliary Division RIC*, Red Coat Publishing, Newtownards, 2018
McCarthy, C, *Cumann na mBan and the Irish Revolution*, Collins Press, Cork, 2007
McCoole, S, *Easter Widows*, Doubleday Ireland, Dublin, 2014.
McCullagh, D, *De Vallera, Rise (1882—1932)*, Gill Books, Dublin, 2017
McGarry, F, *Eoin O'Duffy: A Self-Made Hero*, Oxford University Press, Oxford, 2005
McGarry, F, Rebels: *Voices from the Easter Rising*, Penguin Books, 2012
McGarry, F, *The Rising, Ireland Easter 1916*, Oxford University Press, Oxford, 2010
McGowan, J, *In the Shadow of Benbulben*, Aeolus Publications, Manorhamilton, 1993
McHugh, R, ed., *Dublin 1916*, Arlington Books, London, 1966
McIvor, A, *A History of the Irish Naval Service*, Irish Academic Press, 1994
Meakin, G, ed., *Forgotten History, the Kilcoole Gunrunning*, Kilcoole Heritage Group, 2014
Mitchell, A, *Roger Casement*, O'Brien Press, Dublin, 2013
Mooney, T, *Cry of the Curlew: the Déise Brigade and the War of Independence*, De Paor, Dungarvan, 2012
Morrison, G, Coogan, TP, *The Irish Civil War*, Weidenfeld & Nicholson, London, 1998
Morrison, G, *Revolutionary Ireland, a Photographic Record*, Gill & Macmillan, Dublin, 2013
Mulcahy, R, *My Father the General: Richard Mulcahy and the Military History of the Revolution*, Liberties Press, Dublin, 2009
Murphy, G, *The Year of Disappearances: Political Killings in Cork 1921—1922*, Gill & Macmillan, Dublin, 2011.
Neeson, E, *The Irish Civil War*, Poolbeg Press, Dublin, 1989
Neligan, D, *The Spy in the Castle*, Prendeville Publishing, London, 1999
Ó Brolcháin, H, *Joseph Plunkett*, O'Brien Press, Dublin, 2012
Ó Comhraí, C, *Revolution in Connacht: A Photographic History 1913—1923*, Mercier Press, Cork, 2013
Ó Conchubhair, B, ed., *Dublin's Fighting Story 1916—21*, Mercier Press, Cork, 2009
Ó Drisceoil, D, *Peadar O'Donnell*, Cork University Press, Cork, 2001
Ó Duibhir, L, *Donegal & the Civil War, The Untold Story*, Mercier Press, Cork, 2011
Ó Gadhra, N, *Civil War in Connacht*, Mercier Press, Cork, 1999
Ó Ruairc, P, *Blood on the Banner, the Republican Struggle in Clare*, Mercier Press, Cork, 2009
Ó Ruairc, P, *Revolution: A Photographic History of Revolutionary Ireland 1913—1923*, Mercier Press, Cork, 2011
Ó Ruairc, P, *The Battle for Limerick City*, Mercier Press, Cork, 2010
Ó Ruairc, P, *Truce*, Mercier Press, Cork, 2016
O'Brien, P, *A Question of Duty, the Curragh Incident 1914*, New Island, Dublin, 2014
O'Brien, P, *Arbour Hill Cemetery*, Kilmainham Tales, Dublin, 2012
O'Brien, P, *Blood on the Streets, 1916 & the Battle for Mount Street Bridge*, Mercier Press, Cork, 2008
O'Brien, P, *Royal Hospital Kilmainha*m, Kilmainham Tales, Dublin, 2015
O'Brien, P, *Shootout, the Battle for St Stephen's Green, 1916*, New Island, Dublin, 2013
O'Callaghan, J, *Con Colbert*, O'Brien Press, Dublin, 2015
O'Callaghan, J, *The Battle for Kilmallock*, Mercier Press, Cork, 2011
O'Connor, D, Connolly, F, *Sleep Soldier Sleep: The Life and Times of Pádraig O'Connor*, Miseab Publications, 2011
O'Donoghue, F, *No Other Law, the Story of Liam Lynch and the Irish Republican Army*, 1916—1923, Irish Press, 1954
O'Dwyer, M, *Brigadier Dinny Lacey, by the men who knew him*, Cashel Folk Village, Co. Tipperary, 2004
O'Faolain, S, *Constance Markievicz*, Cresset Women's Voices, London, 1987
O'Farrell, M, *1916, What the People Saw*, Mercier Press, Cork, 2013
O'Farrell, M, *50 Things you didn't know about 1916*, Mercier Press, Cork, 2009
O'Farrell, M, *The 1916 Diaries*, Mercier Press, Cork, 2014
O'Farrell, P, *The Seán Mac Eoin Story*, Mercier Press, Cork, 1981
O'Farrell, P, *Who's Who in the Irish War of Independence and Civil War, 1916—1923*, Lilliput Press, Dublin, 1997
O'Malley, CKH, Horgan, T, ed, *The Men will Talk to Me: Kerry Interviews by Ernie O'Malley*, Mercier Press, Cork, 2012
O'Malley, CKH, Ó Comhraí, C, ed, *The Men will Talk to Me: Galway Interviews by Ernie O'Malley*, Mercier Press, Cork, 2013
O'Malley, MC, *Military Aviation in Ireland 1921—45*, University College Dublin Press, Dublin, 2010
O'Reilly, T, *Rebel Heart; George Lennon: Flying Column Commander*, Mercier Press, Cork, 2005
Pinkman, JA, *In the Legion of the Vanguard*, Mercier Press, Cork, 1998
Quinn, J, *The Story of the Drumboe Martyrs*, McKinney, Letterkenny, 1958
Regan, JM, *The Irish Counter-Revolution 1921—1936*, Gill & Macmillan, Dublin, 1999
Riccio, R, *AFVs in Irish Service since 1922: From the National Army to the Defence Forces*, MMP Books, Petersfield, Hampshire, 2010
Riccio, R, *Irish Coastal Landings 1922*, MMP Books, Petersfield, Hampshire, 2012
Riccio, R, *The Irish Artillery Corps since 1922*, MMP Books, Petersfield, Hampshire, 2012
Ryan, G, *The Works, Celebrating 150 Years of Inchicore Works*, Dublin, 1996
Ryan, M, *The Day Michael Collins was Shot*, Poolbeg Press, Dublin, 1998
Ryan, M, *The Real Chief: Liam Lynch*, Mercier Press, Cork, 2005
Ryan, M, *Tom Barry: IRA Freedom Fighter*, Mercier Press, Cork, 2012
Ryle Dwyer, T, *Michael Collins and the Civil War*, Mercier Press, Cork, 2012
Ryle Dwyer, T, *Tans, Terror & Troubles, Kerry's Real Fighting Story*, Mercier Press, Cork, 2001
Share, B, *In Time of Civil War: The Conflict on the Irish Railways 1922—23*, The Collins Press, Cork, 2006
Spindler, K, *The Mystery of the Casement Ship*, Kribe-Verlag, Berlin, 1931
Stiles, D, *Portrait of a Rebellion*, CreateSpace Independent Publishing, 2012
Valiulis, MG, *Portrait of a Revolutionary, General Richard Mulcahy and the Founding of the Irish Free State*, Irish Academic Press, Dublin, 1992
Walsh, M, *In Defence of Ireland: Irish Military Intelligence 1918—45*, The Collins Press, Cork, 2010
Yeates, P, *A City in Civil War, Dublin 1921—4*, Gill & Macmillan, Dublin, 2015
Yeates, P, *A City in Wartime, Dublin 1914—18*, Gill & Macmillan, Dublin, 2011
Yeates, P, *Lockout, Dublin 1913*, Gill & Macmillan, Dublin, 2013
Younger, C, *Arthur Griffith*, Gill & Macmillan, Dublin, 1981
Younger, C, *Ireland's Civil War*, Fontana Press, London, 1986

Glossary

Act of Union	This came into effect on 1 January 1801 and united the kingdoms of Great Britain and Ireland, thus creating the 'United Kingdom of Great Britain and Ireland'.
Active Service Unit (ASU)	IRA Active Service Units were established at the end of December 1920 in Dublin. There were four companies, each assigned to one of the city battalions. These Volunteers were full-time and paid a salary.
ADRIC	Auxiliary Division of the Royal Irish Constabulary. Recruiting for this paramilitary force began in July 1920.
Amiens Street Railway Station	Opened in 1844, renamed Connolly Station in 1966.
Anglo-Irish Treaty	The Anglo-Irish Treaty signed on 6 December 1921 by Irish plenipotentiaries and representatives of the British Government. It provided for the establishment of an Irish Free State. The six-county entity given the name Northern Ireland was entitled to opt out, which it immediately did.
Ardfheis	National convention.
Black and Tans	A nickname (after a name used for the beagles of the Scarteen Hunt, Co. Limerick) applied to the (mostly British) ex-servicemen recruited to the RIC from early 1920 onwards. They were initially clad in a mixture of khaki and green uniforms, due to a shortage of RIC uniforms.
B-Specials	A name commonly given the Ulster Special Constabulary (USC). This was a paramilitary reserve special constable police force, established in October 1920 in what was soon to become the new entity, Northern Ireland.
Cumann na mBan	Founded in early 1914, this republican women's auxiliary corps supported the objectives of the Irish Volunteers. *Cumann na mBan* participated strongly during the Rising and War of Independence as an active, but non-combatant, support organisation.
Commandant	A military rank used in Ireland, equivalent to 'Major' in some other armies.
Curragh Camp	The Curragh has been a place of military assembly on the flat plains of County Kildare for centuries. In the early 20th century it was a principal base of the British Army; now the main training centre for the Irish Defence Forces.
Dáil Éireann	The first *Dáil* (an assembly or parliament) met on 21 January 1919. It was established by Sinn Féin MPs (who won a majority of Irish seats) elected to the UK parliament in the December 1918 UK general election.
D&SER	Dublin & South Eastern Railway.
DMP	Dublin Metropolitan Police. An unarmed urban police force in Dublin, merged into the Garda Síochána in 1925. The 'G' Division (its detectives were popularly known as 'G-men') was a plain-clothes section which had gathered intelligence on Irish republicanism since the time of the Fenians.
Fenians	A revolutionary movement, originating in the new Irish immigrant population of the USA in the mid-19th century. Its objective was the establishment of an independent Irish Republic. See 'IRB'.
Fianna Éireann	Irish nationalist youth organisation founded by Countess Markievicz and Bulmer Hobson in 1909.
Flying Column	Permanent units of the IRA engaged in fighting the guerrilla war, usually operating from remote areas in the countryside. These were established after August 1920.
Free State	The State (known as the Irish Free State or in Irish *Saorstát Éireann*), a self-governing dominion of the British Empire, established on 6 December 1922 under the terms of the Anglo-Irish Treaty, replacing the (transitional) Provisional Government established in January 1922. Its remit covered 26 counties of Ireland. It existed until 1937 when, after a referendum, a new constitution, which replaced that of 1922, was approved. Ireland declared itself a republic under the Republic of Ireland Act 1948. This came into effect on 18 April 1949.
Frongoch Camp	A former POW camp (originally a distillery) for captured Germans in Merionethshire, North Wales. It was used after the 1916 Rising to intern most of the Republican prisoners.
GAA	Gaelic Athletic Association, founded in 1884 as a sporting and cultural organisation for promoting and organising Gaelic games.
GHQ	General Headquarters.
GNR (I)	Great Northern Railway (Ireland).
Government of Ireland Act (1920)	Also titled 'An Act to provide for the better government of Ireland'. This became law on 23 December 1920. It divided Ireland into two parts. 'Northern Ireland' comprised the six north-eastern counties. 'Southern Ireland' was to comprise the remaining 26 counties. Each entity was to have a bicameral parliament with limited powers. A Northern Ireland parliament was opened on 22 June 1921, in accordance with the Act.
GPO	General Post Office, on the western side of Lower O'Connell (formerly Sackville) Street in Dublin. It was headquarters of the Irish Post Office. The Republican forces set up their headquarters here during Easter 1916.
GS&WR	Great Southern & Western Railway.

Home Rule	Policy aiming at the establishment of a parliament and government in Dublin to legislate for Irish domestic affairs, thus repatriating some aspects of government from Westminster.
ICA	Irish Citizen Army. It was founded in November 1913 as a workers' defence militia. After Jim Larkin's departure to the USA, it was organised and directed by James Connolly. The ICA participated strongly in the Rising.
Igoe Gang	The IRA name for a group of RIC men from around the country, assembled in Dublin under the leadership of Head Constable Eugene Igoe. It had been established as the 'Intelligence Company' by Brigadier-General Ormonde Winter, chief spymaster in Dublin Castle.
Irish Parliamentary Party (IPP)	It was formed in 1882 by Charles Stewart Parnell. Its MPs promoted three Home Rule Bills in the decades that followed. After the split over Parnell, John Redmond emerged as its leader.
IRB	Irish Republican Brotherhood. A secret oath-bound society, prepared to use force to establish an independent Irish Republic, which represented the continuation of the Fenian tradition. The organisation dissolved itself in 1924.
Irish Volunteers	A nationalist militia founded in November 1913 at the Rotunda in Dublin to 'secure the rights and liberties common to all the people of Ireland'. After the outbreak of WWI in 1914, as the Redmond majority departed with the objective of supporting the British war effort, the remainder of radical nationalists, effectively under the IRB, reorganised and made plans for a rising.
Kingstown	Renamed Dún Laoghaire in 1922.
L&NWR	London and North Western Railway.
Lord Lieutenant	The representative of the British sovereign in Ireland (also known as the Viceroy). His residence was the Viceregal Lodge in the Phoenix Park. (Now *Áras an Uachtaráin*, official residence of the President of Ireland.)
MGWR	Midland Great Western Railway.
Munitions Crisis	The crisis arising from the refusal of Irish railwaymen, from mid-May 1920, to carry men and equipment of the Crown forces – an initiative that lasted until December of that year.
Northern Ireland	A constituent unit of the United Kingdom of Great Britain and Northern Ireland. It comprises six Irish counties – Antrim, Armagh, Down, Fermanagh, Derry (shired as Londonderry) and Tyrone.
OC	Officer Commanding.
Queenstown	Renamed Cobh in 1922.
RAF	The Royal Air Force, formed on 1 April 1918 (formerly the Royal Flying Corps). RAF planes were deployed at aerodromes across Ireland during the War of Independence.
RIC	Royal Irish Constabulary, an armed police force in Ireland (outside of Dublin), in existence up to 1922.
RPR&MC	Railway Protection, Repair and Maintenance Corps, established in October 1922, a unit of the National Army.
Sackville Street	Renamed O'Connell Street in 1924.
SDU	South Dublin Union. In 1916 it was a large complex of buildings (hospitals, asylums, convents, churches and ancillary buildings) on 20 hectares. The site now accommodates St James's Hospital.
Shemus	Ernest Forbes (1879–1962), an English cartoonist who worked for the *Freeman's Journal,* published in Dublin. Over the period 1920-24 he produced some 300 cartoons. During the War of Independence his work exposed the flaws of the blundering British campaign in Ireland. He took a pro-Treaty stance during the Civil War.
Sinn Féin	Founded in 1905, under the leadership of Arthur Griffith, who wished to establish a national legislature in Ireland. Griffith and the organisation did not participate in the Rising, despite it being dubbed the 'Sinn Féin Rising' at the time. It was restructured in 1917 to take a more radical nationalist and republican direction.
Squad	A small unit (of tough and resilient Volunteers, who soon gained expertise in assassination) established in 1920 by Michael Collins, to counter British intelligence efforts to crush and destroy the IRA and *Sinn Féin*.
Society of United Irishmen	Formed in 1791, this non-sectarian radical organisation was inspired by the French and American revolutions. It had the objective of establishing a sovereign, independent Irish Republic. It was central to the rebellion of 1798.
TD	*Teachta Dála* (member of parliament, *Dáil Éireann*).
The O'Rahilly	Michael Joseph O'Rahilly. A founding member of the Irish Volunteers.
Unionism	In the Irish context, it is an ideology which supports political union between Ireland and Great Britain.
UVF	Ulster Volunteer Force. Founded in January 1913, it was a unionist militia, based in Ulster, with the objective of blocking Home Rule in Ireland.
Westland Row Railway Station	The first railway terminus in Dublin (1834), renamed Pearse Station in 1966.
Whippet Tank	A popular name given to the medium Mk A tank used in WWI and deployed in Ireland. Confusingly, the nickname was also applied to the fast and agile Rolls-Royce armoured car.

Index

A

Act of Union 13, 19
Aiken, Frank 261, 354
Allman, Dan 208
Aloysius, Father 112
American Commission of Inquiry on Conditions in Ireland 192
Amiens Street 56
An Claidheamh Soluis 34
Anglo-Irish Treaty 233, 235, 247, 252, 255-266, 268-9, 271-274, 276, 277-279, 281, 282-284, 287-8, 291-293, 296, 298, 300, 302- 309, 311-314, 316, 318-320, 324-326, 329, 331, 333, 335-337, 339-342, 344-5, 347, 352-3, 355

Anti-Treaty IRA 260-1, 269, 271, 273-4, 276-279, 282, 284, 291, 293, 302, 329, 333, 342, 344
Arbour Hill 45, 106, 359
Army Air Service (known as the 'Army Air Corps' from October 1924) 309-10
Arvonia 314-15, 317, 345
Asgard 29, 30
Ashbourne 116, 182
Ashe, Thomas 79, 129
Ashtown ambush 144
Asquith, Herbert 45, 99, 100, 104
ASU 196
Athlone 270, 274
Aud 38-40, 42
Austin armoured car 156
Auxiliaries 116-7, 147, 159, 160, 167, 170-1, 174-5, 178, 180, 183-186, 188, 195-6 198, 201, 203, 205, 206, 209, 210, 216, 218, 221, 225, 228, 236

B

Baggallay, Captain 203
Baggot Street 203
Bailieboro 241
Balbriggan 167
Baldonnel 309, 310
Ballast Office, Dublin 279
Ballincollig 197, 206
Ballsbridge 149
Ballykinlar camp 181
Ballymacelligot 170
Ballymullan Barracks 348-9
Ballyseedy 261, 348-350
Ballyturin House 217
Ballyvoyle Viaduct 329
Banbridge 157
Bandon 206-7
Bantry 166
Barrett, Richard 341
Barrington, Winifrid 217
Barrow Railway Bridge 331
Barry, Kevin 164, 203
Barry, Tom 164-5, 184-5, 206, 237, 248, 359
Barton, Robert 234, 249, 254
Béal a' Ghleanna 131
Bealnablath 321-324
Beggar's Bush Barracks 72, 178, 236, 261, 268-9, 339
Belfast 56, 117, 230, 233, 240, 276, 284
Belfast Boycott 234, 284

Bell, Alan 149
Belleek 281
Benbulben 337-8
Black and Tans 147, 199
Blackwater, River 158
Blessington 299
'Block', the 260, 288, 291-2, 294, 296-7
Bloody Sunday 173, 176, 181, 203
Boland, Harry 133, 137-8, 242
Boland's Bakery 71, 73, 126
Bootle 219
Boundary Commission, the 277, 358
Bowen-Colthurst, John, Captain 44, 63-65
Brennan, Michael 271, 302
Breen, Dan 136, 139, 144, 174
Bristol F.2B fighter 309, 310
Britain 13, 20, 31-2, 37, 118-9, 136, 139, 142, 219, 250
British Empire 234-5, 249, 252, 256-7
British Labour Party 192
Brixton Gaol 161, 163
Brooke, Frank 158
Brugha, Cathal 63, 77-8, 125, 138, 234, 247, 250, 272, 280, 292, 296
Bryan, Thomas 196, 203
Busteed, Frank 197
Byrne, Vinnie 139

C

Café Cairo 175
Caherciveen 41, 335, 349
'Cairo Gang' 175
Capel Street 154
Capuchins 161, 285, 290
Carolan, John, Professor 174
Carrickmines 217
Carrowkennedy 225
Carson, Sir Edward 25
Casement, Sir Roger 13, 37, 40, 45, 114, 165, 203
Castle Barracks, Limerick 304
Cavan 241
Ceannt, Éamonn 76, 95, 102
Childers, Erskine 29, 254, 307, 339, 360
Chippewa Tribe 140
Churchill, Winston 272, 281, 284
Church Street 66, 68-70, 285, 287
City Hall, Dublin 44, 54-5, 161, 186-7, 244, 267
Civic Guard 357
Civil War 235, 242-3, 247-8, 255, 259, 261, 269, 285, 293, 310, 331, 344-346, 348, 357-8, 360
Clancy, Peadar 179
Clancy, Seoirse 205
Clan na Gael 32
Clanwilliam House 72, 74-5
Clare 56, 126, 155, 158, 168, 194, 238, 271
Clarke, Kathleen 263
Clarke, Thomas 32, 93, 98, 101-2
Clashmealcon 353
Clogheen 210
Clonakilty 212
Clonbanin 202
Clonfin 198
Clonliffe Road 180
Clonmult 201
Coade, James 64
Cobh (Queenstown) 319, 356
Colbert, Con 77, 102
Collins, Michael 116, 123, 129, 130, 134, 137-139, 146, 149, 157, 173, 176,

179, 216, 227-8, 234-5, 249, 253-4, 256, 260, 266-7, 272, 277, 281, 283, 307, 313, 320,
Coolboreen 217
Connolly, James 43-49, 51, 54, 88, 90-1, 94, 105
Connolly, Seán 54
Cork 54, 79, 104, 116, 117, 131, 139, 141, 148, 157, 161-2, 184, 186-189, 192, 194, 197, 200-202, 205-207, 210, 212, 224-226, 232, 239, 260-1, 270-2, 276, 305, 307, 313-4
Cork Examiner 318
Cosgrave, WT 76, 265, 267, 307, 325, 343, 355
Craig, Sir James 230-1
Criminal Investigation Department (CID) 261, 346, 352
Croke Park 176, 180
Crossbarry 206-7
Crossley Tender 153, 184, 202, 225, 321
Crown Alley central telegraph exchange 56
Cumann na mBan 92, 143, 244-246, 247-8, 286
Cumann na nGaedheal 261, 355
Cumming, HR, Brigadier-General 202
Curragh Camp 56, 280
Custom House 44, 52, 220-222

D

Dáil Éireann 116, 135, 138, 143, 173, 234, 251-2, 259, 262-265
Dalton, Emmet 216, 280, 321,
Daly, Edward 68, 102
Democratic Programme of *Dáil Éireann* 135
Derry 131
De Valera, Éamon 73, 99, 116, 117, 126-7, 130, 137-8, 140, 173, 191, 220, 231, 234-5, 248, 249-252, 257, 356
Devins, Seamus 338
Devoy, John 22, 38
Dickson, Thomas 64-5
Dillon's Cross 186
Donegal 131
Down 181
Downing Street 249, 253
Doyle, Patrick 203
Dripsey 197
Drishanbeg 200
Drogheda 314
Dromkeen 199
Drumboe Castle 350
Drumcondra 174, 203
Dublin 43-45, 51-2, 54, 56-58, 62-3, 74, 76, 79, 80, 82, 94, 99, 106-7, 110, 112, 116-7, 122-3, 130, 133, 137, 139, 143, 146, 149, 151-2, 154-5, 158, 160, 164, 170-172, 174-176, 178-182, 181-2, 188, 191, 195-6, 203, 216-218, 220-223, 227, 229, 231, 241, 250, 256, 259-261, 263, 266-268, 272-3, 346-7
Dublin and Blessington Steam Tramway 299
Dublin and South Eastern Railway 158
Dublin Castle 15, 43-4, 54, 58, 62, 94, 133, 143, 149, 170-172, 175-6, 181, 183, 216
Dublin Fire Brigade 107, 112, 294
Dublin Guard 278
Dublin Metropolitan Police (DMP) 30, 54-5, 96, 125, 143, 146, 228, 243
Duffy, George Gavan 254

Duggan, Éamon 237, 254
Dundalk 230

E

Earlsfort Terrace 263-4
Easter Rising 43, 45, 109, 115, 121, 125, 245, 250
Eighteen-pounder field gun 243, 314, 344
Ellis, John 165, 203-4
Ennis 156
Ennis, Tom 209, 221
Enniscorthy 79
Ennistymon 168
Essex Regiment 200, 206-7, 212, 226

F

Fenians 13, 20-22, 124-5
Fenit 38, 306, 311, 313, 317, 335
Fermoy 141, 166
Fianna Éireann 24, 29, 30, 125, 245, 325
First Southern Division 211
FitzGerald, Desmond 307
Four Courts 44, 57, 68-70, 91, 95, 124, 229, 259, 260, 271, 273, 283-287, 289-291, 293, 311-4, 341, 358
Flood, Frank 196, 203
Freemasons' Hall 277, 279
French, John, Field Marshal Lord 133, 144, 145, 148, 158
Frongoch Camp 115, 118, 123, 148, 245
Furlong, Matt 241

G

Gaelic Athletic Association 143
Gaelic League 24, 34, 37, 76, 143
Galway 79, 183, 217, 183
'G' Division, DMP 146
General Post Office, Dublin 43-47, 49, 51, 56-58, 82, 84, 85, 88, 90, 108-9, 113, 121, 273, 297
George V, King 117, 230, 235, 230
'German Plot' 138
Germany 13, 28, 31, 37-8, 132, 136, 204
Glasnevin Cemetery 114, 203, 261, 324, 360
Gloucestershire Regiment 224
Gort 183, 215, 217
Government of Ireland Act 117, 145, 191, 230
Gifford, Grace (Plunkett) 101, 267
Granard 198
Granville Hotel, Dublin 296, 300
Great Famine 13, 20
Great Northern Railway (Ireland) 57, 81
Great Southern and Western Railway 83, 326-7, 329, 333
Greenwood, Sir Hamar 151, 153, 172, 188, 194
Gresham Hotel 177, 291
'Grey Ghost' Lancia 332-3
Griffith, Arthur 35, 234, 249, 253-4, 265, 274, 320

H

Hackett, Rosie 244
Hales, Seán 261, 340
Hammam Hotel 291, 295
Haulbowline 272, 335
Headford Junction 208
Helga 44, 52-3, 73
Heuston, Seán 43-4, 46, 102
Higginson, Brigadier-General 237

Ho Chi Minh 163
Hogan, Seán 139
Holohan, Garry 66, 67, 209
Holyhead 162
Home Rule 13, 23, 25, 31, 122, 128, 145
Hornibrook family 276
Howth 29, 30, 37
Hurley, Charlie 207

I

Ibberson, Geoffrey, Lieutenant 213
Igoe Gang 227
Inchicore 83
Irish Brigade 37, 40
Irish Bulletin 171
Irish Citizen Army 26, 43-4, 46-7, 54-5, 59, 60-62, 244
Irish Convention 115, 128
Irish Free State 235, 257, 261, 268-9, 280, 312, 342, 345, 348, 350, 352, 356-358
Irish Labour Party 192, 260-1, 282, 355
Irish Parliamentary Party 13, 23, 25, 122, 124, 127-8, 132, 134-5
Irish Republic 46, 48-9, 51, 91, 116, 135, 140
Irish Republican Army (IRA) 116-7, 137, 139, 141, 146, 148, 157-8, 161, 168-9, 172, 174-176, 178, 180, 182, 184-5, 189, 196-7, 199-202, 207-213, 217, 219, 220-222, 223-228, 232-237, 239-242, 244-255, 259-261, 263, 269,
Irish Republican Brotherhood, (IRB) 13, 20, 22, 27, 32, 36, 38, 41, 43, 48, 58, 76, 101, 105, 134
Irish Volunteers 13, 26-29, 31, 33, 35-6, 41, 43, 46, 115, 130-1, 143, 245
Irish War News 51

J

Jacob's Factory 44, 57-8, 95, 112-3
Jervis Street Hospital 180
Johnson, Thomas 181

K

Kearns, Linda 238
Kenmare 312
Kent, Thomas 104
Keogh, Tom 39, 336
Kerry 39, 40, 66, 79, 189, 202, 208, 215, 261, 306-7, 311, 347, 349
Kildare 131, 229, 277, 357
Kilkenny 127, 134, 194
Kilmainham Gaol 45, 100-1, 105, 182, 258, 356
Kilmallock 157, 305, 306
Kilmichael 184-186
Kilroy, Michael 225
King John's Castle, Limerick 271
Kingsbridge (now Heuston) Railway Station 56, 80
Kingstown (now Dún Laoghaire) 44, 51, 72-3, 252
Kinsale 200, 206
Knocklong 139, 203
Knockmealdown Mountains 352
Knocknagoshel 347-8

L

Lacey, Denis 168

Lady Wicklow 311, 314, 317, 318
Lancia armoured vehicle 225, 229, 281, 287, 290, 292-3, 308, 314, 316, 333
Laverton, Hazel 281
Lea-Wilson, Percival, Captain 93, 157
Lee Enfield SMLE Mk III 242, 295, 323
Lee Metford carbine 131, 147
Leenane 225
Lemass, Noel 346
Leonard, Joe 216
Lewis machine gun 224, 243
Leyland Eight touring car 321, 323
Liberty Hall 42-44, 46, 52-54
Limerick 79, 122, 137, 158, 166, 189, 199, 205, 217, 271, 282, 302-3,
Lincoln Gaol 137
Lindsay, Mary 197
Linenhall Barracks 70
Lisburn 148, 166
Listowel 157
Liverpool 191, 219
Lloyd George, David 117, 122, 128, 132, 145, 148, 162, 188, 191, 229-231, 234-5, 249, 250, 252, 254, 256, 257
London 169, 177, 209, 231, 234-5, 249, 250, 252-3, 256
London and North Western Railway Hotel 209
Long, Walter 145
Longford 168, 198
Louth 79
Lowe, William, Brigadier-General 56-7, 74, 92
Lucas, Cuthbert, Brigadier-General 158
Lynch, Liam 141, 169, 211, 261, 302, 304, 340, 342, 351-2
Lynn, Kathleen 54-5, 244
Lyons, Timothy 'Aeroplane' 353

M

MacBride, John 102
MacCormack, Patrick 177
Mac Curtain, Tomás 148, 359
MacDermott, Seán 32, 35-6, 93, 96, 105, 244
MacDonagh, Thomas 58, 94-5, 98, 102
Mac Eoin, Seán 168, 198, 216, 234, 225, 270, 274, 278
MacIntyre, Patrick 65
MacNeill, Brian 338
MacNeill, Eoin 13, 27, 41, 138, 338, 358
Macready, Nevil, General Sir 117, 151, 194, 231
Macroom 197, 206, 276
MacSwiney, Muriel 341
MacSwiney, Terence 117, 161-3, 359
Magazine Fort, Dublin 66
Maguire, Tom 213, 360
Maher, Patrick 203
Mallin, Michael 43, 46, 59, 95-8, 102
Malone, Michael 72, 75
Mallow 169, 198, 200, 208
Markievicz, Constance, Countess 24, 59, 95, 100, 134, 245, 263, 325, 341
Mansion House, Dublin 117, 130, 132, 135, 138, 211, 231, 234-5, 251
Marlborough (now McKee) Barracks 164, 345
Marrowbone Lane 76-7
Martial Law 193, 194
Maryborough (now Portlaoise) 258, 327
Mater Hospital, Dublin 174
Mauser C96 semi-automatic pistol 242
Maxwell, John, General Sir 44-5, 94, 97, 99, 100, 122
Mayo 213, 225

McCartan, Pat 173
McDonnell, Mick 139, 144, 149
McGarry, Seán 137
McGuinness, Joseph 124
McKee, Dick 164, 179
McKenna, Kathleen 171
Mee, Jeremiah 157
Meelin, Co. Cork 194
Mellows, Liam 79, 341
Mendicity Institution 43-4, 46
Menevia 311, 345
Midland Great Western Railway 326, 328
Midleton 193-4, 201
Milltown Malbay 168
Monaghan 160
Monk's Bakery, Dublin 164
Monteith, Robert 40
Moore Street 44-5, 89-92, 109, 244
Moran, Patrick 204
Mountjoy Gaol 116, 150, 164-5, 196, 203-4, 216, 234, 238, 284, 341
Mount Street 44, 71-2, 74-5
Moylan, Seán 194, 224
Mulcahy, Richard 130, 172-3, 232, 244, 255, 272, 313, 325, 354
Mullingar 332
Munitions Crisis 152, 153

N

National Army (in 1922, Army of the Provisional Government) 260-1, 269, 274, 284, 288, 292, 296, 303-306, 312-3, 318, 320, 324, 334-5, 337-8, 344-5, 354-5
Nenagh 166
Newport, Co. Mayo 217
New York 140, 210
Nire Valley 351
Northern Ireland 145, 191, 230, 277
North King Street 68, 70
Northumberland Road 72, 74-5, 178
North Wall 68, 209, 313, 345

O

O'Callaghan, Michael 205
O'Carroll, Richard 64
O'Connell Bridge 47, 83, 111
O'Connell, JJ 260, 280, 284
O'Connor, Pádraig 268, 273, 287, 288, 290, 293, 339, 341, 347, 360
O'Connor, Rory 273, 248, 293, 341
O'Connor 'Scarteen', Tom 312
O'Daly, Paddy 66, 139, 146, 158, 268
O'Donovan Rossa, Jeremiah 22, 36, 129
O'Donnell, Patrick, Bishop 128
O'Dwyer, Edward, Bishop 122
O'Duffy, Eoin 280, 303, 305, 313
O'Farrell, Elizabeth 45, 92, 95, 244
O'Hannigan, Donncha 199
O'Hanrahan, Michael 102
O'Higgins, Kevin 248, 265, 357, 360
O'Kelly, Seán T 136
O'Malley, Ernie 169, 271
Ordnance Barracks, Limerick 303
Oriel House 261, 346

P

Pallasgreen 199
Paris Peace Conference 116, 134, 136
Passage West 315,-6

Pearse, Patrick 33-35, 43, 45, 49, 51, 58, 70, 88, 91-2, 94, 98, 102, 119, 138, 158
Pearse, William 12, 16, 22, 26, 35, 102
Peerless armoured car 156, 195, 216, 222
Pentonville Prison 45, 114
Percival, Arthur, Major 226
Pettigo 281
Phoenix Park 66-7, 357
Playfair, George 66-7
Plunkett, George Noble, Count 124-5, 234, 249
Plunkett, Joseph 98, 101-2
Poblacht na hÉireann 286, 307-8, 319, 339, 341
Pollard, Hugh, Captain 170-1
Portobello (now Cathal Brugha) Barracks 44, 62, 280, 272, 313
Price, Leonard, Captain 178
Proclamation of Irish Republic 43, 46, 48-9, 58, 98, 106
Provisional Government 259-261, 266, 267-269, 271-2, 274, 284, 287, 294, 297, 299, 303, 311, 314, 318, 320, 325-6, 337, 340, 357
Public Record Office, Dublin 260, 287, 289
Public Safety Act 339

Q

Queenstown (now Cobh) 39, 162, 315, 319
Queenstown Dry Docks 315

R

RAF 117, 215, 281
Railway Protection, Repair & Maintenance Corps 319, 326, 332-3
Rathcoole, Co. Cork 225
Redmond, John 13, 25, 31, 124
Richmond Barracks 45, 77, 93, 95-98, 104
Rineen ambush 168
Rogers Brothers foundry 241
Rolls Royce armoured car 202, 271, 287, 293, 294, 314, 321, 337
Roscommon 124, 144
Royal College of Surgeons 44, 59, 95, 244-5
Royal Fusiliers 208
Royal Irish Constabulary (RIC) 40, 79, 104, 116, 131, 136-7, 139, 142, 144, 146-148, 153, 156-7, 159, 166-168, 183, 193, 196, 198-9, 210, 212-3, 218, 225, 228, 240
Royal Navy 250, 261, 335
Ryan, Bernard 203
Ryan, Min 244

S

Sackville Street (now O'Connell) Street 44-5, 47, 49, 51, 53, 82, 84, 93, 107-8, 260, 289, 291, 293-295, 297-8
Savage, Martin 144
Shelbourne Hotel 44, 59
Shannon, River 271
Sheehy-Skeffington, Francis 44, 63
Shemus (pseudonym of Ernest Forbes) 188, 194, 230, 264, 273, 282
Sherwood Foresters 44, 73-75
Sinn Féin 35, 80, 107, 115-6, 121, 124, 126-128, 130, 132-135, 142-3, 148-9, 173, 230, 251, 355
Skibbereen 322
Skinnider, Margaret 244
Sliabh na mBan 321, 322

Sligo 274, 337-8, 344
Sligo 'Noble Six' 338
Soloheadbeg 136, 139, 144
Somerville, Hugh 335
South Dublin Union (SDU) 44, 57, 76-78, 95
South Staffordshires 70
Spies 227, 228
'Squad', the 66, 96, 139, 174, 158, 221
Stack, Austin 249
St Enda's School 34-5, 138
Strickland, Peter, Major-General Sir 189
Strickland Report 188
St Stephen's Green 43-4, 46, 48, 57-62

T

Talbot Street 174
Templemore Barracks 166, 271
Thomastown 168
Thomond Bridge 271
Thornton, Frank 228
Tipperary 136, 168, 180, 189, 217
Tolka Bridge 196
Tourmakeady 213
Tralee 170, 200, 210
Traynor, Oscar 273, 291, 341
Traynor, Thomas 203
Treacy, Seán 139, 174
Trinity College, Dublin 44, 57, 80-1, 128
Truce 160, 233, 234, 236-241, 248, 232
Tudor, Henry, Major-General Sir 151, 157, 159
'Typhoid Plot' 172, 173

U

Ulster Special Constabulary (B Specials) 276, 277, 281
Ulster Volunteer Force (UVF) 13, 25-6, 28
Unionists 13, 25, 116, 122, 128, 134, 145, 191, 230-1
United Services Club 59
United States 140
Upnor 272
Upper Pembroke Street 178
Upton 200, 206

V

Viceregal Lodge 144
Vickers machine gun. 243
Vico Road, Killiney 170
Victoria (now Collins) Barracks, Cork 186, 189

W

War of Independence 45, 115, 141, 146, 176, 215, 241-2, 245, 263, 293, 308, 310, 340, 349, 360
Waterford 194, 215, 239, 300, 329, 331
Wellington (now Griffith) Barracks 274
Wesleyan Chapel, Fermoy 141
West Cork 131, 184, 206, 212, 226, 260, 319, 321-2, 339, 340
Westland Row (now Pearse) Station 57, 72, 123
Westport 311, 225
Wexford 11, 194, 342
Whelan, Thomas 203-4
Wicklow 311, 314, 317-8, 336, 339, 346
Wilson, Henry, Field Marshal Sir 260, 283
Winter, Ormonde, Brigadier-General 179, 227
Woods, Herbert 276

368